THE

PROPHECY

PUZZLE

Fitting prophecy from the whole Bible into the book of Revelation

By Joseph Ebenhoe

The Prophecy Puzzle

Copyright © 2008, 2010, 2018 by Joseph R. Ebenhoe

The Prophecy Puzzle
Fitting prophecy from the whole Bible into the book of Revelation
By Joseph R. Ebenhoe

ISBN: 9781549718120

All rights reserved solely by the author. All contents are original and do not infringe upon the legal rights of any other person or works. Anyone is free to use any portion of this book, as long as it is not for profit.

All Scripture quotations are from the King James Version unless otherwise stated.

The Prophecy Puzzle

Contents

Introduction: v

CHAPTER 1: John's Introduction to the Glorified Christ Jesus – Revelation 1:1 – 3 1

CHAPTER 2: Grace and Peace from the Father, Son and Holy Spirit – Revelation 1:4 – 8 9

CHAPTER 3: The Introduction to the Letter Written to the Seven Churches – Revelation 1:9 – 20 21

CHAPTER 4: The Letter to the Seven Churches – Revelation 2:1 – 3:22 31

CHAPTER 5: Coming up to Date – Recent Fulfillments of Prophecy 99

CHAPTER 6: The Heavenly Scene – Revelation 4:1 – 5:14 105

CHAPTER 7: An Outline of End-time Events 123

CHAPTER 8: The Timing of the Events of the Seven-year Tribulation According to Revelation 6:1 – 11:19 127

CHAPTER 9: The Timing of Events According to Revelation 12:1 – 16:21 199

CHAPTER 10: Timing of Events According to Revelation 17:1 – 19:21 237

CHAPTER 11: The Judgment and the Millennium Kingdom – Revelation 20:1 – 15 255

The Prophecy Puzzle

CHAPTER 12: The New Heavens and the New Earth – Revelation 21:1 – 22:21 269

CHAPTER 13: The Historic View of the Seven Churches 279

CHAPTER 14: The Complete Timeline According to the Book of Revelation 301

Closing Comments: 313

The Prophecy Puzzle

INTRODUCTION

Thank you for picking up this book. I truly hope you will find it thought provoking and edifying. Most of you who pick up this book I assume will be familiar with the Bible and believe it is the Word of God. If that is you I am sure you will enjoy this book very much, but if that is not you I especially encourage you to read on, because it is my hope that you will come to appreciate the Bible for the amazing book that it is; actually I should say books, because it is actually a compiling of 66 different books. The Bible is an amazing book in many ways, but one of its greatest wonders is prophecy. The apostle Peter said we have the great truth of prophecy to prove that the Bible is the Word of God and that Jesus of Nazareth is the Christ.

2 Peter 1:19 (KJV)

"We have also a more sure word of prophecy; whereunto ye do well that ye take heed, as unto a light that shineth in a dark place, until the day dawn, and the day star arise in your hearts:"

The purpose of this book, as the subtitle suggests, is to take "end-time" prophecies of the whole Bible and place them into the book of Revelation giving a clear picture of the end-time events. At the time of my writing this I have a two-year old boy. He can take puzzle pieces that should <u>not</u> fit together and somehow get them to mush together, but the final picture is distorted. In order to prevent this from happening with our picture of end-time events we need to start at the beginning of the book of Revelation and go through it verse by verse, being sure to keep things in context. Also to prevent a distorted understanding I would strongly suggest reading through the whole

The Prophecy Puzzle

book of Revelation from the beginning to the end before you begin this book, so it is fresh in your mind.

There is just one last point to be made before we begin this journey through this fascinating subject of prophecy and that is to be a good Berean and check to make sure what is said is what Scripture truly says (Acts 17:11).

In order to have a good understanding of any story one must know its background. There are several facts that need to be established first in order to achieve that understanding; such as, who the author was, to whom he wrote and the time he wrote it.

The Apostle John was the author of the book of Revelation, but we are not sure of when he wrote it. There are two views. One view is that it was written between 65 A.D. and 69 A.D. Those who believe this do so because of such facts as:

- If one translates Nero Caesar's name in Hebrew the sum of the letters adds up to 666 (Rev. 13:18).
    - This of course is only relevant if that is the meaning of the "666", which we will discuss in depth when we arrive there.
    - Nero was certainly a type of anti-Christ. He severely persecuted Christians, especially after blaming them for the burning of Rome in 64 A.D.
- John makes no mention of the destruction of the temple, which happened in 70 A.D.
- It provides an early (but incomplete) fulfillment of some of the prophecies made by John (Rev. 1:3, "the time is **at hand**").

The Prophecy Puzzle

- o Prophets often gave some prophecies pertaining to the near future along with those that would be fulfilled later on.
    - This gave some evidence that the prophecy was truly from YHWH and would indeed be fulfilled.
        - YHWH (Yahweh) is the "name" of the God of the Bible; the one, true, living, eternal, self-existent God – Exodus 3:15.

The other view is that it was written around 95 A.D. Those who believe this do so for the following reasons:

- They do not believe the early dating gives John enough time to have established ministries to the seven churches (Revelation 2:1 – 3:22).
- They do not believe the churches would have had time to decay as Sardis and Laodicea had done.
- Irenaeus who was a student of Polycarp, who was a student of the apostle John, said that John received this vision around this time.
- Nero wasn't in the habit of sending Christians to the island of Patmos, but Emperor Domitian who reigned from 81 A.D. to 96 A.D. was known to do that.
- John doesn't mention the destruction of the temple, because he wasn't told to write about the past. He was told to write about the things that are, and the things to come in the future (Rev. 1:19). So why would he write about the temple being destroyed?
    - o John does allude to a new temple in Rev. 11:1 – 2.
    - o This must be a new temple, for what reason would there be for measuring it again, if it was the existing temple in Jerusalem at that time. They already know its measurements.

The Prophecy Puzzle

- I have never heard of anyone questioning the need for a new temple. I think if the temple were standing in Jerusalem at the time of the writing of Revelation, someone in John's day would have raised that question.

If one is a full preterist or amillennialist one must insist on the early dating of the book of Revelation, because according to those views all or most of the book of Revelation was fulfilled in 70 A.D. For premillennialists like myself the date it was written doesn't matter that much, because we believe that most of the prophecies in the book of Revelation will take place sometime in the future and Christ Jesus will rule for a literal 1000 years from the Throne of David in Jerusalem. There is one thing that no one argues about and that is that the book of Revelation was written during a time when Caesar worship was being enforced, and Christians were being persecuted and killed because they refused to bow before Caesar.

The question might be asked, why should we spend our time studying end-time events and the book of Revelation? We have at least five good reasons to read the book of Revelation:

1) God promises to bless all who read **and heed** the things written in it (Revelation 1:3).
2) It is encouraging, because it shows that Christ Jesus wins in the end.
3) It's the fulfillment of our prayers, if we ever prayed, "Thy kingdom come".
4) It helps bring the rest of the Bible into focus. It gives us God's whole plan, "the big picture".
5) Prophecy is important: <u>One fourth</u> of the Bible is prophetic in nature.

The Prophecy Puzzle

A great example of the importance of prophecy is Daniel 9:25.

Daniel 9:25

> "Know therefore and understand, that from the going forth of the commandment to restore and to build Jerusalem unto the Messiah the Prince shall be seven weeks, and threescore and two weeks: the street shall be built again, and the wall, even in troublous times."

- It will be 69 weeks (173,880 days) from the issuing of the decree to rebuild Jerusalem until the Messiah is presented in Jerusalem.

- Nehemiah 2:1 – 8: This is the issuing of that decree (Mar. 14, 445 B.C.).
    - 173,880 days from Mar. 14, 445 B.C. is April 6, 32 A.D., which is also the **10th of Nisan**.
        - This is the day on which the lambs to be sacrificed for the Passover are inspected for blemishes (Luke 19:41 – 44).
    - Christ Jesus' "triumphal entry" happened on that day. He was being inspected as the Lamb of God.
        - For detailed information on this read, "The coming Prince" by Sir Robert Anderson.
- In Luke 24:25 Christ Jesus states that they should have <u>known</u> **and** <u>believed</u> the prophets.
    - With that in mind we should note that there are <u>eight times</u> as many prophecies about Jesus' <u>second</u> coming than His first.

The Prophecy Puzzle

I have just one last point to make before we actually begin to look at the book of Revelation. Although the book of Revelation has many illustrations that might seem confusing to us on the surface we must not be quick to dismiss them or spiritualize them. It must be realized that much of it is in code and that the code to understand it is given throughout the Bible. The book of Revelation has a little more than 400 verses in it, yet it has over **800** references to the Old Testament.

CHAPTER ONE

John's Introduction to the Glorified Christ Jesus – Revelation 1:1 - 3

****

Revelation 1:1 – 3

"The Revelation of Jesus Christ, which God gave unto him, to shew unto his servants things which must shortly come to pass; and he sent and signified it by his angel unto his servant John:"
2 Who bare record of the word of God, and of the testimony of Jesus Christ, and of all things that he saw."
3 Blessed is he that readeth, and they that hear the words of this prophecy, and keep those things which are written therein: for the time is at hand."

This book is about **Christ Jesus**. It is the revealing of Jesus Christ for who He truly is, YHWH. Now, don't slam the book shut. I am not saying that Jesus Christ is the Father. No, Jesus Christ is the second person of the triune God, who is YHWH. This will be discussed further later on in the book. The book of Revelation also tells of Jesus Christ's

The Prophecy Puzzle

kingdom on the earth. It tells everything from how His reign was acquired, all the way through to the new heavens and earth (eternity).

I would like to make some observations of Jesus Christ as we see Him here. He is still walking in perfect submission to the Father as He did during the entire time of His "earthly ministry".

>Luke 22:41 – 42
>
>"And he was withdrawn from them about a stone's cast, and kneeled down, and prayed, Saying, Father, if thou be willing, remove this cup from me: nevertheless not my will, but thine, be done."
>
>John 5:19
>
>"Then answered Jesus and said unto them, Verily, verily, I say unto you, The Son can do nothing of himself, but what he seeth the Father do: for what things soever he doeth, these also doeth the Son likewise."
>
>1 Corinthians 15:28
>
>"And when all things shall be subdued unto him, then shall the Son also himself be subject unto him that put all things under him, that God may be all in all."

Jesus Christ is still being obedient and doing only what the Father gives Him to do. He is our perfect example of submission (Phil. 2:5 – 15). And no, His submission doesn't mean that He isn't God (YHWH). Just

The Prophecy Puzzle

as the Father is God (YHWH), so is Christ Jesus. As mentioned earlier, we will discuss this in more detail as we reach the verses that directly touch on this issue.

Some might think this next point has nothing to do with the book of Revelation, but it actually has everything to do with it. John in this passage is described as being Jesus Christ's servant (**bondservant**). This is an important point, because according to this passage Christ Jesus is only revealed to those who are His bondservant. Historically a bondservant was a servant who had served his time of service, but chose to remain a servant to his master forever (Deuteronomy 15:12 - 17). The question each one of us must ask ourselves is, are we bondservants of Jesus Christ? Anyone who is a Christian should be a bondservant, because to be a Christian is the giving of one's life to Jesus Christ as one's Savior and LORD (God). We are called to **surrender** our lives to Christ Jesus, not make a **commitment** to Him.

In Revelation 1:1 John makes reference to "the things, which must shortly take place" and again in v. 3 he says that "the time is at hand (near)", but did these things happen back then? What does John mean by "the time is near"? There has been much debate over these questions for centuries and many positions have developed from the attempts to answer this question. We will take a very brief look at four of them here.

- Preterism
- Amillennialism
- Postmillennialism
- Premillennialism

The Prophecy Puzzle

Preterism is the belief that everything written in the Bible has already happened in the past. Even the rapture of the church and Christ Jesus' return to earth all happened in 70 A.D. In my opinion preterism doesn't have a leg to stand on. Acts 3:19 – 22 eliminates preterism as a possibility.

Acts 3:19 – 23

> "Repent ye therefore, and be converted, that your sins may be blotted out, when the times of refreshing shall come from the presence of the Lord;
> 20 And he shall send Jesus Christ, which before was preached unto you:
> 21 Whom the heaven must receive until the times of restitution of all things, which God hath spoken by the mouth of all his holy prophets since the world began.
> 22 For Moses truly said unto the fathers, A prophet shall the Lord your God raise up unto you of your brethren, like unto me; him shall ye hear in all things whatsoever he shall say unto you.
> 23 And it shall come to pass, that every soul, which will not hear that prophet, shall be destroyed from among the people."

In v. 21 it states that Jesus Christ **must** remain in heaven until the time of restoration of <u>all things</u> comes upon the earth. It is clear that this period of restoration of <u>all things</u> has not yet been realized on the earth. Also if preterism is true there is no reason to celebrate "the Lord's Supper", because we are told to only celebrate it <u>until</u> Jesus Christ returns (1Cor. 11:26). If preterism is correct everything in the

The Prophecy Puzzle

Bible has already happened, which would mean that the age of grace is over as well and if the age of grace is over, I have no hope.

Amillennialism is the most held view in the church today. At least two-thirds of churches today hold to it. Most mainline denominations – Catholic, Orthodox, Lutheran, Reformed, etc. are amillennial.

- They do <u>not</u> believe that Christ Jesus will set up a thousand-year reign on "this earth" from "this Jerusalem."

- In general they believe:
    - The book of Revelation is largely symbolic language and much of the text must be spiritualized to understand it.
    - The nation of Israel has forfeited all the promises and blessings God had given it, because they rejected Jesus of Nazareth as their Messiah and gave Him over to be crucified.
    - The church has received all the promises and blessings that the nation of Israel forfeited.
        - The Church is now the representation of Israel upon the earth.
    - We are now living in the millennium age.
        - Jesus Christ is reigning on earth through the church.
        - Satan is bound by Christ Jesus and is not able to deceive the nations because of the working of the Holy Spirit through the Word of God and the church.
    - At sometime in the future Jesus Christ will return to judge the living and the dead and at that time everyone

will either go to hell or spend eternity in the presence of God.

Amillennialism is orthodox, but is an incomplete understanding of Scripture. It is correct in some of what it asserts, but incorrect in what it denies.

Postmillennialism is the belief that Christ Jesus will return after the Millennium kingdom. According to this view the Church will spread the gospel throughout the world and one day bring in the kingdom of God on earth and after that Jesus Christ will return to judge the living and the dead.

This view in my opinion is a little dangerous, because they could receive the false Messiah (anti-Christ) as Jesus Christ. When the false prophet creates a one-world religion they might, if they are not truly grounded in the Word of God, think this is the world peace brought about by the advancing of the gospel (a social gospel). If they are deceived they would take part in this false world-religion.

We see this false world-religion being developed all around us today. The ecumenical movement is very popular and I believe will one day lead to the one-world religion, which will be lead by the false prophet.

Premillennialism is held by most Evangelicals and is encapsulated by the following beliefs:

- That sometime in the future:
    - The church will be raptured.
    - The earth will be judged through the outpouring of the wrath of God.

The Prophecy Puzzle

- o   After which time Jesus Christ will sit on the throne of David and will reign along with His saints on the earth, over all the people who were not killed during the great tribulation for a period of one thousand years (the Millennium Kingdom).
- o   Then after the thousand-year reign the final judgment occurs.
- o   Then eternity in the new heavens and new earth.

The greatest problem premillennialists have is Revelation 1:1 and 1:3 where it is stated that these things will happen shortly and soon. To understand this, I would suggest we need to keep in mind what it says in Psalm 90:4:

> "For a thousand years in thy sight are but as yesterday when it is past, and as a watch in the night."

To the LORD a thousand years is like a nights watch or even shorter yet, a day that has past. If you are as old as I am, you know how fast the days in the past fly by; so two thousand years is nothing to Him.

If the early dating of the book of Revelation is correct then it could be argued that many of these events did happen in 70 A.D., shortly after John had written them. But it needs to be emphasized that they would have been only a **partial** or **incomplete** fulfillment of them, which were to validate the later and complete fulfillment still to come. As I stated earlier, this is a common practice with Bible prophecy. Here is a good example.

The Prophecy Puzzle

Isaiah 7:14

Therefore the Lord himself shall give you a sign;
Behold, a virgin shall conceive, and bear a son, and
shall call his name Immanuel.

This had a near, incomplete fulfillment in the time of Isaiah's life. The birth of his son was the fulfilled it (Isaiah 8:1 – 4). But that wasn't the true fulfillment of it for in the gospel of Matthew it tells us it is about the miracle birth of Christ Jesus.

Matthew 1:18 – 23

Now the birth of Jesus Christ was on this wise: When as his mother Mary was espoused to Joseph, before they came together, she was found with child of the Holy Ghost.
19 Then Joseph her husband, being a just man, and not willing to make her a publick example, was minded to put her away privily.
20 But while he thought on these things, behold, the angel of the Lord appeared unto him in a dream, saying, Joseph, thou son of David, fear not to take unto thee Mary thy wife: for that which is conceived in her is of the Holy Ghost.
21 And she shall bring forth a son, and thou shalt call his name JESUS: for he shall save his people from their sins.
22 Now all this was done, that it might be fulfilled which was spoken of the Lord by the prophet, saying,
23 Behold, a virgin shall be with child, and shall bring forth a son, and they shall call his name Emmanuel, which being interpreted is, God with us.

The Prophecy Puzzle

CHAPTER TWO

Grace and Peace from the Father, Son and Holy Spirit – Revelation 1:4 – 8

****

Revelation 1:4 – 6

"John to the seven churches which are in Asia: Grace be unto you, and peace, from him which is, and which was, and which is to come; and from the seven Spirits which are before his throne;
5 And from Jesus Christ, who is the faithful witness, and the first begotten of the dead, and the prince of the kings of the earth. Unto him that loved us, and washed us from our sins in his own blood,
6 And hath made us kings and priests (kingdom of priests) unto God and his Father; to him be glory and dominion for ever and ever. Amen."

The Prophecy Puzzle

John begins his letter to the seven churches by giving them the greeting of grace and peace. Grace was the common greeting in Greek and peace (shalom in Hebrew) was the common greeting in Hebrew. That is a nice greeting coming from anyone; but it amazing when one stops to realize that this is coming from YHWH, the one true living God.

The most important thing to notice in this passage is that it is from YHWH, the Triune God - the "Trinity" (v. 4b – 5a):

- "Him who is and who was and who is to come" - God the Father.
- The "seven Spirits who are before the throne" - Holy Spirit.
    - The number seven is symbolic of complete or perfect.
- Christ Jesus.

I don't believe it was an accident that **God describes Himself** as He does in these opening verses. He knows that the most common error about Him is that His triune nature is misunderstood. Throughout the book of Revelation YHWH's triune nature is emphasized. This only makes sense, because as I stated earlier the book of Revelation is about the revealing of Jesus Christ (YHWH).

In this passage we learn the following things about Christ Jesus. He is:

- The faithful witness:
    - Jesus Christ revealed everything the Father gave Him to reveal to us. Nothing more, nothing less! (John 5:19).
- The first-born of the dead:
    - Others such as Lazarus had risen from the dead before Jesus Christ did, but not in a glorified resurrected body, never to die again.

The Prophecy Puzzle

- - -
            - The resurrection is proof that Jesus of Nazareth is the Messiah (Acts 13:32 – 37, Romans 1:4).
        - It is a reference to His status (a title, like king), not just a reference to His being the first to rise from the dead with a glorified body (Colossians 1:15).
            - We see this demonstrated elsewhere in the Bible such as with Ephraim, who in Jer. 31:9 is said to be YHWH's "first-born". We know that is a figure of speech indicating their position with YHWH, because many people and nations were born long before Ephraim came into existence.
            - If one wants to make Ephraim refer to the man instead of the nation we see according to Genesis 41:50 – 52 he was the second-born son of Joseph, not the first.

- The Ruler of the kings of the earth (Rev. 19:16).
- The One who loved/loves us.
    - His love is continually on all who have called upon Him as their Savior and LORD (Romans 8:31 – 39).
- The One who released and cleansed us from our sin.
    - By the shedding of His Blood on the cross (Hebrews 10:14, 1Peter 1:18 - 19).
- The One who has made us a kingdom of priests.
    - We (born-again Christians) are indeed priests and I believe there are correlations between the duties of the Old Testament priests and Christians today. Here are some comparisons:

The Prophecy Puzzle

<u>PRIESTLY DUTIES</u> for the O.T. priests (sons of Aaron) and N.T. priest (Christians):
- UPKEEP OF TEMPLE:
    - O.T. priests: Num. 3:38; 4:5 – 15, Josh. 3:6 – 17
    - N.T. priests (Christians): 1Cor. 6:19 – 20
- KEEP THE LIGHT ON:
    - Exodus 27:20 – 21
    - Matthew 5:14 – 16
- BURNING INCENSE:
    - Exodus 30:7 – 8
    - Revelation 5:8, 8:3
- OFFER SACRIFICES:
    - Leviticus 1:1 – 17
    - Romans 12:1, Philippians 4:18, 1Peter 2:5
- BLESS PEOPLE:
    - Numbers 6:23 – 27
    - Romans 10:13 – 15
- PURIFY THE UNCLEAN:
    - Leviticus 15:15 – 31
    - 1 Thessalonians 2:4, Acts 15:6 – 11
- DIAGNOSING DISEASE:
    - Leviticus 13:2 – 59
    - Ephesians 5:11, 1Corinthians 5:9 – 13, Gal. 5:19 – 21
- BLOWING TRUMPETS:
    - Numbers 10:1 – 10
    - Hebrews 10:24 – 25, Ephesians 6:10 – 12
- TEACH:
    - Leviticus 10:11
    - Matthew 28:19

The Prophecy Puzzle

There is one last point that needs to be emphasized from this passage in Revelation and that is that Jesus Christ is the one who deserves and will receive all the glory and dominion forever and ever.

The next two verses we read, Revelation 1:7 – 8 truly proclaim the whole book of Revelation in a nutshell.

Revelation 1:7 – 8

"7 Behold, he cometh with clouds; and every eye shall see him, and they also which pierced him: and all kindreds of the earth shall wail because of him. Even so, Amen.
8 I am Alpha and Omega, the beginning and the ending, saith the Lord, which is, and which was, and which is to come, the Almighty."

The three main events of the book of Revelation are:
1. The return of Christ Jesus to the earth in view of everyone.
2. The coming of YHWH's wrath on the earth, which will result in the grieving and wailing of those on the earth at that time.
3. The complete revealing of YHWH; Father, Son and Holy Spirit.

I would like to look at the revealing of YHWH. The text itself gives us a hint of the plurality of the one speaking in verse eight. Some believe this is God the Father speaking, while others believe this is Jesus Christ speaking. The truth is that it could be either one.

Those who believe that God the Father is saying v. 8 would look to verses like Rev. 1:4, which describes God the Father as the One who is, was and is to come.

The Prophecy Puzzle

Revelation 21:22

"And I saw no temple therein: for the Lord God
Almighty and the Lamb are the temple of it."

We see that there is a distinction made between "the Almighty" and the Lamb. So "the Almighty" in Rev. 1:8 would have to be God the Father.

Those who believe that God the Son, Jesus Christ is the one speaking would state that grammatically it would refer to the one most recently being spoken of, which was Jesus Christ in v. 7. They would also look to verses such as:

Revelation 2:8

"And unto the angel of the church in Smyrna write;
These things saith the first and the last, which was
dead, and is alive;"

In this verse it is clear that Christ Jesus speaking, because God the Father has never been dead. Their point is that "the first and last" means the same thing as "the Alpha and the Omega", so it must be Jesus Christ speaking in Rev. 1:8.

The confusion arises because of the plurality of YHWH, which will be revealed more fully throughout the book of Revelation.

Most of the remainder of the book of Revelation is simply giving more detail of these two events mentioned in verses 7 and 8, the coming of Jesus Christ in judgment and the revealing of YHWH. This is a common method in Jewish writing called parallelism and we will see it repeated several times throughout the book of Revelation.

The Prophecy Puzzle

Before we move on I would like to take a moment to demonstrate that this idea of YHWH being more than one person is not something new, only found in the book of Revelation. Here are a few verses/passages that reveal that there is more than one individual who are YHWH.

Genesis 1:1

"In the beginning God created the Heaven and the earth."

- The word translated "God" here is "Elohim", which is actually the plural noun for God, "Gods".

- We have a plural noun used with a singular verb. That should at the very least cause us to stop and take note of it.

Genesis 1:26

"And God said, Let us make man in our image, after our likeness: and let them have dominion over the fish of the sea, and over the fowl of the air, and over the cattle, and over all the earth, and over every creeping thing that creepeth upon the earth."

- Here we have God (Elohim) using plural pronouns to refer to Himself.

- Again we have plural pronouns being used with singular verbs.

- Incidentally the "us" and "our" cannot refer to the angels, because we are not made in the image of angels, but of God.
    - Gen. 1:27: "His (singular) image."

The Prophecy Puzzle

Genesis 19:24

"Then the LORD (YHWH) rained upon Sodom and upon Gomorrah brimstone and fire from the LORD (YHWH) out of heaven;"

- Here we have two YHWHs. One is in heaven and one on the earth.

- The key word here is "from". YHWH rained brimstone from YHWH.

1 Samuel 3:21

"And the LORD appeared again in Shiloh: for the LORD revealed himself to Samuel in Shiloh by the word of the LORD."

- YHWH appeared in Shiloh revealing himself as "the word of YHWH," who is Jesus Christ (John 1:1, Rev. 19:13).

Psalms 149:2

"Let Israel rejoice in <u>him</u> that made him: let the children of Zion be joyful in their King."

- In the Hebrew "him" is in the plural. It literally says, "Let Israel rejoice in <u>them</u> who made him."

The Prophecy Puzzle

Jeremiah 23:5 – 6

"Behold, the days come, saith the LORD, that I will raise unto David a righteous Branch, and a King shall reign and prosper, and shall execute judgment and justice in the earth.
6 In his days Judah shall be saved, and Israel shall dwell safely: and this is his name whereby he shall be called, THE LORD OUR RIGHTEOUSNESS."

- The righteous branch, the King who will reign is Christ Jesus. In verse 6 we are told that His name is the LORD (YHWH) our Righteousness."
- Also in support of this we see in Phil. 2:9, "Wherefore God also hath highly exalted him, and given him a name which is above every name:"
    - Note it does **not** say that Jesus' name was made higher than all others, but He was **given** the name which is higher than all others.
    - Whose name is higher than any other?
        - There only can be one name above all others.
        - That name is YHWH.
            - Ps 148:13, "Let them praise the name of the LORD (YHWH): for his name alone is excellent (sagab: exalted); his glory is above the earth and heaven. (Parenthesis added)
    - Christ Jesus is given the name YHWH, for He is YHWH (the self-existent, eternal God); as is the Holy Spirit and the Father.

The Prophecy Puzzle

Before I leave Revelation 1:7 – 8, I would like to make sure that no one overlooks three little words at the end of verse 7, they are, "Even so, Amen". They could be translated as "So be it! Yes it is so, so be it! Their purpose is to emphasize that YHWH is God and He is righteous and sovereign, and therefore is fully authorized to carry out the judgments in this book. This is plainly stated later in Revelation 19:1 – 6, 11.

I think this would be a good time to read Psalm 96 for I believe it is the perfect lead into a study on the book of Revelation.

Psalms 96

> "O sing unto the LORD a new song: sing unto the LORD, all the earth.
> 2 Sing unto the LORD, bless his name; shew forth his salvation from day to day.
> 3 Declare his glory among the heathen, his wonders among all people.
> 4 For the LORD is great, and greatly to be praised: he is to be feared above all gods.
> 5 For all the gods of the nations are idols: but the LORD made the heavens.
> 6 Honour and majesty are before him: strength and beauty are in his sanctuary.
> 7 Give unto the LORD, O ye kindreds of the people, give unto the LORD glory and strength.
> 8 Give unto the LORD the glory due unto his name: bring an offering, and come into his courts.
> 9 O worship the LORD in the beauty of holiness: fear before him, all the earth.

The Prophecy Puzzle

10 Say among the heathen that the LORD reigneth: the world also shall be established that it shall not be moved: he shall judge the people righteously.
11 Let the heavens rejoice, and let the earth be glad; let the sea roar, and the fulness thereof.
12 Let the field be joyful, and all that is therein: then shall all the trees of the wood rejoice
13 Before the LORD: for he cometh, for he cometh to judge the earth: he shall judge the world with righteousness, and the people with his truth."

The Prophecy Puzzle

The Prophecy Puzzle

CHAPTER THREE

The Introduction to the Letter Written to the Seven Churches – Revelation 1:9 – 20

****

Revelation 1:9

"I John, who also am your brother, and companion in tribulation, and in the kingdom and patience of Jesus Christ, was in the isle that is called Patmos, for the word of God, and for the testimony of Jesus Christ."

We find John imprisoned on the island of Patmos. He was there for two reasons, the word of God (the Bible) and the testimony of Jesus Christ.

The Prophecy Puzzle

Many religions use the Bible today. In fact the "New-agers" love the Bible, but they take it out of context and twist the clear meaning of the Scriptures. Most people today do not have too much of a problem with the Bible, unless one insists on it being the true infallible Word of God. But what really gets people in an uproar is if someone says that Jesus Christ is God in the flesh (Emanuel - Mat. 1:23, 1 John 4:3) and that He is the **only way** to the Father (John 14:6, Acts 4:12). John of course believed and professed both of these facts and they are the reason he was imprisoned.

The fact that Christ Jesus is God in the flesh is such a crucial truth that Satan has attached it probably more than any other. But the LORD has given the clarity if we look closely. Take 1 John 4:2 for example.

> 1 John 4:2
>
> "Hereby know ye the Spirit of God: Every spirit that confesseth that Jesus Christ is come in the flesh is of God:"

Note that it says that one must confess that Jesus Christ **is come** in the flesh. Most modern translations miss the whole idea of Jesus Christ coming in the flesh. They just say one must confess Jesus, but which Jesus? What about Jesus? Of the few modern translations that include His coming in the flesh, most have it in the past tense, missing the point that Jesus Christ is in the flesh **today**. Most importantly that He rose **bodily** from the grave, not just spiritually (Luke 24:37 – 43, John 20:27). The Greek is clearly in the perfect tense indicating something that happened in the past and continues on into the future. There is one modern translation that I know of that does a good job of translating this verse. It is the International Standard Version (ISV):

The Prophecy Puzzle

1 John 4:2 ISV

"This is how you can recognize God's Spirit: Every spirit who acknowledges that Jesus the Messiah has become human—and remains so—is from God."

The **bodily** resurrection of Jesus Christ is an essential doctrine of the Christian faith, and it is constantly being attacked by Satan.

Another essential of Christianity is the divinity of Jesus Christ. If this is something you struggle with I strongly recommend Dr. Robert Morey's book, "The Trinity – Evidence and Issues". We already looked at this issue, but you might like to also look at: Isaiah 9:6; 43:10, 11; Micah 5:2; John 1:1; 20:28; Romans 9:5; Col. 2:9; Heb. 1:5 – 8.

The divinity of Jesus Christ is not the only controversy in this small passage. Verse 10 brings up two additional points of debate.

Revelation 1:10

"I was in the Spirit on the Lord's day, and heard behind me a great voice, as of a trumpet,"

The first point of debate is what does John mean by, "I was in the Spirit". A literal translation of the Greek would be, "I became a spirit." I think it is referring to John being allowed into the "dimension of heaven," the spiritual realm if you will. This would be similar to what we see Steven experiencing in Acts 7:55 – 56 and Paul in 2 Corinthians 12:2 – 4.

The Prophecy Puzzle

The other point of controversy is what John meant by, "The Lord's Day." Some believe this means, "the day of the Lord (the Great tribulation). This is not the case. John uses the "the Lord's Day" just as we do today as a reference to Sunday (or Saturday for some).

Sunday was the day, which the early church met on to worship in recognition of Jesus Christ rising from the dead on the first day of the week (John 20:19, Acts 20:7). So John was simply saying that he was praying on Sunday. But this is a minor issue and truly not worth arguing over.

Revelation 1:11

> "Saying, I am Alpha and Omega, the first and the last: and, What thou seest, write in a book, and send it unto the seven churches which are in Asia; unto Ephesus, and unto Smyrna, and unto Pergamos, and unto Thyatira, and unto Sardis, and unto Philadelphia, and unto Laodicea."

Jesus Christ gave John instructions to send this letter to <u>all seven churches</u>. Note that it is a single letter (scroll) "send **it** to the seven churches". It does not say "them". This is important to note, because it is essential for the correct understanding of the letter. Each church would have received and read the whole letter as it was passed from church to church in the order they were listed in verse eleven.
This fact gives us insight into the multiple levels of meaning within this letter, such as:

- The whole letter had relevance to each church (Revelation 3:22).

The Prophecy Puzzle

- The portion of the letter written to each individual church applies to it individually.
- The whole letter was written to "those who have an ear".
    - So the whole letter could apply to any individual.
- Finely it is believed by some that the seven letters together in the order they are given, layout the entire history of the Christian church.
    - We will go into this in greater detail in chapter thirteen.

Revelation 1:12 – 20

"12 And I turned to see the voice that spake with me. And being turned, I saw seven golden candlesticks;
13 And in the midst of the seven candlesticks one like unto the Son of man, clothed with a garment down to the foot, and girt about the paps with a golden girdle.
14 His head and his hairs were white like wool, as white as snow; and his eyes were as a flame of fire;
15 And his feet like unto fine brass, as if they burned in a furnace; and his voice as the sound of many waters.
16 And he had in his right hand seven stars: and out of his mouth went a sharp twoedged sword: and his countenance was as the sun shineth in his strength.
17 And when I saw him, I fell at his feet as dead. And he laid his right hand upon me, saying unto me, Fear not; I am the first and the last:
18 I am he that liveth, and was dead; and, behold, I am alive for evermore, Amen; and have the keys of hell and of death.

The Prophecy Puzzle

> 19 Write the things which thou hast seen, and the things which are, and the things which shall be hereafter;
> 20 The mystery of the seven stars which thou sawest in my right hand, and the seven golden candlesticks. The seven stars are the angels of the seven churches: and the seven candlesticks which thou sawest are the seven churches."

There is so much here, this passage alone could be a book in and of itself. Let's start off with what John sees. The first thing John sees is a group of seven candlesticks (lamp-stands). These lamp-stands represent the seven churches (v. 20).

It is important to point out that the lamp-stands <u>hold</u> the light-source. They are not the light source. This is important, because the church as a whole or we as individual Christians are not the source of light, but simply the vessel YHWH chooses to use to bear <u>His</u> light.

Next John sees Jesus Christ. Jesus Christ is dressed in the attire of the high priest (v. 13; Lev. 16:4, 24 – 25). This is significant, because **Jesus Christ is our high priest** today and forever (Heb. 4:14).

John sees Jesus Christ having white hair (v. 14), which symbolizes purity (Isaiah 1:18). He also has eyes like flaming fire, which are often said to represent His omniscience and ability to see into the heart of a person, but I cannot find any Scripture to validate that view. Looking at Revelation 19:12 – 15 and other verses like Exodus 24:17, Deut. 4:24 and 9:3; I believe the correct understanding of the eyes like flaming fire is that they indicate that **Jesus Christ is coming in Judgment**.

The Prophecy Puzzle

Some have linked Jesus Christ's feet of glowing white brass to judgment as well, because brass is also a symbol of judgment, I do not believe that is what is being communicated here. The Greek word is "chalkolibanon," which literally means "white brass". According to Suidas, it was "more precious than gold." It is believed to have been a mixture of gold, silver, and brass. Based on this understanding I believe the point being made about **Jesus Christ's feet is that they are pure**. As I mentioned earlier white is symbolic of purity. The high priest entered the Holy of Holies with bare feet, just as Jesus Christ's feet are and they are white symbolizing His perfect holiness (purity). From the description given us in these two verses it is indicating that **Jesus Christ is pure (holy) from head to toe** and He is coming in judgment.

John also gives us a description of Jesus Christ's voice in v. 15b. He says that it is loud, like the sound of many waters. If you have ever been to Niagara Falls you have a hint of what John is speaking of here. But more important than just being loud it is similar to how YHWH describes His own voice.

Job 40:9

"Hast thou an arm like God? or canst thou thunder with a voice like him?"

John's description of Jesus Christ also has a double-edged sword coming out of His mouth. This of course is not a literal sword, but it is symbolic of the Word of God (Ephesians 6:17, Hebrews 4:12).

The Prophecy Puzzle

Let's summarize the meaning of how Christ Jesus appears to John.
1. Jesus Christ is our high priest.
2. He is coming in judgment.
3. He is holy from head to foot.
4. He speaks with the voice of God, because He is God.

What John sees with Jesus Christ is also important. Thankfully they are explained to us in v. 20. The seven lamp-stands (candlesticks) are the seven churches (v. 11). The seven stars that He is holding are the seven angels of the seven churches. There is some debate over if these are literal angels or something else. The word "angel" is a transliteration of a transliteration and it really simply means "messenger". There are cases when it means a spiritual being, but the context usually makes that clear. Here I believe it is referring to the pastors of each of the churches.

John's reaction to seeing all of this is one of such fear that he falls down as if he was dead. This is a common reaction when people encounter the living God (Gen. 17:3, Job 42:6, Ez. 1:28, 3:23). This reaction is often followed with YHWH comforting the individual as Jesus Christ does here as He touches John.

This passage is filled with important facts and issues to understand, but understanding the meaning of how Jesus Christ describes Himself has to be near the top. He describes Himself as:
- The "first and the last" indicating that He is God (YHWH) (v. 17).
  - The eternal one (Exodus 3:14, Isaiah 43:10).
- The living one, who has conquered death (v. 18a).
  - The source of eternal life (Isaiah 9:6, 1Cor. 15:54 – 57, 1 John 5:11 – 12).

The Prophecy Puzzle

- The one who was dead (v. 18b).
    - Reference to Jesus Christ's sacrificial death / crucifixion.
- The one who has the keys to death and hell (v. 18c).
    - He has power and control over death and hell (John 5:22, Revelation 20:11 – 14).

The overall point of these two verses is that Jesus Christ is God (YHWH). And it is because of this fact that John is told to write:
- The things that he had seen (chapter one).
- The things that are (chapters two and three).
- The things that will happen in the future (chapters four through twenty-two).

The Prophecy Puzzle

The Prophecy Puzzle

CHAPTER FOUR

The Letter to the Seven Churches –
Revelation 2:1 – 3:22

****

As I mentioned before, the letter to the seven churches has <u>four</u> dimensions to it:

1. It is written to the specific church mentioned in the letter.
2. It has a message to all seven churches as a whole, for each church would receive the whole letter, which contained all seven messages. So each section addressed to a specific church can apply to all churches then and **<u>now</u>** (v. 7).
3. It is written to "all who have an ear," that is to us as individuals.

The Prophecy Puzzle

4. The fourth dimension is debatable, but it would seem that they do give an outline of church history.

Revelation 2:1 – 7

"Unto the angel of the church of Ephesus write; These things saith he that holdeth the seven stars in his right hand, who walketh in the midst of the seven golden candlesticks;
2 I know thy works, and thy labour, and thy patience, and how thou canst not bear them which are evil: and thou hast tried them which say they are apostles, and are not, and hast found them liars:
3 And hast borne, and hast patience, and for my name's sake hast laboured, and hast not fainted.
4 Nevertheless I have somewhat against thee, because thou hast left thy first love.
5 Remember therefore from whence thou art fallen, and repent, and do the first works; or else I will come unto thee quickly, and will remove thy candlestick out of his place, except thou repent.
6 But this thou hast, that thou hatest the deeds of the Nicolaitans, which I also hate.
7 He that hath an ear, let him hear what the Spirit saith unto the churches; To him that overcometh will I give to eat of the tree of life, which is in the midst of the paradise of God."

According to Jesus Christ the church in Ephesus was doing five things correctly.

The Prophecy Puzzle

1. They were working for the advancement of the kingdom.
2. They were persevering in their faith.
3. They did not accept evil within their fellowship.
4. They tested the teachings of the preachers against the Holy Scriptures.
5. They hated the deeds of the Nicolaitans.

I think we need to examine these more closely to understand exactly what Jesus Christ meant.

The first one is fairly straightforward. They were working to advance the kingdom of heaven. They were witnessing to nonbelievers and strengthening each other.

Secondly, Jesus Christ commends them for keeping their faith even when persecution and the pressures of the world had come against them.

Thirdly, Jesus Christ commends them for not allowing evil to run free in their congregation, as we see happening in the Corinthian church (1Cor. 5:1 – 2) and too many churches today.

Fourthly, they were testing the preachers to see if what they said agreed with the Word of God. It is crucial that we continually test all teachings by comparing them to the Word of God **in context**. Paul praises the Bereans for doing exactly that (Acts 17:11). I cannot emphasize "**in context**" enough. The Bible can be made to say most anything when it is taken out of its original context.

Jesus Christ also brings up the point that some were coming to them saying that they were apostles, but were not true apostles. This is an

The Prophecy Puzzle

issue that might step on a few toes, but I feel it is an important enough issue to express my opinion.

It is my belief based on Scripture that there have been only twelve apostles of Christ Jesus. Yes in the general sense of the meaning of the word anyone who is sent out from a church is an apostle. Some refer to these apostles as "Apostles of the Church", but they are different from the "Apostles of Christ." I'm speaking of the position of authority and leadership, which the twelve apostles (the Apostles of Christ) had. When John died, that was the end of **the** apostles. Here in this passage anyone claiming to be an apostle in the sense of the twelve apostles is said to be a false apostle; the same is said of them in 2Cor. 11:13. Also in Rev. 21:14 it makes reference to the "**twelve** names of the **twelve** apostles". One last point to make on this issue is that I do not know of anyone in the past or present that possesses and consistently practices the "signs of an apostle" - "signs and wonders and miracles" (2Cor. 12:12).

The last thing they were doing correctly will take a little more study to understand. What does it mean that they hated the deeds of the Nicolaitans? There are some who try to say that what the Nicolaitans were guilty of was sexual immorality, but that cannot be the case, because in Rev. 2:14 and 15 they are viewed as separate problems. In v. 14 John condemns the committing of sexual immorality and then in v. 15 he condemns the teaching of the Nicolaitans. So the teaching of the Nicolaitans must be something different than the sexual immorality of v. 14. The same reasoning will lead to the conclusion that the doctrine of Balaam and the doctrine of the Nicolaitans cannot be the same thing. I believe the correct understanding of what the Nicolaitans were doing, that YHWH hated, is found in the meaning of the name. The name, Nicolaitans is formed from two words in the Greek, "*nikao*", which

The Prophecy Puzzle

means, "to conquer", and "*laos*", which means, "the laity or people". So from that we can conclude that the Nicolaitans were forming a group (clergy), which ruled over the laity.

In and of itself that doesn't seem so terrible that YHWH should hate it so, but let us look at this a little deeper. The natural result of having a clergy above the laity is that the laity now has to go to or through the clergy to get to God. And if there is one thing YHWH hates is someone putting themselves between Him and his people. Let's look at a couple verses that make this point.

Galatians 4:17

> "They zealously affect (desire) you, but not well; yea, they would exclude you, that ye might affect (desire) them."

Paul is referring to the Judaizers who were trying to persuade the Christians to be circumcised and follow them instead of Paul and the gospel of Grace he had shared with them. The ultimate purpose of people putting themselves between God and people is always the same, and that is to draw people to themselves so they can guide (control) them. Coincidently, this seems to always result in some kind of financial gain for those in power as well. This type of leadership is completely contrary to the instructions YHWH has given us in His Word.

Matthew 23:8 – 10

> "But be not ye called Rabbi: for one is your Master, even Christ; and all ye are brethren.

The Prophecy Puzzle

> 9 And call no man your father upon the earth: for one is your Father, which is in heaven.
> 10 Neither be ye called masters: for one is your Master, even Christ."

Mark 10:42 – 44

> "But Jesus called them to him, and saith unto them, Ye know that they which are accounted to rule over the Gentiles exercise lordship over them; and their great ones exercise authority upon them.
> 43 But so shall it not be among you: but whosoever will be great among you, shall be your minister:
> 44 And whosoever of you will be the chiefest, shall be servant of all."

YHWH has made it abundantly clear that there is only one mediator between God and mankind.

1 Timothy 2:5 – 6

> "For there is one God, and one mediator between God and men, the man Christ Jesus;
> 6 Who gave himself a ransom for all, to be testified in due time."

As verse six alludes to Jesus Christ had to die a horrible death on a cross in order to make that access to the Father possible. This fact was demonstrated to be true by the veil that separated the Holy of Holies being torn from the **top** to the bottom when Jesus Christ died.

The Prophecy Puzzle

Matthew 27:50 – 51

> "Jesus, when he had cried again with a loud voice, yielded up the ghost.
> 51 And, behold, the veil of the temple was rent in twain from the top to the bottom; and the earth did quake, and the rocks rent;"

Because of Christ Jesus' sacrificial death, and **only** because of it, we can go directly to the Father.

Hebrews 4:14 – 16

> "Seeing then that we have a great high priest, that is passed into the heavens, Jesus the Son of God, let us hold fast our profession.
> 15 For we have not an high priest which cannot be touched with the feeling of our infirmities; but was in all points tempted like as we are, yet without sin.
> 16 Let us therefore come boldly unto the throne of grace, that we may obtain mercy, and find grace to help in time of need."

For someone to prevent someone else from going directly to the Father by putting themselves between God and that person is unthinkable. This is especially true when we remember what YHWH had to do to provide this precious access.

Now we need to look at what they did wrong. Jesus Christ says they did only one thing wrong. They had left their first love (v. 4). But again, what does that mean? How was it evident in their lives?

The Prophecy Puzzle

There have been many answers given, but I believe the best answer is the combining of two popular answers. On one side of the coin is our love for God and on the other side of that same coin is how we express that love – our love for our fellow Christian.

There is something to be said for the feelings of love. The hating of being apart, the joy and comfort of being in the presence of a loved one and that could be part of what Jesus Christ is speaking of here. He is simply saying that they are not spending enough time with Him in prayer and study of His Word.

Any man who has been married for any length of time knows firsthand what Jesus Christ is talking of here. When a wife comes to her husband and says:

- "I want us to spend more time together."
- "I want us to just talk more."
- "I want to be part of your world."

They are saying what Jesus Christ could be expressing to the Church in Ephesus and to us.

The other side of that same coin is summed up in 1 John 4:20 – 21:

> 1 John 4:20 – 21
>
> "If a man say, I love God, and hateth his brother, he is a liar: for he that loveth not his brother whom he hath seen, how can he love God whom he hath not seen? 21 And this commandment have we from him, That he who loveth God love his brother also."

The Prophecy Puzzle

Their first love was a love for God, but one of the ways, that love is expressed is by loving the believers around you (John 13:34 – 35). Loving each other is the greatest witness we can have in our community. I personally think the church spends too much time, money and energy trying to "love" the people outside the church and not nearly enough on loving those within the church (John 13:34 – 35). This could have been the problem with the Christians in Ephesus.

They were doing all the right things and held to all the right doctrines, but they were so busy learning and doing they didn't have time to love each other or spend time talking with God. It is very hard to love someone if you don't even know his/her name. It is very hard to love someone if you have no idea what his/her needs might be. It is very hard to love someone if you don't have time to talk to them. I think one of Satan's greatest ploys is to keep us so busy doing good things that we don't have the time or energy to really love God or others.

Jesus Christ tells them to remember and to do the things they used to do. Depending on which side of the coin one is on they could be such things as:

- Spending more time alone with YHWH in prayer and Bible study and reading.
- Talking with each other.
- Helping each other.
- Truly loving each other.
    - To love someone is to be involved in their life.
    - To take the time to truly share in the joy and sorrow in their life.

The Prophecy Puzzle

Jesus Christ tells them exactly what will happen if they do not correct this problem. They will lose their lamp-stand (church Rev. 1:20). Remember John 13:34 - 35? Our greatest witness to our community is our love for each other. If we don't love each other the light in our lamp-stand begins to go out. If this is not corrected eventually the church will disappear. A lamp-stand without a light in it might look pretty, but beyond that it is useless.

On the bright side (maybe a little pun intended☺), the one who overcomes will receive eternal life (1:7). If that is the case it is of the utmost importance that we know how to overcome. To answer that let's look at some Scriptures:

John 16:33

> "These things I have spoken unto you, that in me ye might have peace. In the world ye shall have tribulation: but be of good cheer; I have overcome the world."

Christ Jesus is the only person who has ever truly overcome the world.

1 John 4:4

> "Ye are of God, little children, and have overcome them: because greater is he that is in you, than he that is in the world."

The Prophecy Puzzle

1 John 5:11 – 12

> "11 And this is the record, that God hath given to us eternal life, and this life is in his Son.
> 12 He that hath the Son hath life; and he that hath not the Son of God hath not life."

One overcomes by receiving and trusting in the only one who has overcome, Jesus Christ. He is our Savior and LORD (Master/God).

I heard Adrian Rogers tell a story that illustrated the truth of these passages well.

A wealthy man had one child, a son, but his son before he got married or had any children died at war. Some years later the wealthy man's wife died and then he died as well. His will gave instructions that all of his belongings should be auctioned off and that the proceeds should be given to charities. The will also stated that the auction should start with his extensive art collection and that the first painting to be auctioned off was to be a portrait of his son.

The painting of his son wasn't anything special. It wasn't painted by anyone famous. But as ordered by the will, the auctioneer started the auction with the portrait of this man's son. No one wanted to bid on it, except for an old man who was a friend of the family. He had known and loved the man's son when he was just a boy, he bid on the painting and the auctioneer said, "Sold!" Then the auctioneer stated that the auction was over, because the will had stated that whoever bought the picture of the son got everything.

The Prophecy Puzzle

That is how it works with God the Father and all people today. If we receive His Son as our Savior and LORD, we become heirs with Him.

Romans 8:16 – 17

> "The Spirit itself beareth witness with our spirit, that we are the children of God:
> 17 And if children, then heirs; heirs of God, and joint-heirs with Christ; if so be that we suffer with him, that we may be also glorified together."

As we read the message to each of these churches we will notice that Jesus Christ describes Himself differently to each of the churches. This is because each description relates to the situation within each church.

To the church in Ephesus Jesus Christ describes Himself as, "The One who holds the seven stars in His right hand, the One who walks among the seven golden lamp-stands." I believe He does so because it communicates to them that He is holding them in His hands. This should comfort and encourage them to continue to hold to their faith even if it means persecution. Secondly, He tells them that He is in their midst. This too should be a comfort to them. His being with them should encourage them to do what He told them to do, to spend more time with Him in prayer and to love one another, because He is there with them.

In the introduction I stated that each message related to more than just the church it addressed, but to all of the churches. This letter relates to all churches in that <u>all churches</u>:

The Prophecy Puzzle

- Can fall into to the trap of becoming too busy to spend time with God, or knowing and loving their fellow believers.
- Must hold fast to the true faith even during times of persecution.
- Must have members who love each other or it will lose its witness in the community and eventually dissolve (die).

All those things are true for the individual as well. We must be involved in the lives of other believers. It has often been said that a burning hot charcoal, if separated will go out. We need to be an active part of a healthy loving church. That means more than showing up on Sunday mornings. That means being part of the ministry of the church where we are exercising our Spiritual gift(s).

We (if we're born-again) all have at least one Spiritual gift. **For the good of the church** (the body of Christ) we must be exercising it (1Cor. 12:1 – 27). That is the best way we can serve others in our church.

Being part of a church, means knowing and caring about the people in the church. In large churches one can't know and love everyone, but we can know and love someone. I'm also a big believer in small-group Bible studies as a way of getting to know people and being involved in ministry.

Lastly, as we study each church we will discover that the name of each church also relates to the conditions within the church. For example the meaning of the word "Ephesus" is "Maiden of Choice" or "Darling". I think it shows how God the Father feels toward His Son's bride (Revelation 21:1 – 3, 27). For that matter, it also could be referring to how Jesus Christ feels toward His bride – the Church (Rev. 21:9).

The Prophecy Puzzle

We will not discuss the "historic timeline" aspect of the seven churches until Chapter 13.

> Revelation 2:8 – 11
>
> "And unto the angel of the church in Smyrna write; These things saith the first and the last, which was dead, and is alive;
> 9 I know thy works, and tribulation, and poverty, (but thou art rich) and I know the blasphemy of them which say they are Jews, and are not, but are the synagogue of Satan.
> 10 Fear none of those things which thou shalt suffer: behold, the devil shall cast some of you into prison, that ye may be tried; and ye shall have tribulation ten days: be thou faithful unto death, and I will give thee a crown of life.
> 11 He that hath an ear, let him hear what the Spirit saith unto the churches; He that overcometh shall not be hurt of the second death."

Jesus Christ has some good things to say about the church in Smyrna. He said that they were holding to their faith in Him, even under extreme persecution, and that even though they were physically poor, they were spiritually rich.

It is believed that the Christians in Smyrna were being persecuted from both the Jews and the Romans. The Jews had been persecuting them because they had left the Jewish faith, and the Romans would have been persecuting them because they would not worship the emperor as a god.

While the New Testament never directly mentions emperor worship, it was practiced during that time. It is believed that the Roman emperor Caligula (A.D. 37 – 41) was the first to start the practice. He proclaimed himself as a god and had temples built for him. His subjects were required to worship him. It should be pointed out that the people were free to worship any other god they wanted to as long as they also worshiped the emperor as a god. Because of this most people had no problem with the law, but for Christians it was a huge problem.

The practice of emperor worship was loosely enforced at this time, but Smyrna was a stronghold of emperor worship and because the Christians would not worship the emperor as a god they were persecuted.

Now let's look at the persecution from the Jews and the "Synagogue of Satan". This is not the first time Jesus Christ referred to someone being of the "Synagogue of Satan". The first time He did was in eighth chapter of the Gospel of John.

John 8:39 – 44:

> "They answered and said unto him, Abraham is our father. Jesus saith unto them, If ye were Abraham's children, ye would do the works of Abraham.
> 40 But now ye seek to kill me, a man that hath told you the truth, which I have heard of God: this did not Abraham.

> 41 Ye do the deeds of your father. Then said they to him, We be not born of fornication; we have one Father, even God.
> 42 Jesus said unto them, If God were your Father, ye would love me: for I proceeded forth and came from God; neither came I of myself, but he sent me.
> 43 Why do ye not understand my speech? even because ye cannot hear my word.
> 44 Ye are of your father the devil, and the lusts of your father ye will do. He was a murderer from the beginning, and abode not in the truth, because there is no truth in him. When he speaketh a lie, he speaketh of his own: for he is a liar, and the father of it."

Jesus Christ said that these Jews who were trying to kill Him were **of the devil**. Their persecuting Jesus Christ revealed that they were of the devil; and when Paul was persecuting Christians, Jesus Christ stated that he was actually persecuting Him (Acts 9:4). So likewise these Jews who were persecuting the Christians are seen as being of the devil (of the Synagogue of Satan). It must be made perfectly clear that neither Jesus Christ nor I am saying that all Jews are of the devil. Estimates are that as many as the first one hundred thousand Christians were Jewish. What makes anyone of the devil in this context is their persecution of Christians.

Jesus Christ had nothing negative to say to this church. He doesn't report anything that they did wrong. This is the kind of report we all long to receive someday – "Well done good and faithful servant" (Luke 19:17).

The Prophecy Puzzle

Jesus Christ does have what could be seen as discouraging news for them. He tells them that they will be experiencing severe persecution for ten days. But along with the harsh news Jesus Christ encourages them, telling them not to fear. He encourages them to keep their faith, reminding them that even if they are martyred they will receive a crown of life in the next life.

There has been much discussion over what is meant by having ten days of tribulation. Does it mean ten literal days? Does it mean ten periods of persecution? One view is that the days are actually years. If so, it could be referring to the ten years of persecution of Christians by Diocletian. Another view is that it relates to ten different Roman Emperors who lived between 100 A.D. and 313 A.D. I'm not sure and I don't think it is worth arguing over.

Now for the practical application of this letter let's look at how it relates to all churches and to us. Churches as well as individuals must stand for the true faith, even if it means being imprisoned or put to death. I know that sounds so foreign here in the United States, at least at the time that I'm writing this; but I'm afraid soon it will be illegal to read portions of the Bible such as Romans chapters one and two from the pulpit, because it will be considered "hate speech". I've read that such a law already exists in Canada today and some pastors have been fined and even imprisoned.

As individuals we must be reminded that our lives are more than what we see. We have an eternal life, and an eternal purpose! We must be willing to sacrifice temporary comforts for eternal rewards. That means we might have to be sent to prison for attending a church that refuses to compromise the truth of the Bible. It might mean we will be put to death for not denying Christ Jesus. Whatever it means we need to be

The Prophecy Puzzle

prepared for that possibility and have made up our minds before that time is upon us that we will stand with Jesus Christ until the end, no matter what.

<blockquote>

2 Corinthians 13:5 – 6

"Examine yourselves, whether ye be in the faith; prove your own selves. Know ye not your own selves, how that Jesus Christ is in you, except ye be reprobates? 6 But I trust that ye shall know that we are not reprobates."

2 Timothy 4:7

"I have fought a (the) good fight, I have finished my course, I have kept the faith:"

</blockquote>

A Christian's faith is tested in many different ways; persecution is only one of them. The form of the test is not what is important. What is important is that we fight the good fight as Paul did, keeping our faith until the end. We must never lose confidence in the Salvation we have in Christ Jesus (Rom. 6:23; Hebrews 7:25 – 27, 10:14). It is in that confidence that the strength to face death and not deny our LORD is found.

I believe the reason Christ Jesus describes Himself as the <u>first and the last</u>, <u>who was dead</u>, <u>and has come to life</u>, is because of the severe persecution being experienced in the church in Smyrna. Many of those receiving this letter might have to die for their faith. Jesus Christ wanted to remind them that He died, but now He lives; and if they truly believe in Him they too will live again, eternally (John 11:25).

The Prophecy Puzzle

Christ Jesus reminds them of this by stating that the one who overcomes has nothing to fear from the "second death", which is eternity in the lake of fire (Rev. 20:14 – 15). It has been said, "If you are only born once, you will die twice; if you are born twice, you will only die once." One more time, one overcomes the world by being born of God (born-again), by trusting in Jesus Christ as one's personal Savior and LORD.

1 John 5:4

> "For whatsoever is born of God overcometh the world: and this is the victory that overcometh the world, even our faith."

As we face difficulties and even death we must remember that Jesus Christ was dead, but now He lives forevermore, and if we trust in Him we too have nothing to fear from death. We have eternal life.

The name "Smyrna" also has great significance. It means "myrrh" and it is a quite fitting description of this church. Myrrh is a spice that is crushed in order to release its beautiful aroma; once crushed it was used to embalm (preserve) the bodies of deceased people. The church at Smyrna was crushed even to the point of death for some and I believe their faith was like a fine aroma to God. Even though this church was being crushed, its perseverance resulted in more and more people being "eternally preserved" in Christ Jesus.

The Prophecy Puzzle

Revelation 2:12 – 17

"And to the angel of the church in Pergamos write; These things saith he which hath the sharp sword with two edges;
13 I know thy works, and where thou dwellest, even where Satan's seat is: and thou holdest fast my name, and hast not denied my faith, even in those days wherein Antipas was my faithful martyr, who was slain among you, where Satan dwelleth.
14 But I have a few things against thee, because thou hast there them that hold the doctrine of Balaam, who taught Balac to cast a stumblingblock before the children of Israel, to eat things sacrificed unto idols, and to commit fornication.
15 So hast thou also them that hold the doctrine of the Nicolaitans, which thing I hate.
16 Repent; or else I will come unto thee quickly, and will fight against them with the sword of my mouth.
17 He that hath an ear, let him hear what the Spirit saith unto the churches; To him that overcometh will I give to eat of the hidden manna, and will give him a white stone, and in the stone a new name written, which no man knoweth saving he that receiveth it."

Jesus Christ starts His letter to the church in Pergamos by praising them for keeping their faith and confession of Him, even in the face of death. He even mentions by name a Martyr from their church, Antipas. We don't know anymore about Antipas other than what is given here, but what a great honor it is to be publicly referred to by Jesus Christ as "My faithful martyr." It is an honor few, if any of us would chose for

The Prophecy Puzzle

ourselves, but I pray that each of us if ever faced with the choice of denying Christ Jesus and live, or profess Christ and die; would have the faith to boldly profess Christ Jesus as our Savior and LORD.

There is much debate over what Jesus Christ meant by "where Satan dwelleth" (has his throne/seat). Some believe He refers to Pergamos this way, because it was the headquarters of Emperor Worship. Others say that it is because it was the location of the throne to Zeus. Still others believe He was referring to the original Babylonian religion that had been founded by Nimrod (Gen. 10:8 – 9; 11:1 – 4) that thrived there as well. All of these facts are true, but which is the one that caused Jesus Christ to refer to Pergamos as where Satan has his throne? I don't think anyone knows for sure. Perhaps it was because all these things were true of Pergamos. In any case it seems that Satan does have a headquarters on the earth from which he runs his operation. Satan is not omnipresent like God, but can only be in one place at any given moment.

Next we need to look at what Christ Jesus says they did wrong. The first problem He addresses is that they held to the doctrine of Balaam. Balaam was an interesting character who we read about in the book of Numbers, chapters 22 through 24. If that were all we knew of Balaam he would be a hero, but there is more written of him.

Numbers 31:16

> "Behold, these caused the children of Israel, through the counsel of Balaam, to commit trespass against the LORD in the matter of Peor, and there was a plague among the congregation of the LORD."

The Prophecy Puzzle

Here we learn that Balaam told the Moabites that they should entice the Israelite men with their women so they would worship Baal instead of YHWH. This would result in YHWH becoming angry with Israel and His judging them.

2 Peter 2:15

> "Which have forsaken the right way, and are gone astray, following the way of Balaam the son of Bosor, who loved the wages of unrighteousness"

Balaam ended up betraying "God's people" for money and the results of his actions were that the Israelites fell into idolatry and sexual immorality (Num. 25:1 – 3, 31:15 – 16).

What does that mean exactly for the church in Pergamos? What exactly did holding the doctrine of Balaam look like? We're not sure; most believe that some were teaching one could participate in the activities taking place at the pagan temples which involved idolatry and much sexual immorality. This is clearly what is referred to in Rev. 2:14. They probably justified their actions through their Gnostic beliefs. They believed that the flesh was evil and the spirit was good, and therefore only what affected the spirit mattered. They taught one could sin all they wanted to in the flesh, as long as they were "spiritually healthy". When one thinks about it, it isn't much different from today's views of "spirituality" with its new morality where not recycling will condemn you, but sexual immorality is almost impossible to commit.

While it is not stated here, others believe following Balaam's example is a reference to the idea that God's blessing can be purchased (2 Peter

The Prophecy Puzzle

2:15). If that was the case, the doctrine of Balaam would have been seen by the selling of "blessings" and "indulgences", similar to what we see in the Roman Catholic Church, the "Word of Faith Movement" and many others today.

The second point of contention Jesus Christ had with the church in Pergamos was that some held to the doctrine of the Nicolaitans. As we remember from the church in Ephesus, this meant the clergy was ruling over the people (laity) and putting themselves between the "laity" and YHWH. As we discussed earlier this is something YHWH hates (Hebrews 4:14 – 16, 1 Peter 5:1 – 3).

Jesus Christ's instructions to them were simple. They were to Repent! That meant they were to stop introducing pagan teachings into the church like those the Gnostics were teaching, leading people into immoral and destructive behavior. They were to stop "selling God's blessing" (if that was what they were doing). They also had to stop placing individuals in the church as "clergy" above the "laity," in essence putting them between the common person and God.

Christ Jesus warns them that if they do not correct these problems He would fight against them with the sword of His mouth. Which means He would use the Holy Scriptures against them (Eph. 6:17). Jesus Christ would do this by bringing people who knew the Bible to this church to teach the Word of God. Then the church would do one of two things, it would either dissolve as the true Christians leave or the church as a whole would repent and a true revival would take place.

Jesus Christ encourages those who hold onto the Truth (the over-comers), by telling them that they will receive "hidden manna" a "white

The Prophecy Puzzle

stone" and a "new name." But what do these mean and how are they encouraging?

There are at least two possibilities to what Christ Jesus is referring to by the "hidden manna". Some believe He was referring to Himself (John 6:48 – 63), implying that having <u>Him</u> within them results in eternal life. The problem I have with this view is that He says that He will give them "hidden manna" sometime in the future. Since they are Christians, they already have Christ Jesus living within them. Others believe He is making reference to His promise to sustain them because they would not eat the meat sacrificed to idols like the "Balaamites" were promoting (Rev. 2:14).

I think the best explanation is found in John 4:31 – 34 where Jesus Christ makes reference to having secret food. He goes on to explain that the food He is referring to is to do the will of the Father. In the same way Jesus Christ will give the faithful Christians the grace and faith to do the will of the Father.

The white stone also could have different meanings, but most believe it represents a declaration of innocence. While there isn't any Scripture that depicts the use of the white stone in the Bible, we do have the use of white depicting forgiveness or the wiping away of sin in Isaiah 1:18, ".... though your sins be as scarlet, they shall be as white as snow...." If this is the correct understanding of what Jesus Christ means He is telling the true Christians that they will be declared innocent having been cleansed of all of their sin. While technically one has already been declared innocent when they receive Christ Jesus as their Savior and LORD (Romans 5:9 – 11, 8:1), we have not yet stood before God and been declared innocent, and I believe that is what Christ Jesus is referring to here.

The Prophecy Puzzle

What makes this stone even more interesting is that it has a new name written upon it, which is only known by the one who receives it.

> Isaiah 56:3 – 5
>
> "Neither let the son of the stranger, that hath joined himself to the LORD, speak, saying, The LORD hath utterly separated me from his people: neither let the eunuch say, Behold, I am a dry tree.
> 4 For thus saith the LORD unto the eunuchs that keep my sabbaths, and choose the things that please me, and take hold of my covenant;
> 5 Even unto them will I give in mine house and within my walls a place and a name better than of sons and of daughters: I will give them an everlasting name, that shall not be cut off."

His saints will receive a new name just like Abram became Abraham and Sarai became Sarah (Gen. 17:5, 15). Interestingly, the "ah" added to Abram and Sarai in the Hebrew means "spirit." So you could say their new names symbolized the receiving of the Holy Spirit. The new name represents a new relationship with God. It is an eternal relationship, which starts by us receiving eternal life in Christ Jesus and His Holy Spirit living within us (Eph. 1:13 – 14).

I find it truly intriguing to see how Jesus Christ's description of Himself gives added insight into the church He is addressing. Here He describes Himself as the one with a double-edged sword. I believe this is because this church has left the clear doctrines of the Bible (the Holy Scriptures) and He is going to use them against the leaders of this church, which will result in either revival or destruction.

The Prophecy Puzzle

This letter refers to all churches and to us as individuals in that it is a warning not to serve the LORD for the wrong reasons, especially not for personal profit. This is not something to nod our heads to in agreement, without ever examining our lives. I encourage each of us to take a moment to do just that right now. I would hate for any of us to arrive in heaven to only see all of our "good works" burned up before us, because they were all wood, hay and stubble (1Cor. 3:12 – 15).

There are two other warnings all churches and we as individuals must take heed of and they both deal with the gospel of grace. The first is to never compromise the gospel of grace. One cannot mix grace with works/religion. We must always have our guard up against religion. Religion is always tempting to us because it is rooted in human effort, and that is appealing to us, because it relates to our sense of pride.

Ephesians 2:8 – 9

"For by grace are ye saved through faith; and that not of yourselves: it is the gift of God: 9 Not of works, lest any man should boast."

I cannot emphasize that enough. It clearly teaches in Romans 11:6, it's either by grace or works, but **it cannot be both**.

The final warning is against the abuse of grace.

Romans 6:11 – 18

"Likewise reckon ye also yourselves to be dead indeed unto sin, but alive unto God through Jesus Christ our Lord.

12 Let not sin therefore reign in your mortal body, that ye should obey it in the lusts thereof.
13 Neither yield ye your members as instruments of unrighteousness unto sin: but yield yourselves unto God, as those that are alive from the dead, and your members as instruments of righteousness unto God.
14 For sin shall not have dominion over you: for ye are not under the law, but under grace.
15 What then? shall we sin, because we are not under the law, but under grace? God forbid.
16 Know ye not, that to whom ye yield yourselves servants to obey, his servants ye are to whom ye obey; whether of sin unto death, or of obedience unto righteousness?
17 But God be thanked, that ye were the servants of sin, but ye have obeyed from the heart that form of doctrine which was delivered you.
18 Being then made free from sin, ye became the servants of righteousness."

Unfortunately this is a problem in the church today. Too many churches and individuals either out of ignorance or hardness of heart believe that there is absolutely no correlation between salvation and lifestyle. They preach and believe that as long as you have "believed in Jesus Christ" and "asked Him into your heart" you're going to heaven. **If** one is sincere, yes they will, but the Bible is very clear that a true faith will change one's worldview and **behavior**.

The Prophecy Puzzle

1 John 3:10 – 11

"In this the children of God are manifest, and the children of the devil: whosoever doeth not righteousness is not of God, neither he that loveth not his brother.
11 For this is the message that ye heard from the beginning, that we should love one another."

1 Corinthians 6:9 – 11

"Know ye not that the unrighteous shall not inherit the kingdom of God? Be not deceived: neither fornicators, nor idolaters, nor adulterers, nor effeminate, nor abusers of themselves with mankind,
10 Nor thieves, nor covetous, nor drunkards, nor revilers, nor extortioners, shall inherit the kingdom of God.
11 And such were some of you: but ye are washed, but ye are sanctified, but ye are justified in the name of the Lord Jesus, and by the Spirit of our God."

Did you see the encouragement in verse 11? "And such **were** some of you:" YHWH has the power to change anyone. We cannot change ourselves, nor do we need to clean ourselves up before we come to Jesus Christ to be saved. He does the "cleaning" of our behavior after we've been caught; but it might be more accurate to state that we are given a new heart at the moment of conversion and the change in attitude and behavior is evidence of that new heart. That doesn't mean we won't struggle with sin, but it does mean we will not embrace it and live in it.

The Prophecy Puzzle

In Phil. 1:6 it says that Jesus Christ will be faithful to complete the work which He began in us. We are also assured that all who sincerely call out to the LORD, Jesus Christ for salvation will be saved (Romans 10:13). So the point is that if anyone calls out to Jesus Christ to be saved from the coming judgment, believing that Jesus Christ is God in the flesh and that His death was complete payment for the debt their (the individual's) sin deserves, he/she is saved and the Holy Spirit is united with their spirit (He indwells them). And, if the God of the universe(s) is living within someone, He should be evident to others and to oneself. That is the point James is making in James 2:14 – 18.

James 2:14 – 18

> "What doth it profit, my brethren, though a man say he hath faith, and have not works? can faith save him?
> 15 If a brother or sister be naked, and destitute of daily food,
> 16 And one of you say unto them, Depart in peace, be ye warmed and filled; notwithstanding ye give them not those things which are needful to the body; what doth it profit?
> 17 Even so faith, if it hath not works, is dead, being alone.
> 18 Yea, a man may say, Thou hast faith, and I have works: shew me thy faith without thy works, and I will shew thee my faith by my works."

That is why in 2Corinthians 13:5 Paul tells each of us to examine ourselves to see if Jesus Christ truly dwells inside us. If one can comfortably walk in sin, either by denying that something is a sin, which God clearly states is a sin in the Bible, i.e. **any kind** of sex

The Prophecy Puzzle

outside of marriage, or simply ignores sin, not caring what God thinks; they need to check their faith as Paul instructed.

2 Corinthians 13:5

"Examine yourselves, whether ye be in the faith; prove your own selves. Know ye not your own selves, how that Jesus Christ is in you, except ye be reprobates?"

Moving on, the meaning of the word "Pergamos" is "Mixed Marriage". It seems rather self-evident that it is referring to how the Christian church started to mix with the culture and pagan religions around it, incorporating false doctrines and sinful practices.

Revelation 2:18 – 29

"And unto the angel of the church in Thyatira write; These things saith the Son of God, who hath his eyes like unto a flame of fire, and his feet are like fine brass;
19 I know thy works, and charity, and service, and faith, and thy patience, and thy works; and the last to be more than the first.
20 Notwithstanding I have a few things against thee, because thou sufferest that woman Jezebel, which calleth herself a prophetess, to teach and to seduce my servants to commit fornication, and to eat things sacrificed unto idols.
21 And I gave her space to repent of her fornication; and she repented not.

The Prophecy Puzzle

22 Behold, I will cast her into a bed, and them that commit adultery with her into great tribulation, except they repent of their deeds.
23 And I will kill her children with death; and all the churches shall know that I am he which searcheth the reins and hearts: and I will give unto every one of you according to your works.
24 But unto you I say, and unto the rest in Thyatira, as many as have not this doctrine, and which have not known the depths of Satan, as they speak; I will put upon you none other burden.
25 But that which ye have already hold fast till I come.
26 And he that overcometh, and keepeth my works unto the end, to him will I give power over the nations:
27 And he shall rule them with a rod of iron; as the vessels of a potter shall they be broken to shivers: even as I received of my Father.
28 And I will give him the morning star.
29 He that hath an ear, let him hear what the Spirit saith unto the churches."

Jesus Christ has many good things to say about the church in Thyatira and really only addresses one problem with it, though it is a very large problem.

He says that they have done the following things correctly:
- They have good deeds.
- They're doing good things, even great things.
- They have love and faith, even persevering in their faith and devotion to YHWH.

The Prophecy Puzzle

Jesus Christ gave this church many good complements and each of them represented an important characteristic of a healthy church, but they had that one problem. This very large problem the church in Thyatira had was that they tolerated the woman Jezebel. Note it doesn't say that the church as a whole followed her ways, just that they **tolerated** her presence. They didn't promote her teaching; they simply looked the other direction. They ignored the problem while she led people astray.
They should have stopped her in order to protect the church. The pastor and elders of a church have two main functions, to protect and feed the people in the church (John 21:15 – 17).

That brings us to the question of, what did Jezebel do that was so terrible? Well, we can start by reading about her in the book of First Kings chapters 16 – 19. I trust that you will take the time to read those chapters on your own. I will list some of the verses that directly pertain to our study of Jezebel.

 1 Kings 16:31 – 33

> "And it came to pass, as if it had been a light thing for him to walk in the sins of Jeroboam the son of Nebat, that he took to wife Jezebel the daughter of Ethbaal king of the Zidonians, and went and served Baal, and worshipped him.
> 32 And he reared up an altar for Baal in the house of Baal, which he had built in Samaria.
> 33 And Ahab made a grove; and Ahab did more to provoke the LORD God of Israel to anger than all the kings of Israel that were before him."

The Prophecy Puzzle

Jezebel not only promoted the worship of Baal, but also of Astarte. We get that from verse 33. The word translated "grove" literally means "Asherah", which was associated with the worship of the goddess Astarte. She was supposed to be the mother of Baal and the chief goddess of Tyre. When we dig a little deeper we find that Astarte is just one of the many names of the **Queen of Heaven** spoken of in the book of Jeremiah (7:18, 44:17 – 25).

Jeremiah 44:17

> "But we will certainly do whatsoever thing goeth forth out of our own mouth, to burn incense unto the **queen of heaven**, and to pour out drink offerings unto her, as we have done, we, and our fathers, our kings, and our princes, in the cities of Judah, and in the streets of Jerusalem: for then had we plenty of victuals, and were well, and saw no evil." (Emphasis mine)

 She is also worshipped as the goddess Ishtar, Venus and Diana to name a few. If you would like to study this subject more I strongly suggest reading the book, "Queen of All" by Jim Tetlow, Roger Oakland and Brad Myers. There is also a very good DVD, titled "Messages from Heaven" produced by www.eternal-productions.org. It can also be viewed on YouTube.

The worship of Baal and Astarte involved sexual immorality and if we remember back to what Jesus Christ said against this church was that they **tolerated** this woman Jezebel. Unfortunately that is exactly what too many churches are doing today. Many churches today turn a blind eye to all kinds of sexual immorality, even by their leaders.

The Prophecy Puzzle

Jesus Christ addresses two different groups in the church in Thyatira. The first group is made up of those who have followed Jezebel. He tells them to repent! Repentance here means they would turn away from the worship of false/pagan gods and goddesses, and to turn away from sexual immorality. Again they are not to just turn away from these sins, but they are to stand against these sins within the church. Jesus Christ also warns these people and Jezebel that if they don't repent they will be judged.

The second group is made up of those who have not followed Jezebel. Jesus Christ doesn't have anything new to tell them, other than to keep up the good work and to hang in there, UNTIL HE COMES!

This is the first mention of His return to any of the churches. I believe this is the first mention of Christ's return or the rapture in the book of Revelation. We will discuss the rapture and its timing in detail later on in the book. But for now I would like to make just two observations. Though we haven't yet looked at the historical aspect of the seven churches, when we do we will discover that it seems that the first three churches cease to exist before the rapture occurs. Those living during the time of the last four churches will either be raptured or go into the great tribulation.

We also have the first mention of the Millennium Kingdom in verse 26, where these Christians will receive their reward. They will serve Christ Jesus as He reigns with a rod of iron from the throne of David for 1000 years.

Now I should probably just move on, without looking at the details of Rev. 2:26 – 28, because I have a different understanding than most; but as the book goes on you will see that is something I'm not very good at doing. The "He" in verse 27 is a reference to Jesus Christ and it is referring back to Psalm 2:

Psalm 2:8 – 9

> "Ask of me, and I shall give thee the heathen for thine inheritance, and the uttermost parts of the earth for thy possession.
> 9 Thou shalt break them with a rod of iron; thou shalt dash them in pieces like a potter's vessel."

I believe what Jesus Christ is saying, is that the person who overcomes, keeping their faith until the end, will reign with Him with a rod of iron. As I just stated the "He" in verse 27 is referring to Jesus Christ and He will reign over the nations with a rod of iron. I believe the breaking into pieces (Ps. 2:9) is referring to the wrath that will be poured out with the coming of the great tribulation. It needs to be pointed out that the great tribulation refers only to the last half of the seven-year tribulation (Matthew 24:21).

Back to the letter, it relates to all churches and to us as individuals in that we all need to flee sexual immorality (1Cor. 6:18 – 20). And, we as individuals and churches, must do more than just stay clear of false doctrines, we <u>must</u> <u>fight</u> them and prevent them from entering the church. God was angry with the people in the church of Thyatira, because they <u>tolerated</u> false teaching <u>within their church</u>. Yes, we need to be careful not to go overboard. We can't be leaving churches because we don't agree with them over a few secondary issues. I don't believe there is a church in the world that I agree with on every single issue discussed in the Bible, but on the <u>essentials of the Christian faith</u> there must be agreement with Scripture for us to attend that church.

The Prophecy Puzzle

I think now would be as good a time as any to list some essentials of the Christian Faith:

- There is only one God in existence <u>anywhere</u>! His name is YHWH (Isaiah 43:10 – 13; 44:6).
- God exists in the three persons: God the Father, God the "Son" (Jesus Christ) and God the Holy Spirit (Revelation 1:4 - 5).
    - To anyone who would like to study this issue more I recommend the book, "The Trinity – Evidence and Issues" by Robert Morey.
    - It is possibly not to understand this and still be a Christian. The truth is, it is impossible for the finite to understand the infinite. But if someone knowingly argues against the Trinity, that is a problem.
- Jesus of Nazareth was born of a virgin (Mat. 1:18 - 25).
- Jesus of Nazareth is the Messiah (Christ) (Matthew 16:16).
- Christ Jesus is both fully man and fully God (John 1:1, 2, 14, 18; 20:28 Acts 20:28; 2Cor. 5:16; Phil. 2:5 - 7).
- Christ Jesus died and His physical death is full payment of our sins (Acts 20:28; Romans 6:23; 2Corinthians 5:21; Hebrews 10:10 - 14).
- Christ Jesus is the <u>only</u> source of eternal life (John 14:6; Acts 4:12).
- Christ Jesus physically (bodily) rose from the dead as a witness to His dual nature and redemptive work (Luke 24:39 - 43; John 20:26 - 29; Romans 14:9; 1Cor. 15:1 - 8; 2Cor. 5:18 - 20, 1 John 4:3[KJV]).

The Prophecy Puzzle

Getting back to the church in Thyatira, Jesus Christ describes Himself as the Son of God, who has eyes like a flame of fire, and feet like burnished bronze. I think He does so in order to state to the people in the church in Thyatira that He:

- Has authority (v. 27).
- Is holy.
    - His children by His grace will reflect that holiness (v. 23).
- Will someday judge those who don't repent (v. 27).

The word "Thyatira" means "Daughter." I believe this is indicating that it is the offspring of the "Mixed Marriage" of the church of Pergamos, which will make more sense when we look at the historical dimension of the seven churches.

The next church is the church in Sardis.

Revelation 3:1 – 6

> "And unto the angel of the church in Sardis write; These things saith he that hath the seven Spirits of God, and the seven stars; I know thy works, that thou hast a name that thou livest, and art dead.
> 2 Be watchful, and strengthen the things which remain, that are ready to die: for I have not found thy works perfect before God.
> 3 Remember therefore how thou hast received and heard, and hold fast, and repent. If therefore thou shalt not watch, I will come on thee as a thief, and thou shalt not know what hour I will come upon thee.

The Prophecy Puzzle

> 4 Thou hast a few names even in Sardis which have not defiled their garments; and they shall walk with me in white: for they are worthy.
> 5 He that overcometh, the same shall be clothed in white raiment; and I will not blot out his name out of the book of life, but I will confess his name before my Father, and before his angels.
> 6 He that hath an ear, let him hear what the Spirit saith unto the churches."

It is noteworthy that Christ Jesus doesn't record anything that the church in Sardis did correctly. This might be jumping ahead a little, but I believe that is because of one simple truth, ".... without faith it is impossible to please Him:" (Heb. 11:6).

Their problem is that they are religious, but they do not have a saving faith. Look in verse 2; their works are not perfect before God. Why is that? It's because they are works of the flesh, not of the Spirit.

Romans 8:8

> "So then they that are in the flesh cannot please God."

We see this brought out again in Galatians 3:3. The Galatians had been given the same command:

Galatians 3:1 – 11

> "O foolish Galatians, who hath bewitched you, that ye should not obey the truth, before whose eyes Jesus

The Prophecy Puzzle

Christ hath been evidently set forth, crucified among you?
2 This only would I learn of you, Received ye the Spirit by the works of the law, or by the hearing of faith?
3 Are ye so foolish? having begun in the Spirit, are ye now made perfect by the flesh?
4 Have ye suffered so many things in vain? if it be yet in vain.
5 He therefore that ministereth to you the Spirit, and worketh miracles among you, doeth he it by the works of the law, or by the hearing of faith?
6 Even as Abraham believed God, and it was accounted to him for righteousness.
7 Know ye therefore that they which are of faith, the same are the children of Abraham.
8 And the scripture, foreseeing that God would justify the heathen through faith, preached before the gospel unto Abraham, saying, In thee shall all nations be blessed.
9 So then they which be of faith are blessed with faithful Abraham.
10 For as many as are of the works of the law are under the curse: for it is written, Cursed is every one that continueth not in all things which are written in the book of the law to do them.
11 But that no man is justified by the law in the sight of God, it is evident: for, The just shall live by faith."

Many of the people in the church at Sardis had left the true faith and had embraced religion (a system of works intended to please God – but that is impossible).

The Prophecy Puzzle

Jesus Christ did find several faults with the church in Sardis. The first problem He mentions is that they have a name that indicates that they are alive, but they truly were dead. We just discussed this issue. Many people in the church were not born-again. They were not spiritually alive. Yes, they attended church and even served, but it was all the vain work of the flesh. They had embraced religion, and in so doing left the Savior and His indwelling Holy Spirit behind.

To understand verse 2 correctly we will need to look at the Greek. First of all, what is translated as "Be watchful" in the KJV is a little misleading, because it is actually in the present imperative active, which is better conveyed as "Become watchful", as "Young's Literal Translation" translates it. The second word we need to look at in this verse is the one translated in the KJV, "strengthen". It can also mean "confirm", which I believe, better communicates what is intended in this verse. Next, I would like to look at the word "lŏipŏu" in the Greek, which is translated in the KJV as "the things which remain." Most often this word is translated in such a way to convey personhood. Such as in Rev. 2:24, "the **rest** in Thyatira," or in Rev. 11:13, "the **remnant** were affrighted". I believe it should be translated as such here in Rev. 3:2.

If I could be so bold, in an attempt to bring out the true meaning of this verse, I would like to offer the following paraphrase: "**Wake up**, and **confirm** the **remnant**, those who are ready to die; for I have not found your works perfect before God."

Now with those changes made let's look at the meaning of this passage. Jesus Christ is telling them to wake up! To come to their senses and realize that they need to stop ridiculing and persecuting the few true born-again believers left in their church and embrace them. They need

The Prophecy Puzzle

to become one of them. They need to be born-again, because they cannot work their way into heaven.

Verse 3 expands upon why they need to do this. It is because their works are in the flesh and as we mentioned earlier, it is impossible to please God in the flesh (Romans 8:8). They might be very good in the eyes of people, but not even the best of them can stand justified before God. As Jesus Christ goes on to explain they need to repent and remember back to what they had heard in the beginning – the gospel of grace, just as the Galatians were told to do (Gal. 3:1 – 11).

In verse 3 Jesus Christ also warns them that if they do not repent He will come in judgment at a time they don't know. Once again this will have further significance when we look at the historical dimension of these letters to the seven churches.

Their need to turn from a religion of good works to salvation by grace in Christ Jesus our LORD is further emphasized by Jesus Christ in verse 4. There He explains to them that those few that are born-again, holding to the truth of salvation by grace through faith, not of works are the ones who are truly justified before Him.

Now without understanding the significance of garments in the Bible one could miss the true meaning of verses 4 and 5, but I think a short study on garments will bring out the full meaning.

Revelation 3:4 – 5

> "4 Thou hast a few names even in Sardis which have not defiled their garments; and they shall walk with me in white: for they are worthy.

The Prophecy Puzzle

5 He that overcometh, the same shall be clothed in white raiment; and I will not blot out his name out of the book of life, but I will confess his name before my Father, and before his angels."

Matthew 22:10 – 13

"So those servants went out into the highways, and gathered together all as many as they found, both bad and good: and the wedding was furnished with guests. 11 And when the king came in to see the guests, he saw there a man which had not on a wedding garment: 12 And he saith unto him, Friend, how camest thou in hither not having a wedding garment? And he was speechless.
13 Then said the king to the servants, Bind him hand and foot, and take him away, and cast him into outer darkness; there shall be weeping and gnashing of teeth."

The actions of the king seem rather severe unless we realize that the man would have been offered a "wedding robe" as he arrived. The man either refused the robe or entered the banquet in an illegitimate way. **The wedding garment represented his right to be there.**

Isaiah 61:10

"I will greatly rejoice in the LORD, my soul shall be joyful in my God; for he hath clothed me with the garments of salvation, he hath covered me with the robe of righteousness, as a bridegroom decketh himself

The Prophecy Puzzle

with ornaments, and as a bride adorneth herself with her jewels."

Revelation 6:11

"And white robes were given unto every one of them; and it was said unto them, that they should rest yet for a little season, until their fellow servants also and their brethren, that should be killed as they were, should be fulfilled."

The white robes are **gifts** from God. They represent the **gift** of righteousness (salvation).

Revelation 7:13 – 14

"And one of the elders answered, saying unto me, What are these which are arrayed in white robes? and whence came they?
14 And I said unto him, Sir, thou knowest. And he said to me, These are they which came out of great tribulation, and have washed their robes, and made them white in the blood of the Lamb."

The robes are made white by the blood of Jesus Christ, which was shed for each of us, which brings us to the point in Rev. 3:4 and it is a very important point. **One defiles their robe, by trying to add their own righteousness, via good works, sacraments, etc. to the gift of righteousness offered to all through Jesus Christ** (Romans 3:21 – 26, 6:23, Eph. 2:8 – 9).

The Prophecy Puzzle

Galatians 2:16 – 21

> "Knowing that a man is not justified by the works of the law, but by the faith of Jesus Christ, even we have believed in Jesus Christ, that we might be justified by the faith of Christ, and not by the works of the law: for by the works of the law shall no flesh be justified.
> 17 But if, while we seek to be justified by Christ, we ourselves also are found sinners, is therefore Christ the minister of sin? God forbid.
> 18 For if I build again the things which I destroyed, I make myself a transgressor.
> 19 For I through the law am dead to the law, that I might live unto God.
> 20 I am crucified with Christ: nevertheless I live; yet not I, but Christ liveth in me: and the life which I now live in the flesh I live by the faith of the Son of God, who loved me, and gave himself for me.
> 21 I do not frustrate the grace of God: for if righteousness come by the law, then Christ is dead in vain."

As I stated earlier this is an issue of utmost importance, because most of the members of this church are not born-again believers and that means if they don't repent and trust in Christ Jesus <u>alone</u> as their Savior and LORD, they will spend eternity in the lake of fire.
In Romans we are told that we can't mix works and grace. In Galatians 5:4 it says that if we add works to grace we have severed ourselves from Christ Jesus. We must humbly receive salvation as a **gift** from God.

The Prophecy Puzzle

Galatians 5:2 – 4

> "Behold, I Paul say unto you, that if ye be circumcised, Christ shall profit you nothing.
> 3 For I testify again to every man that is circumcised, that he is a debtor to do the whole law.
> 4 Christ is become of no effect unto you, whosoever of you are justified by the law; ye are fallen from grace."

Back in Revelation 3:5 Jesus Christ again reassures the true believers (the overcomes) that they will be made righteous (receive a white garment) and have eternal life (have his name in the book of life). Remember that one overcomes by being born of God (born-again) through faith in Christ Jesus (1 John 5:4).

The way verse 5 is worded often raises the issue of eternal security. This is a subject I would like to overlook, but I cannot, at least not until I give a brief opinion on the issue.

I think the Bible is clear that one is saved by grace through faith (Eph. 2:8 – 9). The key, which is often overlooked, is that salvation is by grace, but received through faith. This is not a faith that exists for only a moment in time, but one that lasts through good times as well as bad. I think this is made clear several places in Scripture, but the most obvious is in Luke 8:4 – 15, the "Parable of the Sower".

Luke 8:11 – 15

> "Now the parable is this: The seed is the word of God.

> 12 Those by the way side are they that hear; then cometh the devil, and taketh away the word out of their hearts, lest they should believe and be saved.
> 13 They on the rock are they, which, when they hear, receive the word with joy; and these have no root, which for a while believe, and in time of temptation fall away.
> 14 And that which fell among thorns are they, which, when they have heard, go forth, and are choked with cares and riches and pleasures of this life, and bring no fruit to perfection.
> 15 But that on the good ground are they, which in an honest and good heart, having heard the word, keep it, and bring forth fruit with patience."

Verse 12 makes it very clear that ultimately the issue is salvation. The seed is taken away so they will not be saved. In verse 13, the people believe at first, but when temptation or trials come they abandon their faith. The fact that their faith does not survive its testing reveals that it was not a true, genuine, saving faith. Without faith one cannot be saved. **A true saving faith will last until the end!** That is why we see over and over in the book of Revelation the phrase, "He who overcomes…" Paul also makes this point in his last letter to Timothy.

2 Timothy 4:7 – 8

> "I have fought a (**the**) good fight, I have finished my course, I have kept the faith:
> 8 Henceforth there is laid up for me a crown of righteousness, which the Lord, the righteous judge,

The Prophecy Puzzle

shall give me at that day: and not to me only, but unto all them also that love his appearing."

Most translations have translated verse 7 as "the good fight". "Young's Literal Translation" and "the Darby Bible" do so. There is a definite article before "good" in the Greek and it should be **the** good fight, the fight of keeping the faith; which is what Paul goes on to emphasize – "I have kept the faith." The battle is for our faith. The saving faith lasts until the end and a false faith will at some time cease to exist. It is not that one was saved and then loses their salvation, it is just that time and tests reveal the authenticity of one's faith (1 John 2:19). We know this is the case, because we are told in Philippians 1:6 that God will finish the work in a believer that **He** has started. In Matthew 7:21 – 23 we see that it is possible for one to actually live their whole life not recognizing (or perhaps, just not admitting) that their faith is an insincere or false (religious) faith. That is why it is so important that we check the authenticity of our faith now as Paul instructs us to do (2Cor. 13:5).

Once again the name of the church gives added insight to the condition of the church. Here Jesus Christ said they "hast a name that thou livest, and art dead." "Name", in the Greek is ŏnŏma, as in "denomination". All too often we find people saying something like, "I'm saved because I'm a Baptist, Methodist, Catholic," etc. That is the mindset of most of those in the church in Sardis. Being a member of a church does not save anyone. You have to be **in Christ Jesus** to be saved

1 John 5:11 – 12

"And this is the record, that God hath given to us eternal life, and this life is in his Son.

12 He that hath the Son hath life; and he that hath not the Son of God hath not life."

Most of the people in the church in Sardis are religious, but they are not born-again. They are spiritually dead. The church as whole was for the most part a Christian church in name only.

I think this church would have benefited greatly from memorizing Eph. 2:8 – 10. Take note of the order of events:

Ephesians 2:8 – 10

8 "For by grace are ye <u>saved</u> through faith; and that not of yourselves: it is the gift of God: 9 Not of works, lest any man should boast. 10 For we are His workmanship, <u>created in Christ Jesus</u> unto <u>good works</u>, which God hath before ordained that we should walk in them." (Emphasis added)

Salvation comes first and the good works come out of that salvation. They are a result of salvation. They do not contribute in any way in the obtaining of salvation.

Jesus Christ tells them that if they do not wake up, He will come like a thief in the night (Rev. 3:3). This is another indication that these people are not saved. They are in the dark.

1 Thessalonians 5:4 – 5

"But ye, brethren, are not in darkness, that that day should overtake you as a thief.

The Prophecy Puzzle

5 Ye are all the children of light, and the children of the day: we are not of the night, nor of darkness."

To the church in Sardis that received this letter, I think Christ Jesus simply meant that He would come unannounced in judgment upon them. In the historical view I think this is a clear indication that these people will not escape God's wrath. Jesus Christ's return will not catch true believers by surprise, but we will discuss that in more detail later.

As always Jesus Christ gives a unique description of Himself. Here to the church in Sardis, He describes Himself as the one having the seven Spirits of God and the seven stars (pastors). I believe He does this to emphasize the fact that He and the Holy Spirit are one, just as He and the Father are one. I think He does this because the church had at least in some way or fashion held onto Jesus Christ, but had ignored the Holy Spirit. This again is one more piece of evidence that most of the people in this church were not born-again believers, for Romans 8:9 says that "…. if any man have not the Spirit of Christ, he is none of his."

I hate to beat a dead horse, but they do not have the Holy Spirit within them and that is why the church is dead (3:1)! Jesus Christ by saying that the "Seven Spirits of God" are with Him, He is telling the church there in Sardis that they cannot have Him, without being born of the Holy Spirit.

The Holy Spirit is God and He must play a central role in the church as well as the individual. If there is no evidence of His presence in the church or the individual there is great reason to be concerned. One must at that point go back to the Bible and see if he has embraced the right gospel and the true Christ Jesus (2Cor. 11:3 – 15, Galatians 1:8).

The Prophecy Puzzle

I believe Jesus Christ tells them that He has the seven stars (pastors) in His hand in order to have them look to Him for life and guidance instead of the pastors. He wants to remind them that He is in control. He is the one who saves, not their pastors or religion. People who become religious often end up following people instead of following Jesus Christ.

As we went through the text we touched on how these issues are important to both the local church and the individual, but as a quick review:

- We need to always be on our guard not to become comfortable just "doing church".
- We need to be reminded that we are not saved by church attendance. We are saved through a living relationship with the Savior.
    - We each must be born-again (John 3:3) and be trusting in Christ Jesus <u>alone</u> for our salvation (Eph. 2:8 – 9). We cannot trade Jesus Christ for religion!
- We can't substitute following a pastor for following Jesus Christ.
- We need to have the Holy Spirit living within us and be listening for and to Him (Romans 8:9 – 14).

The name, "Sardis" means "Remnant". I think it refers to the few people in this church that still held to the true gospel of Jesus Christ and did not soil their garments with any self-righteousness (religion). Mostly spiritually dead, religious people occupied the church in Sardis, but there was a remnant of true born-again Christians in the church. I believe the fact that "Sardis" means "remnant" adds validity to the interpretation (translation) of Rev. 3:2, which I shared earlier.

The Prophecy Puzzle

Revelation 3:7 – 13

"And to the angel of the church in Philadelphia write; These things saith he that is holy, he that is true, he that hath the key of David, he that openeth, and no man shutteth; and shutteth, and no man openeth;
8 I know thy works: behold, I have set before thee an open door, and no man can shut it: for thou hast a little strength, and hast kept my word, and hast not denied my name.
9 Behold, I will make them of the synagogue of Satan, which say they are Jews, and are not, but do lie; behold, I will make them to come and worship before thy feet, and to know that I have loved thee.
10 Because thou hast kept the word of my patience, I also will keep thee from the hour of temptation, which shall come upon all the world, to try them that dwell upon the earth.
11 Behold, I come quickly: hold that fast which thou hast, that no man take thy crown.
12 Him that overcometh will I make a pillar in the temple of my God, and he shall go no more out: and I will write upon him the name of my God, and the name of the city of my God, which is new Jerusalem, which cometh down out of heaven from my God: and I will write upon him my new name.
13 He that hath an ear, let him hear what the Spirit saith unto the churches."

The Prophecy Puzzle

Before we examine what is said in this passage, I think we should acknowledge what is **not** said in it. Christ Jesus makes no mention of anyone in the church in Philadelphia doing anything wrong. I think that is significant, because it is an indicator that these people have been cleansed by the blood of Jesus Christ and have clothed themselves with **His** righteousness through faith.

Romans 4:4 – 8

"Now to him that worketh is the reward not reckoned of grace, but of debt.
5 But to him that worketh not, but believeth on him that justifieth the ungodly, his faith is counted for righteousness.
6 Even as David also describeth the blessedness of the man, unto whom God imputeth righteousness without works,
7 Saying, Blessed are they whose iniquities are forgiven, and whose sins are covered.
8 Blessed is the man to whom the Lord will not impute sin."

Romans 8:1

"There is therefore now **no condemnation** to them which are in Christ Jesus, who walk not after the flesh, but after the Spirit." (Emphasis added)

Because the blood of Jesus Christ has washed all of their sins away, there are no sins for Him to see (Revelation 7:14). The same is true for

The Prophecy Puzzle

anyone who has trusted in Christ Jesus as their Savior and surrendered to Him as their LORD/God.

On the other hand Jesus Christ does have some compliments for them. He lists three of them in v. 8. The first one is that they have "little power". The second is that they have kept His Word and the third is that they have not denied His Name. Jesus Christ gives them a fourth compliment in v. 10; they have proclaimed Jesus Christ's faithfulness. Now let's look more closely at each of these.

The first one in verse 8 is that they have a little power. That seems like a strange compliment, one would expect Him to say that they have a lot of power, but that is not what He says. Perhaps the truth is that it isn't a compliment, but simply a statement of fact.

There is disagreement over what kind of power He is referring to in this verse. Some believe He is saying that they had very little political or worldly power. While others believe Jesus Christ is referring to spiritual or miraculous power.

The former is certainly true and does fit the immediate context. It is logical that Jesus Christ would give them an open door, because they did not have the power to open it themselves (We will discuss what the open door is later). The latter seems to have some difficulty. Why would Jesus Christ reward them for not having the power for spiritual victories? I would have to side with the former viewpoint.

Next Christ Jesus compliments them on having kept His Word. This would seem to be clear. I believe He is simply saying that they have continued in faith and obedience to Him and His teachings; living a

The Prophecy Puzzle

moral life of love and selflessness and proclamation of the gospel of grace.

The next compliment goes right along with the previous one. They have not denied His name. Remember, it was primarily the Jewish religious leaders who were persecuting these people and the main point of contention they had with the Christians was their proclaiming Jesus of Nazareth as the Messiah. If they simply would have practiced their "religion" without insisting on Jesus of Nazareth being the Messiah and YHWH in the flesh, they could have lived in peace.

We see the same problem today. As long as someone doesn't insist on saying that Jesus Christ is God and the **only** way to the Father, the world doesn't have a problem with him. There isn't any problem praying in public, as long as it isn't in the name of Jesus Christ.

In verse 10 we have some controversy. There truly shouldn't be any controversy, but there is because many of the newer translations, such as the NLT, NIV and NKJV, incorrectly translate it as if the Philadelphian Christians are the ones who are persevering instead of Jesus Christ. The issue on hand is that **Jesus Christ is faithful**.

Psalms 40:10

".... I have declared thy [YHWH's] faithfulness and thy salvation...."

It is God's faithfulness that is of importance (Psalm 106). He is forever faithful and trustworthy! He will do exactly as He has said and promised to do. That is why we can take complete comfort in what Jesus Christ says next in Rev. 3:11, "I am coming quickly". Jesus Christ will return just as He said He would, much to the horror of the scoffers (2Peter 3:3 – 4).

Moving onto the open door mentioned in verse 8. What exactly is Jesus Christ referring to by an "open door"? I think we should see how this term is used elsewhere in the Bible. There are four other references in the Bible to an "open door". Three of the four are referring to opportunities to witness (1Cor. 16:8 – 9, 2Cor. 2:12, Col. 4:3). The other one is Rev. 4:1 and it is referring to God opening the door to heaven for John to pass through. I believe Christ Jesus intends it to be understood in both ways, but at different times. In the immediate context to the church that existed in John's time, He is referring to an opportunity for the Christians at that time to witness, but in the historical view of the letters to the seven churches, which we will discuss later, I believe He is referring to an open door to heaven.

In verse 9 we once again have reference to those in the synagogue of Satan. If we think back to Rev. 2:9 we remember that those who were part of the synagogue of Satan were the Jews who persecuted the church as they had Jesus Christ (John 8:39 – 44). Here we see that they will acknowledge that the Philadelphian Christians are the true followers of God. In other words they will acknowledge that they were in the wrong all along. If we think about it, isn't that exactly what will happen when the Jews at the time of the abomination of desolation cry out to Jesus of Nazareth as their Messiah?

> Hosea 5:15
>
> "I will go and return to my place, till they acknowledge their offence, and seek my face: in their affliction they will seek me early."

The Prophecy Puzzle

Yes, I believe so.

In verse 10 (Rev. 3:10) Jesus Christ makes reference to the hour of testing, which is about to come upon the whole earth. This is clearly a reference to the great tribulation (God's wrath) (2Peter 2:4 – 9). Some try to provide other possibilities for this testing, but they just don't fit.

One view is that it refers to the persecution of the Christians by Trajan, whose attack against the church was said by some to be even more severe than Nero's. That is fine, but it doesn't fit. First of all the time of testing is against those who dwell on the earth (belong to this world). This attack by Trajan was upon the church (believers); the tribulation spoken of in Rev. 3:10 will not be upon the church, but the world (non-believers) (Rev. 13:8, 14).
I'm not sure what this hour of testing referred to in relationship to the church in Philadelphia at the time of John's writing. Some have suggested that it is referring to YHWH giving Christians the power to overcome temptation (1Cor. 10:13). I'm not sure we need to make a different explanation other than the one for the whole church. The Christians who were alive at that time did escape the hour of testing which is to come upon the whole earth, because they died and went into the presence of the LORD at that the time of their death.

I do believe this is ultimately referring to the great tribulation and therefore a very clear indication that these seven letters to the seven churches do layout the history of the church from its beginning to its end, as we will discuss more in chapter 13.

Verse 11 (Rev. 3:11) brings us to Jesus Christ's instructions for those in the church in Philadelphia. He tells them that they should hold on to what they have so they don't lose their crown. The crowns are speaking of their eternal reward for their works. This is a very important issue for them, because neither they nor we want to lose our eternal reward. So we need to know exactly what they are to hold on to in order to keep their eternal reward.

Starting in verse 8 Jesus Christ said that they have an open door that no one can shut. As we discussed earlier that is a reference to having opportunities to witness. So the implication is that they need to continue to take advantage of those opportunities. He also said that they had kept His Word and not denied His Name. In a nutshell this means that they have held to the true gospel and the true Christ Jesus. And lastly in verse 10 they had believed and professed YHWH's perseverance and faithfulness.
If we hold true to the same things that the Philadelphian Christians did we too will have eternal reward and even more than that we will have hope and peace to see us through all that comes in this life as well.

Once again, as always Jesus Christ reassures the one who overcomes that he will have eternal life (v. 12). Notice the many allusions to the permanency of their salvation. This is to comfort and encourage the Philadelphian Christians (and us).
Jesus Christ describes Himself to the church in Philadelphia as the One who is holy, true, having the key of David, who opens and no one will shut and shuts and no one opens. I believe He does this in order to reassure them that they have been right all along and to encourage them to hang in there. The fact that He has the "Keys of David" should also comfort them, because it indicates that He has the authority to give access to the kingdom of God.

The Prophecy Puzzle

The name "Philadelphia" means "brotherly love" and I believe it reflects the most significant attribute of the church in Philadelphia, which is representative of a healthy Christian church; brotherly love. In John 13:35 Jesus Christ tells us that it is our love for one another (fellow Christians) that is the greatest witness to the world. Many think our greatest witness to the world is how we love them, by feeding the poor, etc., but that is not what Jesus Christ said. He said, "By this shall all men know that ye are my disciples, if ye have love, one to another." - John 13:35. I'm sure you don't need me to tell you that it is a lot easier to love a stranger, than it is to love a brother or sister, but that is what we are called to do.

Revelation 3:14 – 22

"And unto the angel of the church of the Laodiceans write; These things saith the Amen, the faithful and true witness, the beginning of the creation of God;
15 I know thy works, that thou art neither cold nor hot: I would thou wert cold or hot.
16 So then because thou art lukewarm, and neither cold nor hot, I will spue thee out of my mouth.
17 Because thou sayest, I am rich, and increased with goods, and have need of nothing; and knowest not that thou art wretched, and miserable, and poor, and blind, and naked:
18 I counsel thee to buy of me gold tried in the fire, that thou mayest be rich; and white raiment, that thou mayest be clothed, and that the shame of thy nakedness do not appear; and anoint thine eyes with eyesalve, that thou mayest see.

The Prophecy Puzzle

> 19 As many as I love, I rebuke and chasten: be zealous therefore, and repent.
> 20 Behold, I stand at the door, and knock: if any man hear my voice, and open the door, I will come in to him, and will sup with him, and he with me.
> 21 To him that overcometh will I grant to sit with me in my throne, even as I also overcame, and am set down with my Father in his throne.
> 22 He that hath an ear, let him hear what the Spirit saith unto the churches."

Once again it is what Christ Jesus doesn't say that has the greatest significance. Just as with the church in Sardis, He doesn't say anything about what the church in Laodicea has done right. I believe that is because the majority of people occupying this church are not born-again believers. We will see ample evidence of this as we continue on in the letter. Remember it is impossible to please God without faith (Hebrews 11:6).

Jesus Christ does have quite a list of problems for the church in Laodicea. For starters He tells them that they are lukewarm and that it makes Him sick (vv. 15 - 16). Some would ask why would Jesus Christ prefer them to be cold over lukewarm. Well, first of all it is much more insulting to God for someone to say that he believes in God's existence, but He's not worth the time to really get to know; than just not believing in Him at all. While that is absolutely true and must cause God great pain, I think there is another reason for Jesus Christ saying that it makes Him sick. I believe it is because lukewarm people in His church give the Church a bad name. The cold person (the unbeliever) is not associated with His Name at all; but the lukewarm claim His Name; but don't necessarily honor His Name. Especially when it comes to His

The Prophecy Puzzle

less popular teaching such as all sex, homosexual or heterosexual outside of a marriage is sin. In fact the gospel itself is seen to be too offensive. Telling people that we are all sinners and in desperate need of a Savior to avoid going to hell, and that we can't save ourselves, but we can only be saved by Christ Jesus; how could anyone expect to fill a church with a message like that?

Chuck Missler says that he believes the commandment, "Thou shall not take the Name of the LORD in vain" is **not** referring to how we use His Name, but rather taking His name as in claiming He is our God, but then not having a changed life that honors Him. I have to agree with him.

I believe there is at least one more reason why Jesus Christ would rather they be cold instead of lukewarm. Lukewarm people are religious. They are self-righteous people and therefore the hardest to reach with the true gospel. They think they are fine the way they are, not in need of anything else in their walk with God. They're good people and they go to church, etc. They believe that God would never send them to hell. They, in their minds deserve eternal life, making the gospel, especially the cross just an insulting foolish idea (1Cor. 1:18).

These lukewarm people in Laodicea probably liked Jesus Christ a lot and even talked about Him often. They probably thought He was a great teacher, maybe even one of the "masters" who came to convey "the Christ consciousness" to mankind. He might even have been thought of as "a god", but not the second person of the only true self-existent God (YHWH). They probably saw Him as someone that could help them achieve **their** goals in life, but not as someone to whom they were to surrender.

The Prophecy Puzzle

This brings us to a related issue. Jesus Christ doesn't say that they weren't doing good things. He just makes no mention of them, because they were all works of the flesh. In fact, my guess would be that they had wonderful plans to feed the hungry, bring in world peace and even had an after school tutor program. After all Jesus Christ did say that they looked good to themselves.

This is the point Jesus Christ is making in verse 17. He said that they were looking to their physical/temporal condition to judge their spiritual/eternal status. They thought since they were a wealthy church and the pews were full every Sunday, that they were doing what was right. I see the same kind of thing in many churches today. They operate by "the rule of pragmatism", but just because something works and by works I mean it fills the church and makes people feel good, doesn't make it true or right.

The issue most often debated in this passage is if these lukewarm people are born-again believers or not. This is a very important issue, because it changes everything. Most, if not all of what I just wrote is not true **if** these lukewarm people are truly saved, born-again people. I believe it is very clear that most if not all of these lukewarm people are not saved, born-again believers. The primary reason I believe this is because of what Jesus Christ tells them to buy <u>from Him</u>: Refined gold, white garments and eye salve. Let's look at these items more closely.

The first item was refined Gold, so they may become eternally rich.

1 Corinthians 3:11 – 15

"For other foundation can no man lay than that is laid, which is Jesus Christ.

The Prophecy Puzzle

> 12 Now if any man build upon this foundation gold, silver, precious stones, wood, hay, stubble;
> 13 Every man's work shall be made manifest: for the day shall declare it, because it shall be revealed by fire; and the fire shall try every man's work of what sort it is.
> 14 If any man's work abide which he hath built thereupon, he shall receive a reward.
> 15 If any man's work shall be burned, he shall suffer loss: but he himself shall be saved; yet so as by fire."

The refined gold would be good works that have some eternal reward. That means they must be works of the Spirit and not of the flesh. It is the motivation behind the good works that determine if there is any eternal reward or not. Our motivation should be to honor and glorify God. I believe these individuals were doing good works for the wrong reasons. They were bringing honor and glory to themselves or maybe even their church, but not to God. But even more importantly, the good works must be built upon the foundation of Christ Jesus. If someone is not saved, their good works are nothing.

This is why Christ Jesus tells them next to buy from Him White garments. White garments were for the purpose of covering their nakedness, which is their self-righteousness, which is really their sinfulness (Matthew 22:9 – 13, Romans 3:21 – 24). We already did a study on garments, but just two passages to refresh your memory.

Isaiah 61:10

> "I will greatly rejoice in the LORD, my soul shall be joyful in my God; for he hath clothed me with the

The Prophecy Puzzle

garments of salvation, he hath covered me with the robe of righteousness, as a bridegroom decketh himself with ornaments, and as a bride adorneth herself with her jewels."

Galatians 3:26 – 27

"For ye are all the children of God by faith in Christ Jesus.
27 For as many of you as have been baptized into Christ have put on Christ."

Jesus Christ is addressing people who are members of the church, but not true born-again Christians, and therefore are walking around in the nakedness of their own self-righteousness. His death paid the penalty for our sins; past, present and future, but we need more than His death, we need His life (Rom 5:10). We need to receive the gift of His perfect righteousness (life) as our covering (white garment). We need to put on Christ. We do this by receiving Him as our Savior and LORD/God (Galatians 3:26 – 29).

One of the best illustrations of this that I have ever heard dealt with the corpse of a person who had died from cancer. Imagine that there was a corpse, which had been filled with cancer lying on a hospital bed before you. Let's say that someone comes along that is able to bring this person back to life. What will happen? The person will very shortly once again die, because his body is still filled with cancer. Another person comes along who has found the cure for cancer. He injects the corpse with the cure and the cancer is gone, but has he helped the corpse? No, it is still dead. One must remove the cancer and bring the corpse back to life. That is what God did. He removed the cancer of sin

The Prophecy Puzzle

through His one sacrifice (Heb. 10:10 – 14), so that anyone who would receive Christ Jesus as his or her Savior and LORD would receive eternal **life** (1 John 5:12).

The last item Jesus Christ tells them to purchase from Him is eye salve, so they can see. It is obvious He is not speaking of physical eyesight, but of spiritual eyesight. The Holy Spirit is the One who gives us spiritual eyesight (John 16:13 – 14, 1Cor. 2:14). Jesus Christ is telling them that they are spiritually blind, because they do not have the Holy Spirit within them (Rom. 8:9). They need to be born-again and then they will receive the Holy Spirit and they will be able to see things as they truly are. I'm afraid these church members were Christian in name only.

The final reason I believe most of the people in this church in Laodicea are not born-again believers is because of what Jesus Christ says in verses 19 and 20. In verse 19 He tells them to be zealous and repent. A lack of enthusiasm for God is a huge red flag. It means one of two things, either one is not a true born-again Christian or he is a Christian who is distracted with the pleasures and problems of this world and is headed to an eternity with very little reward (Mat. 13:22). Before you say, as I hear so many people say, "I just want to get there, I don't care if I'm the very lowest of the low." remember you're talking about eternity. Even the smallest reward becomes enormous when it is multiplied by eternity. The same could be said about losses.

Jesus Christ goes on to tell them to repent, followed by verse 20, which clearly has Jesus Christ on the outside and declaring that if anyone would receive Him for who He is, He would come into him or her. In other words they would be born-again and have eternal life. That

The Prophecy Puzzle

means what they need to repent of is disbelief in the true Christ Jesus and the true gospel of grace.

Jesus Christ ends this letter to the church in Laodicea much the same way He did the others. He again confirms, **as He did with every church**, that those who overcome will receive eternal life (v. 21). When He says that they will be able to sit on His throne with Him, He means that they will be able to reign with Him from the Throne of David (Luke 1:32) during the Millennium Kingdom (Revelation 20:4).

In this letter to the church in Laodicea Jesus Christ describes Himself as the Amen, the faithful and true witness; the beginning (source) of creation. In order to see the significance of these titles we need to look at each one individually.

Amen, means "so be it" or as I think it should be translated, "Yes, it is so, so be it!" So when Jesus Christ refers to Himself as "the Amen," He is telling them that He is the last word on all subjects (Hebrews 12:2). What He says is so. It is so and there is absolutely no compromising His Word. Along with this is the truth that His Word is complete; nothing needs to be added to it like psychology, mysticism, grand experiences, etc. These are not stated as problems in the text, but I believe the implication is there. When we look at the historic dimension of this church we will see them as problems in the "modern day Laodicean church".

Next Jesus Christ refers to Himself as, "the faithful and true witness". By this Jesus Christ is declaring exactly that. He is the true witness of the truth (John 18:37) and He will forever be faithful in the expression of that truth.

The Prophecy Puzzle

The beginning of the creation of God is a little trickier than the other two, primarily because Arians use this verse to wrongly convey that Jesus Christ is a created being. I want to make it clear that Jesus Christ is not a created being. He is the second person of the eternal triune God. The word "beginning" in Greek is "Arche," which means "origin", or "source". What Jesus Christ is trying to communicate to the Laodiceans is that He is the source of all creation (John 1:3).

I believe there is a second reason why Jesus Christ mentions the creation process in this passage. I believe it is because many "modern day Laodicean churches" do not believe the creation account in Genesis. The six-day creation is biblical (Exodus 20:11) and scientifically sound. There are many good books out there that do a great job of providing substantial evidence for this truth, so I will not deal with it other than giving you a website to refer to: www.answersingenesis.org

"Laodicea" means, "Rule of the people". It obviously shows how this church is more concerned with pleasing people instead of pleasing God. They follow the will of the people and the whims of the culture instead of Jesus Christ and His teachings in the Bible (2 Tim. 4:3 - 4). If a church sees itself as being wonderful, spiritually mature and prosperous, <u>but</u> God sees the church as lukewarm; it is obvious that they are trying to please people, not God.

Just as a quick review I would like to recap how Jesus Christ described Himself to the seven churches. He describes Himself as being:
- The One in control and omnipresent (2:1).
- The eternal One who has power over death (2:8).
- The possessor of truth (2:12).
- The One coming in Judgment (2:18).

The Prophecy Puzzle

- One with the Holy Spirit (3:1).
- Faithful and having the power to give entrance into heaven (3:7).
- The author and finisher of the Faith (3:14).

After looking at how Christ Jesus describes Himself, I cannot understand how anyone can walk away not acknowledging that Jesus Christ is God, or at least admitting that He believed Himself to be God.

The Prophecy Puzzle

CHAPTER FIVE

Coming up to Date – Recent Fulfillments of Prophecy

****

Before we can move forward to investigate what the future holds, we should look at prophecies that are given in the Bible, which have been fulfilled in modern times. This will give us a better understanding of where we are in YHWH's plan.

The Prophecy Puzzle

There have been some very significant fulfillments of prophecy in the past century. The first one we will look at is the rebirth of the nation of Israel.

Ezekiel 37:7 – 10

"So I prophesied as I was commanded: and as I prophesied, there was a noise, and behold a shaking, and the bones came together, bone to his bone.
8 And when I beheld, lo, the sinews and the flesh came up upon them, and the skin covered them above: but there was no breath in them.
9 Then said he unto me, Prophesy unto the wind, prophesy, son of man, and say to the wind, Thus saith the Lord GOD; Come from the four winds, O breath, and breathe upon these slain, that they may live.
10 So I prophesied as he commanded me, and the breath came into them, and they lived, and stood up upon their feet, an exceeding great army."

Note in verse 8 that the physical bodies were returned to whole, but there was no breath (spirit) within them. That is exactly how it happened about sixty years ago. In 1948 the physical nation of Israel was reborn, but they have not yet embraced their Messiah, Jesus of Nazareth. They have not yet had the Holy Spirit come to indwell them, they are not born-again, but as verse 10 states, this will happen in the future, when they cry out to Jesus Christ from the great tribulation (Hosea 5:15-KJV, Jer. 31:33 – 34).

The very existence of modern Israel is a miracle itself. On May 13, 1948 there was not a nation named Israel. It did not exist. But on May 14,

The Prophecy Puzzle

1948 there was a nation named Israel, but it immediately found itself surrounded by nations that swore to destroy it. The small and poorly equipped Israeli "army" miraculously prevailed, even though the vastly larger and more powerful armie**s** of the Muslim nation**s** surrounding it immediately attacked. It was without a doubt a modern day miracle. I recommend the videos, "*[Against all Odds](): Israel Survives*" narration by Michael Greenspan and "Miracle of Israel, A Documentary" with narration by Leonard Nimoy (if you can find it).

A prophecy that we see being fulfilled before our very eyes is Isaiah 27:6:

> "He shall cause them that come of Jacob to take root: Israel shall blossom and bud, and fill the face of the world with fruit."

Mark Twain visited the land that is today Israel in 1869 and in his book, "The Firsthand Impressions of a Traveler", he wrote,

> "The hills are barren... The valleys are unsightly deserts fringed with a feeble vegetation that has an expression about it being sorrowful and despondent... It is a hopeless, dreary, heartbroken land."

Today it is a totally different story. Israel is the third largest exporter of fruit in the world. Today one can find fruit that was grown in Israel for sale around the world.

Jesus Christ tells us that when we see Israel starting to blossom, the end is near (Matthew 24:32 - 33). I truly believe "the end" will be here in my lifetime, assuming I have another forty years or so to live. Yes I

The Prophecy Puzzle

know that every generation from the time of Christ thought they would be the last one. Well, one of us has to be right, but I admit that God could put us in a holding pattern for another thousand years. Until we see the peace treaty that gives Israel permission to rebuild their temple, we have no definite idea how close we truly are to the rapture and the end of this age. We will discuss this in much further detail later on in the book.

Another prophecy that is one of my personal favorites is found in Isaiah.

> Isaiah 41:19 – 20
>
> "I will plant in the wilderness the cedar, the shittah tree, and the myrtle, and the oil tree; I will set in the desert the fir tree, and the pine, and the box tree together:
> 20 That they may see, and know, and consider, and understand together, that the hand of the LORD hath done this, and the Holy One of Israel hath created it."

Way back in the time of the Roman Empire the land of Israel started to be stripped of its forests. Before then Israel was a land with many trees, but after the Romans, came the Muslims, the Crusaders and the Turks. All of them cut down the trees of Israel, until there were virtually none left. Israel became the barren land described by Mark Twain, as we just read.

But today the land is once again filled with trees. The Jewish Nation Fund has been planting trees for years and today there are more varieties of trees in Israel than **ever before**. We are not just talking about saplings, but beautiful mature trees – forests once again can be

The Prophecy Puzzle

found in Israel. Isaiah 41:19 has truly been fulfilled. That doesn't mean He will never have to do it again, for during the great tribulation Israel will once again be destroyed; but that doesn't take away from what has happened over the past sixty years or so.

There are many more such prophecies that have been and are being fulfilled in Israel today. If you would like to study this subject more, I recommend the book, "25 Messianic Signs in Israel Today", by Noah W. Hutchings.

The point of this chapter is that there are many prophetic signs being fulfilled today and we need to know where we are in God's timeline so that His day does not come upon us like a thief in the night (1Thes. 5:4).

The Prophecy Puzzle

The Prophecy Puzzle

CHAPTER SIX

The Heavenly Scene – Revelation 4:1 – 5:14

****

Revelation 4:1 – 5:14

"After this I looked, and, behold, a door was opened in heaven: and the first voice which I heard was as it were of a trumpet talking with me; which said, Come up hither, and I will shew thee things which must be hereafter.
2 And immediately I was in the spirit: and, behold, a throne was set in heaven, and one sat on the throne.

The Prophecy Puzzle

3 And he that sat was to look upon like a jasper and a sardine stone: and there was a rainbow round about the throne, in sight like unto an emerald.
4 And round about the throne were four and twenty seats: and upon the seats I saw four and twenty elders sitting, clothed in white raiment; and they had on their heads crowns of gold.
5 And out of the throne proceeded lightnings and thunderings and voices: and there were seven lamps of fire burning before the throne, which are the seven Spirits of God.
6 And before the throne there was a sea of glass like unto crystal: and in the midst of the throne, and round about the throne, were four beasts full of eyes before and behind.
7 And the first beast was like a lion, and the second beast like a calf, and the third beast had a face as a man, and the fourth beast was like a flying eagle.
8 And the four beasts had each of them six wings about him; and they were full of eyes within: and they rest not day and night, saying, Holy, holy, holy, Lord God Almighty, which was, and is, and is to come.
9 And when those beasts give glory and honour and thanks to him that sat on the throne, who liveth for ever and ever,
10 The four and twenty elders fall down before him that sat on the throne, and worship him that liveth for ever and ever, and cast their crowns before the throne, saying,

The Prophecy Puzzle

11 Thou art worthy, O Lord, to receive glory and honour and power: for thou hast created all things, and for thy pleasure they are and were created.

5:1 And I saw in the right hand of him that sat on the throne a book written within and on the backside, sealed with seven seals.

2 And I saw a strong angel proclaiming with a loud voice, Who is worthy to open the book, and to loose the seals thereof?

3 And no man in heaven, nor in earth, neither under the earth, was able to open the book, neither to look thereon.

4 And I wept much, because no man was found worthy to open and to read the book, neither to look thereon.

5 And one of the elders saith unto me, Weep not: behold, the Lion of the tribe of Juda, the Root of David, hath prevailed to open the book, and to loose the seven seals thereof.

6 And I beheld, and, lo, in the midst of the throne and of the four beasts, and in the midst of the elders, stood a Lamb as it had been slain, having seven horns and seven eyes, which are the seven Spirits of God sent forth into all the earth.

7 And he came and took the book out of the right hand of him that sat upon the throne.

8 And when he had taken the book, the four beasts and four and twenty elders fell down before the Lamb, having every one of them harps, and golden vials full of odours, which are the prayers of saints.

9 And they sung a new song, saying, Thou art worthy to take the book, and to open the seals thereof: for thou

The Prophecy Puzzle

wast slain, and hast redeemed us to God by thy blood out of every kindred, and tongue, and people, and nation;
10 And hast made us unto our God kings and priests: and we shall reign on the earth.
11 And I beheld, and I heard the voice of many angels round about the throne and the beasts and the elders: and the number of them was ten thousand times ten thousand, and thousands of thousands;
12 Saying with a loud voice, Worthy is the Lamb that was slain to receive power, and riches, and wisdom, and strength, and honour, and glory, and blessing.
13 And every creature which is in heaven, and on the earth, and under the earth, and such as are in the sea, and all that are in them, heard I saying, Blessing, and honour, and glory, and power, be unto him that sitteth upon the throne, and unto the Lamb for ever and ever.
14 And the four beasts said, Amen. And the four and twenty elders fell down and worshipped him that liveth for ever and ever."

When looking at chapter four we need to remind ourselves that in some circumstances John is trying to describe the indescribable. It is almost as impossible for John to describe what he sees as it is for the finite to comprehend the infinite. Keeping this in mind might help us deal with the frustration we might experience as we study these final chapters of the Bible.

In 4:1 John clearly states that what he now sees is "after these things". In Revelation 1:19 John was told to write, three things: The things he had seen (past events), the things that are, and the things that will

The Prophecy Puzzle

happen in the future. It is obvious this means after the situation with the churches he just wrote about in Revelation 2:1 – 3:22, but that could be understood to mean two different things.

It could mean after the **present** time that John had written to the churches, meaning the first century A.D. This is the simplest understanding. It means that the things John is going to describe from this point on are things that will happen sometime in the future; that is after the time John wrote the book of Revelation, be it 69 or 95 A.D.

The second view takes this to mean after the "church age" as defined by the historic view. According to this view, these things John describes here must take place after the rapture of the church. That is after the end of the "church age". For this view to be correct the "historic view" of the seven churches must also be embraced.

The supporters of this view understand John's being called up to heaven in verse one to represent the rapture. They would argue that the voice that sounded like a trumpet is the last trumpet referred to in 1 Corinthians 15:51 - 52. Those against this understanding would say the text clearly states that it was a voice that sounded like a trumpet. It was not a trumpet. They would argue that the calling up of John was for him alone and did not refer to the rapture of the church.

I believe the first view is the correct one. John is referring to **the time he wrote the book** of Revelation in the first century. The timing of the rapture will be discussed further throughout the remainder of this book, but for now let's try to describe what John actually sees. I believe it is obvious that he is seeing the throne of God in heaven. There he sees a representation of God the Father. We need to be careful here. I am not saying that God the Father has a physical body for we are

The Prophecy Puzzle

clearly told in John 4:24 that He is spirit. What that exactly means could easily fill another book and never achieve a complete understanding, but for now let's just say that John sees a **representation** of the Father.

So the representation of God the Father that John sees looks like jasper and sardius stones. In other words He <u>looked like</u> a man made of a semi-transparent stone, similar to a diamond or ruby. Some of the stone was brilliant "clear color" (jasper - Rev. 21:11) and the rest of it was a transparent fiery red color (sardius).

Remembering the opening point I made in this chapter, how can John describe God? For that matter how does God present Himself to John in a way that he can at least in part understand what he is seeing? I'll let you think about that. I'm not sure what the significance is but, the jasper stone was the last stone in the breastplate of the high priest and the sardius was the first. The jasper represented Benjamin, Israel's last-born son (Ex. 28:20) and the sardius represented Reuben, Israel's firstborn. It is possible and perhaps likely there is something symbolic here. Perhaps it illustrates that YHWH is the God of **all** of Israel, or perhaps it is symbolic of His being the First and the Last (Revelation 11:11, 17; 2:8; 22:13).

There was an emerald colored rainbow around the throne as well. It has been suggested that it is symbolic of God's righteous judgment and His promise of peace, similar to the rainbow that He gave Noah after the flood as a symbol of the promise that He would never again destroy the earth by a worldwide flood (Gen. 9:12). I honestly don't think that is it. I've read other suggestions about what this emerald rainbow means, but to be honest in my opinion they have very little biblical support.

The Prophecy Puzzle

One point that might be of significance is that the third stone in the breastplate of the high priest was an emerald and it would have represented Levi. The Jewish priesthood was made up of Levites, so one could suggest that they represented God's grace, in His providing a way for people to worship Him and seek His forgiveness. So the emerald rainbow surrounding God's throne could be expressing that it is a throne of grace (Hebrews 4:16). I like what Jon Courson says in regards to this topic in his *Application Commentary*:

> "We are invited to come boldly unto the throne of *grace* (Hebrews 4:16). I am totally convinced that grace is not the beginning thing—it's the whole thing. God is looking for people to bless who won't take credit by saying, "It's my praying or witnessing, my disciplined spirituality or intense study," but rather, "It's only grace that has brought me thus far." You see, grace is the only thing that truly allows the LORD to get all the glory. That's why His is a throne of grace. *Amazing* grace."

The twenty-four elders we see around the throne represent the church. We know this for the following reasons:
- They are clothed in white garments.
    - Christians are clothed in white garments (Rev. 3:5, Mat. 22:9 - 13).
- They are wearing crowns.
    - As a rule only people receive crowns (2 Tim. 4:8, James 1:12).
    - The only exception to that rule is Revelation 12:1, but it is clear from the context that this crown is symbolic.

The Prophecy Puzzle

- When we look at the visions of heaven in the Old Testament the twenty-four elders are never mentioned, indicating that the church is not yet there (Is. 6:1 - 4, Ezekiel 1 and Ezekiel 10).
- One of the few other places we find the number "24" in the Bible is 1 Chronicles 24:1 – 19, where the sons of Aaron who are the O.T. priests are divided up into twenty-four divisions.
    - The twenty-four priests from the twenty-four divisions represented all the priests.
    - We are N.T. priests (Rev. 1:6) and the twenty-four elders (priests) present before the throne represent all Christians.
        - It is even possible that every Christian will have their turn to be one of the twenty-four elders.
- They claim to have been redeemed by God (Rev. 5:9 KJV).
    - Only people are redeemed.
- They claim to have been made kings and priests (Rev. 5:10 KJV) just as Christians have been (Rev. 1:6).
- They claim that they will reign on earth (Rev. 5:10 KJV) just as Christians will do (2 Tim. 2:12, Rev. 20:4).

Those who hold to the pre-tribulation rapture of the church use this to prove that the church is raptured before any of the tribulation starts in chapter six, because the twenty-four elders are already there in chapter four. But it doesn't prove that at all. It simply establishes the fact that there are Christians in heaven at that time. That should be obvious, because being absent from this body means to be present with the Lord (2Corinthians 5:8). Anytime after the resurrection of Christ Jesus, we would expect to see the church (saints) represented in heaven.

The rest of what we find before the altar is thankfully clearly explained for us from other places in the Bible. In Rev. 1:20 we saw that the lamps represented the seven churches and from Rev. 1:4, 5:6 & Is. 11:2 we saw that "the Seven Spirits of God" is another name for the Holy Spirit. Lastly, we see throughout the Bible the presence of lightning and thunder is usually associated with the presence of God and His coming judgment.

Once again those who hold to the pre-tribulation rapture of the church would use the fact that we see the Holy Spirit before the throne at this time to support their position. They would state since the Holy Spirit is before the throne, He can no longer be indwelling the church on the earth, and therefore the church age must be over.

Those who hold to any of the other views would simply restate the earlier arguments and add that the Holy Spirit is God and therefore omnipresent. He can be with the believers in heaven who have died up to that point in time and still be with those alive on the earth.

The understanding of the "sea of glass like unto crystal" in verse six; might not be as clear as it is, but we might gain some insight by looking at the tabernacle, because many believe there is a correlation between the throne of God and the tabernacle in the Old Testament. If this is true, there might be some correlation between the molten sea before the entrance of the tabernacle (1 Kings 7:23) and this sea of glass. The priests washed themselves in the molten sea before they offered sacrifices to YHWH. In Rev. 15:2 we see saints standing on the sea of glass. If this is all correct it could be symbolic of the blood of Christ Jesus, because just as the priests had to wash before they entered the temple, the people had to be washed in the blood of the Lamb before they can stand before the throne of God. Some would use the Word of God in place of the blood, because we do stand on the authority and infallibility of the Word of God as well. It can also be said, that we are

The Prophecy Puzzle

washed by the Word of God (Eph. 5:26); but for what it is worth, I believe it is referring to being washed in the blood of the Lamb.

Moving onto some of the most interesting characters before the throne of God, the four living creatures; they are hard to describe, but I'll do my best. To begin with the word translated, "beast" (creature) is "zoa" in the Greek. It is the word from which we get "zoo". Most believe these "creatures" are cherubim/seraphim as seen in Ezekiel (1:10, 28:13 - 17). I also believe that, but I think they are special or unique in that they are representative of, if not actually the guardians of the throne. I believe that for three reasons: Because of where they are, what they have and what others like them have done.

First, these creatures are at the center of the "sea of glass" right next to, but <u>not on</u> the throne. They are <u>encircling</u> the throne. This would be the logical place for guardians of throne to be. Secondly, they are covered with eyes enabling them to see in all directions. Being able to see in all directions at the same time would be a very useful ability for a guard to possess. Finally, we see similar creatures being used as guards, such as at the entrance of the Garden of Eden (Genesis 3:24).

Some believe that originally there were five of these living creatures and that Satan was the fifth. The reason this is believed is because each living creature seems to correlate to a category of living creatures on earth. That could be why they are called "Zoa" in the Greek, because they represented the whole "animal" kingdom.

According to this theory the one with the face of a lion represents the <u>wild</u> warm-blooded animals. The one with the face of an ox represents the domesticated warm-blooded animals. The one with the face of an eagle represents the birds and the one with the face of man represents

The Prophecy Puzzle

mankind. That would leave the cold-blooded animals with no one to watch over or represent them. Incidentally Satan is said to have a face of a serpent (Gen. 3:1 – 13) and is often described as a dragon. It would be logical that he would have been the fifth cherub around the throne and would have watched over and represented the cold-blooded animals.

This view is also supported by Habakkuk 1:14. There it states that the cold-blooded animals do not have a ruler (watcher/seraphim) over them. The reason they don't would seem to be fairly obvious; Satan was that ruler, but he was cast out of that position when he rebelled against YHWH (Ezekiel 28:13 – 16).

What these creatures say is also significant; for they <u>continually</u> say, "Holy, holy, holy, is the Lord God, the Almighty, who was and who is and who is to come." That is their way of giving honor and glory to God. Do you think it would be wise for us to follow their example and continually praise God?

It's not known for sure why the creatures repeat "holy" three times but some suggest it is a way to emphasize God's holiness. While others believe it is a way of proclaiming the Trinity; one holy for each: God the Father, God the Son and God the Holy Spirit.

Before we move on I would like to take a moment just to think about the meaning of the word "holy". It is "aylos" in the Greek and literally means sacred, pure or blameless. It comes from the root "ayos" which means "awful thing". I would define holy as, "Something so great and so pure it strikes fear in the core of one's being (Is. 6:5)."

The Prophecy Puzzle

I'm afraid the church as a whole and I too at times forget that YHWH is holy, holy, holy. Yes He is our Savior, Father and friend, but He is also an almighty, holy, holy, holy God.

Finally we come to observe the one who is on the throne itself. The One sitting on the throne is God the Father (we discussed His appearance early). Now let us focus in on what He is holding. He is holding a scroll, which had writing on both sides of it.

The writing on the outside of the scroll probably stated the requirements needed to open the seals (v. 2). Under Roman law only the appointed heir could open the seals on a will. Jesus Christ is the appointed heir of the world by the Father (Hebrews 1:1 – 2).

Based on the requirements of a kinsman redeemer, some of the requirements listed on the outside of the scroll might be:
- That he is a man (100% human) (v. 3).
    - Jesus Christ is a man (Luke 24:39; 1 John 4:3).
- That he is a descendant of Judah and King David (v. 5).
    - Jesus Christ is both (Matthew 1:1 – 16, Luke 3:23 – 38).
- That he is able to redeem.
    - Jesus Christ was able to redeem us, because He is holy and sinless.
    - He offered His perfect life to redeem our sinful lives (2Corinthians 5:21, Hebrews 10:10 – 14).

The scroll had seven seals on it. It is not by chance the scroll was sealed with seven seals. The number seven in the Bible is symbolic of being perfect or complete. Also, I've read that it was Roman law at that time that wills and official deeds had to be sealed with seven seals.

The Prophecy Puzzle

It has been said that this scroll is the "deed" (will), for this earth. While that might be true, some clarification of what that means is necessary. Some teach that God had given it to Adam and Eve and that they lost it to Satan. That is <u>not</u> true! God the Father is holding the deed in His hand at the time depicted for us in v. 1 and <u>He has always possessed it</u>.

Psalms 50:10 – 12

> "For every beast of the forest is mine, and the cattle upon a thousand hills.
> 11 I know all the fowls of the mountains: and the wild beasts of the field are mine.
> 12 If I were hungry, I would not tell thee: for the world is mine, and the fulness thereof."

There never was a time when God did not own the whole earth (Psalm 104:24; 1Cor. 10:26). When Satan offered Jesus Christ the kingdoms of the earth (Mat. 4:8 – 9), he was referring to the hearts and souls of mankind, not the earth. Satan has blinded the hearts of mankind, but he doesn't own the earth (John 3:5, 36; 8:21 – 24, 44; James 4:4).

Moving on to what else John experiences as he sees this scene in heaven (5:2 – 4). There are two very important points that are made in these verses. First, John began to weep when no one was found to open the seals. The implication of John's weeping is that the opening of this scroll is the only way to bring in the millennium kingdom and then the eternal heavenly kingdom.

The second point is that no one other than Christ Jesus could be found to open the seals, this points to the fact that there is salvation through

The Prophecy Puzzle

no one other than Jesus Christ (John 3:36; Acts 4:12; 1 John 5:11, 12). Without Jesus Christ, humanity has no hope.

As always the appearance of Jesus Christ has great significance. Here He is described as "the Lion of the tribe of Judah, the Root of David." These descriptions point back to Jesus Christ being the kinsman redeemer. Also these are very Jewish titles and I believe they are used to remind us that this is a Jewish book. In order to understand the book of Revelation we must read it from a Jewish mindset.
Christ Jesus is described here as a Lamb, standing as if slain. This is to inform us that He redeemed the world through His death on the cross, being crucified as the **Lamb of God** (Heb. 10:10 – 14, 1Peter 2:24).

Another point that is often overlooked by Christians is that Jesus Christ is still a man today and still has the scars from the wounds He received when He was crucified. It has been said that the only man-made thing that will ever be in heaven are the scars on Jesus Christ.

Some say Jesus Christ no longer has a physical body; but He does (Luke 24:38 – 43, John 20:26 – 27, Acts 1:11). For those who argue that is impossible, because of 1Cor. 15:50 where it says that "flesh and blood cannot inherit the kingdom of God", but it should be noted that Jesus Christ did not say "flesh and blood". He said "flesh and bones". This is a very unusual statement. The only other place a phrase similar to this is used in the Bible is Job 2:5. It would seem that our "glorified bodies" have flesh and bones, but no blood.

This is more than just a theological issue to argue over. It is much more than that and I think the best way to convey that is to share a story that Chuck Missler shares about a dream his friend John had some time

The Prophecy Puzzle

ago. I'm sorry I'm writing the story from memory and I'm sure I'm changing it a little bit, but the point is the same as Chuck Missler made.

In John's dream YHWH was showing him the universe and John was enjoying the tour immensely. He was at awe with the grandeur and beauty of the universe, but then YHWH turned to John and asked him if he had noticed a particular planet. John said "No," but YHWH asked John to look at it more closely and when he did he saw that the planet was filled with vicious dogs. YHWH went on to explain to John that He loved those dogs and that He wanted him to go tell these vicious dogs that God loved them. John of course said, yes he would do that, but YHWH added, "Oh, John when you go to this planet I need you to become a dog in order to tell them of my love and I don't want you to be just any dog, I want you to be a Chihuahua." "Well..." John hesitated, but then he said, "Okay LORD, if that is what you want, I will do it." Then YHWH said, "John, these vicious dogs are going to tear you apart limb-from-limb, but don't worry, after you die I will bring you back to life." John wasn't at all sure that he wanted to do this now, but how could he refuse his LORD. He said, "Okay," but just then YHWH added one last thing. He said, "John I almost forgot to tell you, when I bring you back to life you will be a Chihuahua."

Stop and think about that. Our becoming a dog is nothing in comparison to Jesus Christ leaving the glory He had with the Father in heaven and becoming a human. Yes, He did receive back the glory he had before when He returned to heaven (John 17:5, 24), but that doesn't mean He is not still in a human body today. We cannot begin to appreciate what that alone cost Him and then to add to that the painful and shameful death He experienced for us. His love is truly beyond our comprehension.

The Prophecy Puzzle

I do want to make it clear that when I say that Jesus Christ is a man today, I am not saying that He ever at any time ceased to be God. That is part of the mystery. From the time of His birth Jesus Christ has been fully human and at the same time has always been God (YHWH).

Back to our text in Revelation, the description of Jesus Christ goes on to state that He has seven horns. In the Bible horns are a symbol of power and Jesus Christ having seven horns symbolizes His complete/perfect power.

The seven eyes Jesus Christ has are explained to us, they are the Seven Spirits of God - The Holy Spirit (Is 11:2). The Holy Spirit isn't just with Jesus Christ, but is <u>one</u> with <u>Him</u>. The Holy Spirit is one with Jesus Christ just as Jesus Christ said He and the Father are one (John 10:30). Christ Jesus' location is also very noteworthy. He is on the throne, not just before it like the elders and the four living creatures, but <u>on</u> it <u>with the Father</u>. Jesus Christ is on the throne of God (Rev. 7:17), because He is God (YHWH).

We talked about the elders and the four living creatures before, but we didn't discuss what they are doing before the throne of YHWH. They are falling down before YHWH – The Father, Son and Holy Spirit <u>who are all present on the throne</u> as we just pointed out, and worshiping Him (Them). This is another clear indicator that both Jesus Christ and the Holy Spirit are members of the Godhead, for only God is to be worshipped (Exodus 34:14; Mat. 4:10; Rev. 19:10, 22:8 - 9).

It should also be pointed out why they worship Jesus Christ. They do so, because He is "the Lamb" and for what He did. He was slain in order to purchase for God with His blood, men from every tribe... As I touched on earlier, we cannot begin to understand the sacrifice Jesus Christ made for us.

In addition to the worship, the twenty-four elders, not the four living creatures (Rev. 5:8) worship with harps (music) and present the prayers of the saints before Jesus Christ.

Some denominations use this verse to validate praying to saints, because the twenty-four elders (saints) present the prayers to Jesus Christ, but this does not validate that practice. We need to remember that the twenty-four elders represent all Christians. What we see here is the representation of the worship and prayers of all saints rising up to Jesus Christ (Ps. 141:2). YHWH has made it very clear in other places in the Bible we are to pray only to Him (John 14:6, 13, 16:26, 1 Tim. 2:5, Hebrews 4:14 – 16).

Again the twenty-four elders are representative of all Christians so when it says, "we shall reign on earth" in verse 10, it is referring to all believers. Some translations translate the "us" and "we" of verse 10 as "them" and "they," but that is an incorrect translation based on the "Alexandrian Greek text".

The last thing mentioned in this description of the throne of YHWH is the group of angels around it. We are not sure how many angels there are here, but to say the least there are a lot of them. If we just multiply the base numbers given here we end up with 101,000,000. So it is safe to say that there are more than one hundred million angels and probably many more than that.

Let us take just a moment to summarize what we have seen in chapters four and five. God the Father has the scroll (the deed to the earth) in

The Prophecy Puzzle

His hand and Jesus Christ approaches to take the scroll from the Father's hand. It should be noted that the seven seals are part of the scroll, but **not** part of the **judgments**, because the **judgments** are written **within** the scroll. The events of the seals **must precede** the judgments, which are written on the **inside** of the scroll. This takes us into the topic of the next chapter, the timing of end-time events, including the rapture.

The Prophecy Puzzle

CHAPTER SEVEN

An Outline of End-time Events

****

I previously mentioned a style of writing called parallelism. This style of writing is incorporated many times in the remainder of the book of Revelation. It is of the utmost importance to realize this truth in order to understand the rest of the book of Revelation. Most people have trouble understanding the book of Revelation after this point, because they do not understand that the same story is told three times. Each story has a different focus, but is essentially the same story. The three passages that give us this same story in three slightly different ways are Revelation 6:1 – 11:19, 12:1 – 16:21 and 17:1 – 19:21.

The Prophecy Puzzle

Revelation 6:1 – 11:19, starts with the beginning of the seven-year tribulation and goes through the seventh bowl of wrath and Armageddon. It gives us a detailed description of the first half of the seven-year tribulation, which is described for us through the opening of the seven seals. It also gives us a detailed description of the judgments of the seven trumpets, which occur during the second half of the seven-year tribulation. The marriage supper of the Lamb, the seven bowls of wrath, and the battle of Armageddon are contained in 11:17 – 19.

Revelation 12:1 – 16:21, focuses on Satan and his role in these end-time events, as well as giving us details about the world empire and the false Messiah. This passage could actually be divided into two separate stories itself.
- 12:1 – 6 give a very brief description of the incarnation, Satan's attempt to destroy Jesus Christ, Christ's resurrection and return to heaven and then it jumps to Israel's flight into the wilderness at the time of the abomination of desolation.
- 12:7 picks up the story again at that point giving a more detailed description explaining how Satan was cast down to the earth at the middle of the seven-year tribulation.
- Chapter 13 focuses on Satan's role in the world empire and the rise of the anti-Christ.
- Chapters 14 – 16 are pretty much in chronological order and describe the events, which take place at and after the abomination of desolation, which correspond with the opening of the Sixth Seal (Rev. 6:12 – 17).
  - Chapter 14 starts with the same 144,000 Jews who were sealed at the time of the opening of the sixth seal. At that time we are also given some of the details of other events that happen at the time of or right after the sealing of the 144,000 Jews.

The Prophecy Puzzle

- We are also introduced to three angels at this time.
  - The first goes throughout the world presenting the eternal gospel of grace.
  - The second angel declares that Babylon (that is the world religious system) is destroyed.
    - It is important to note that it is the anti-Christ who destroys it (Rev. 17:16 – 17).
  - The last angel warns everyone not to worship the beast or receive his mark.
    - He also comforts those who will die from this point on for their faith by telling them that God will reward them in the eternal.
  - 14:14 – 20 are a description of the rapture which happens with or right after the above mentioned events, which are followed by the judgments of YHWH which are also represented here.
  - 14:19 – 20 contain the seven trumpets, and the seven bowls of wrath which are described for us in detail in chapters 15 and 16.
    - The battle of Armageddon is included in 16:16 – 21.

Revelation 17:1 – 19:21, focuses on the great harlot and the Babylonian Empire.
- 17:1 – 13 is a description of how the revived Roman Empire and the great harlot (the world religious system), use each other to accomplish their goals leading up to and including the first half of the seven-year tribulation.
- 17:14 tells us how they will work together to persecute Christians during the first half of the seven-year tribulation.

The Prophecy Puzzle

- 17:15 – 18:3 is the announcement of the harlot's (false religious system) destruction.
- 18:4 can be understood in two different ways:
    - That it is a description of the rapture (Rev. 14:14 – 16).
    - That it is a warning to those who had believed after the rapture to leave this false religious/world system.
        - This same announcement is given in Rev. 14:8 and is followed with a warning not to receive the mark of the beast in verse nine.
- 18:5 - 24 goes on to describe the destruction of the actual city of Babylon, which will happen near the end of the great tribulation.
- Chapter 19 focuses on the Marriage Supper of the Lamb and then ends with a detailed description of the battle of Armageddon.

The remainder of the book (Revelation 20:1 – the end) starts with the great white throne judgment and then deals with the remainder of the Millennium Kingdom and ends by describing the new heavens and earth (eternity).

When we see these divisions in the book of Revelation, the puzzle pieces all come together. The remainder of this book will be trying to explain the placement of these puzzle pieces in order to give a clear picture of the end-time events given to us in the Bible.

The Prophecy Puzzle

CHAPTER EIGHT

The Timing of the Events of the Seven-year Tribulation According to Revelation 6:1 – 11:19

****

As I stated in the previous chapter, Revelation 6:1 – 11:19 starts with the beginning of the seven-year tribulation and goes through the seventh bowl of wrath and Armageddon. It gives us a detailed description of the first half of the seven-year tribulation and the judgments of the seven trumpets, which occur during the second half of the seven-year tribulation. The marriage supper of the Lamb, battle of Armageddon, and the bowls of wrath are summarized and contained in 11:17 – 19.

The Prophecy Puzzle

Another passage that corresponds with Revelation 6:1 – 11:19 is Matthew 24:1 – 31. While some would argue that these two passages are not discussing the same events, I believe they are, but you make up your own mind after we go through this chapter together. First let us look at Revelation chapters six and seven.

Revelation 6:1 – 7:17

> "And I saw when the Lamb opened one of the seals, and I heard, as it were the noise of thunder, one of the four beasts saying, Come and see.
> 2 And I saw, and behold a white horse: and he that sat on him had a bow; and a crown was given unto him: and he went forth conquering, and to conquer.
> 3 And when he had opened the second seal, I heard the second beast say, Come and see.
> 4 And there went out another horse that was red: and power was given to him that sat thereon to take peace from the earth, and that they should kill one another: and there was given unto him a great sword.
> 5 And when he had opened the third seal, I heard the third beast say, Come and see. And I beheld, and lo a black horse; and he that sat on him had a pair of balances in his hand.
> 6 And I heard a voice in the midst of the four beasts say, A measure of wheat for a penny, and three measures of barley for a penny; and see thou hurt not the oil and the wine.
> 7 And when he had opened the fourth seal, I heard the voice of the fourth beast say, Come and see.

The Prophecy Puzzle

8 And I looked, and behold a pale horse: and his name that sat on him was Death, and Hell followed with him. And power was given unto them over the fourth part of the earth, to kill with sword, and with hunger, and with death, and with the beasts of the earth.
9 And when he had opened the fifth seal, I saw under the altar the souls of them that were slain for the word of God, and for the testimony which they held:
10 And they cried with a loud voice, saying, How long, O Lord, holy and true, dost thou not judge and avenge our blood on them that dwell on the earth?
11 And white robes were given unto every one of them; and it was said unto them, that they should rest yet for a little season, until their fellowservants also and their brethren, that should be killed as they were, should be fulfilled.
12 And I beheld when he had opened the sixth seal, and, lo, there was a great earthquake; and the sun became black as sackcloth of hair, and the moon became as blood;
13 And the stars of heaven fell unto the earth, even as a fig tree casteth her untimely figs, when she is shaken of a mighty wind.
14 And the heaven departed as a scroll when it is rolled together; and every mountain and island were moved out of their places.
15 And the kings of the earth, and the great men, and the rich men, and the chief captains, and the mighty men, and every bondman, and every free man, hid themselves in the dens and in the rocks of the mountains;

The Prophecy Puzzle

16 And said to the mountains and rocks, Fall on us, and hide us from the face of him that sitteth on the throne, and from the wrath of the Lamb:
17 For the great day of his wrath is come; and who shall be able to stand?
7:1 And after these things I saw four angels standing on the four corners of the earth, holding the four winds of the earth, that the wind should not blow on the earth, nor on the sea, nor on any tree.
2 And I saw another angel ascending from the east, having the seal of the living God: and he cried with a loud voice to the four angels, to whom it was given to hurt the earth and the sea,
3 Saying, Hurt not the earth, neither the sea, nor the trees, till we have sealed the servants of our God in their foreheads.
4 And I heard the number of them which were sealed: and there were sealed an hundred and forty and four thousand of all the tribes of the children of Israel.
5 Of the tribe of Juda were sealed twelve thousand. Of the tribe of Reuben were sealed twelve thousand. Of the tribe of Gad were sealed twelve thousand.
6 Of the tribe of Aser were sealed twelve thousand. Of the tribe of Nepthali were sealed twelve thousand. Of the tribe of Manasses were sealed twelve thousand.
7 Of the tribe of Simeon were sealed twelve thousand. Of the tribe of Levi were sealed twelve thousand. Of the tribe of Issachar were sealed twelve thousand.
8 Of the tribe of Zabulon were sealed twelve thousand. Of the tribe of Joseph were sealed twelve thousand. Of the tribe of Benjamin were sealed twelve thousand.

The Prophecy Puzzle

9 After this I beheld, and, lo, a great multitude, which no man could number, of all nations, and kindreds, and people, and tongues, stood before the throne, and before the Lamb, clothed with white robes, and palms in their hands;
10 And cried with a loud voice, saying, Salvation to our God which sitteth upon the throne, and unto the Lamb.
11 And all the angels stood round about the throne, and about the elders and the four beasts, and fell before the throne on their faces, and worshipped God,
12 Saying, Amen: Blessing, and glory, and wisdom, and thanksgiving, and honour, and power, and might, be unto our God for ever and ever. Amen.
13 And one of the elders answered, saying unto me, What are these which are arrayed in white robes? and whence came they?
14 And I said unto him, Sir, thou knowest. And he said to me, These are they which came out of great tribulation, and have washed their robes, and made them white in the blood of the Lamb.
15 Therefore are they before the throne of God, and serve him day and night in his temple: and he that sitteth on the throne shall dwell among them.
16 They shall hunger no more, neither thirst any more; neither shall the sun light on them, nor any heat.
17 For the Lamb which is in the midst of the throne shall feed them, and shall lead them unto living fountains of waters: and God shall wipe away all tears from their eyes."

The Prophecy Puzzle

In Revelation 6:1 – 2 we see the events that occur with the opening of the first seal. The opening of the first seal marks the beginning of the seven-year tribulation. We are told that when Jesus Christ opens the first seal there will be one who comes onto the world scene riding upon a white horse holding a bow, but note he has no arrows.

Some believe the one on the white horse is Jesus Christ, but if we look at other passages in the Bible we see that is not the case. It is understandable though why this one is mistaken for Jesus Christ, because he is the false Messiah. He comes upon the scene on a white horse, a symbol of a conquering king (Rev. 19:11), but not because of his military strength, but because of his bow. This bow is not a weapon of war, but it is a bow like the rain**bow** YHWH used to symbolize a "peace treaty" with Noah (Gen. 9:13). The Septuagint (the Greek translation of the Old Testament) uses the same Greek word in Gen. 9:13 as is used here in Revelation 6:2.

Genesis 9:13

"I do set my bow in the cloud, and it shall be for a token of a covenant between me and the earth."

We have this understanding confirmed from other passages dealing with the anti-Christ (false Messiah) in the Bible. Again some do argue that these verses do not apply to the false Messiah, but to others who had lived in the past. Yes, they might apply to historical characters in part, but their ultimate fulfillment is in the anti-Christ.

The Prophecy Puzzle

Daniel 8:23

"And in the latter time of their kingdom, when the transgressors are come to the full, a king of fierce countenance, and understanding dark sentences, shall stand up."

Daniel 9:27

"And he shall confirm the covenant with many for one week: and in the midst of the week he shall cause the sacrifice and the oblation to cease, and for the overspreading of abominations he shall make it desolate, even until the consummation, and that determined shall be poured upon the desolate."

Daniel 11:21

"And in his estate shall stand up a vile person, to whom they shall not give the honour of the kingdom: but he shall come in peaceably, and obtain the kingdom by flatteries."

From our passage in Matthew 24 we have Jesus Christ telling us the same thing, but not as a specific individual, but the general warning of the coming of false Messiahs.

Matthew 24:4 – 5

"And Jesus answered and said unto them, Take heed that no man deceive you.

> 5 For many shall come in my name, saying, I am Christ; and shall deceive many."

So the seven-year tribulation begins with a world leader, the false Messiah rising to prominence by negotiating a peace treaty with Israel. It needs to be noted that some things must be in place before this can happen, because we are told in Daniel 7:23 – 24 and Rev. 13:1 - 5 that the "world government" is in place before the rise of the false Messiah. This is actually something that is discussed in detail in the next chapter, but because I think it is important to understand how the false Messiah rises out of an already existing "World Empire" we will look at it briefly now.

Daniel 7:7 – 8

> "After this I saw in the night visions, and behold a fourth beast, dreadful and terrible, and strong exceedingly; and it had great iron teeth: it devoured and brake in pieces, and stamped the residue with the feet of it: and it was diverse from all the beasts that were before it; and it had ten horns.
> 8 I considered the horns, and, behold, there came up among them another little horn, before whom there were three of the first horns plucked up by the roots: and, behold, in this horn were eyes like the eyes of man, and a mouth speaking great things."

Daniel 7:23 – 25

> "Thus he said, The fourth beast shall be the fourth kingdom upon earth, which shall be diverse from all

The Prophecy Puzzle

> kingdoms, and shall devour the whole earth, and shall tread it down, and break it in pieces.
> 24 And the ten horns out of this kingdom are ten kings that shall arise: and another shall rise after them; and he shall be diverse from the first, and he shall subdue three kings.
> 25 And he shall speak great words against the most High, and shall wear out the saints of the most High, and think to change times and laws: and they shall be given into his hand until a time and times and the dividing of time."

In verses 7 and 23 we are introduced to this fourth kingdom-beast and in verses 8 and 24 we see that the horns are ten kings, but <u>after</u> them, another one - the false Messiah (the man-beast) rises. In his coming into power he replaces three of the original world leaders. I do not believe that he was one of the original ten, but he was someone of lesser stature who comes to prominence by forming the peace treaty with Israel – i.e. the small horn (Dan. 7:7 – 8, 11:21).

Revelation 13:1 – 5

> "And I stood upon the sand of the sea, and saw a beast rise up out of the sea, having seven heads and ten horns, and upon his horns ten crowns, and upon his heads the name of blasphemy.
> 2 And the beast which I saw was like unto a leopard, and his feet were as the feet of a bear, and his mouth as the mouth of a lion: and the dragon gave him his power, and his seat, and great authority.

The Prophecy Puzzle

> 3 And I saw one of his heads as it were wounded to death; and his deadly wound was healed: and all the world wondered after the beast.
> 4 And they worshipped the dragon which gave power unto the beast: and they worshipped the beast, saying, Who is like unto the beast? who is able to make war with him?
> 5 And there was given unto him a mouth speaking great things and blasphemies; and power was given unto him to continue forty and two months."

Here we see the same exact thing as in Daniel. We see the kingdom-beast coming out of the sea (the kingdoms of the world) with ten world leaders (horns) (Rev. 17:12). In verse 5 we are once again introduced to the false Messiah – the mouth (the man-beast).

In order to prevent confusion, I think it would be wise to take some time here to identify the ten horns.

Revelation 17:12

> "12 And the ten horns which thou sawest are ten kings, which have received no kingdom as yet; but receive power as kings one hour with the beast."

It is made clear that they are not true kings, because they have authority, but they have no land. One might say that they are representatives, each representing one of the ten regions of the "world government".

The Prophecy Puzzle

There have been many suggestions made about where these "kings" come from, such as the United Nations, the G7, NATO and the European Union. It seems to me that the European Union is the most likely. I've read that they have divided up the world into ten regions and plan to have a director ("king") over each region. I do caution though that things can change quickly on the world front and I would not be dogmatic on any stance at this time.

It has been suggested that the true human powers behind this revived Empire is the Federal Reserve and the International Monetary Fund (IMF). They do have an enormous amount of seemingly unchecked power as they manipulate the currencies of governments around the world, so I'm sure they will have a role in the "world government." On a related note, one thing I do know is that the purpose of this global warming hoax is to finance this global government. A DVD that reveals this truth is "Global Warming or Global Governance?"

So to bring us back to our timeline. We have the Revived Roman Empire, having ten representatives, each representing a tenth of the earth. Shortly after the forming of this world governing body we have what was described for us at the breaking of the first seal - a peace treaty is signed with Israel (it's the world on one side and Israel on the other). The individual who will become the false Messiah is the one primarily responsible for the forming and signing of this treaty.

Sometimes it is assumed that the anti-Christ will come onto the scene proclaiming to be the Messiah. I do not believe that is the case. Jesus Christ said that he would come in his own name, not in the name of God (John 5:43). He doesn't proclaim to be God until the middle of the seven-year tribulation. At the time of his signing this peace treaty with Israel he will be just one more rising political star.

The Prophecy Puzzle

The next event to happen according to the Bible is the opening of the second seal.

Revelation 6:3 – 4

> "And when he had opened the second seal, I heard the second beast say, Come and see.
> 4 And there went out another horse that was red: and power was given to him that sat thereon to take peace from the earth, and that they should kill one another: and there was given unto him a great sword."

With the opening of the second seal we see that while the peace treaty with Israel seems to stay intact wars/battles breakout elsewhere around the world. It should be noted that it is implied that there was worldwide peace for a short time. In any case the Revived Roman Empire with its great military strength is able to stay in power (Dan. 8:24).

Christ Jesus says the same thing in a slightly different manner in Matthew 24.

Matthew 24:6 – 7a

> "And ye shall hear of wars and rumours of wars: see that ye be not troubled: for all these things must come to pass, but the end is not yet.
> 7 For nation shall rise against nation, and kingdom against kingdom:"

The Prophecy Puzzle

In Matthew, Christ Jesus makes mention of the "the end" and that it has not yet come. The end referred to here is the end of this age, the age of grace (the church age). This age ends with the completion of the events that come with the opening of the sixth seal, which includes the rapture. The Jewish day starts with the evening (the coming of darkness) and so, the "Day of the LORD" starts with judgment. But we'll discuss this more later. After the events of the second seal we have the breaking of the third seal, which brings famine around the world.

Revelation 6:5 – 6

> "And when he had opened the third seal, I heard the third beast say, Come and see. And I beheld, and lo a black horse; and he that sat on him had a pair of balances in his hand.
> 6 And I heard a voice in the midst of the four beasts say, A measure of wheat for a penny, and three measures of barley for a penny; and see thou hurt not the oil and the wine."

And we see this too is what is next in the series of events given to us by Jesus Christ in Matthew 24:7.

Matthew 24:7b

> "... and there will be famines,"

Before we move onto the next seal let's discuss the cause of this shortage of food. As today there are droughts and floods, etc. that can create a shortage of food regionally, but the main reason people go without food today is not the shortage of food, but the unwillingness to

The Prophecy Puzzle

distribute the abundance of food in the world. The food is available and often times having been given to be distributed among those in need, but the food cannot get to the people, because they live under a cruel government that will not allow the food to reach them. That is the way the false Messiah runs his government as well (Dan. 11:24).

I am not saying there won't be shortages of food, but I believe part of the problem during this time will be that the government will not allow the food to be distributed to those in need. I believe the end of verse six could be indicating that, because it states that the oil and wine should not be hurt. The oil and wine are believed to be a reference to the wealthy. The wealthy elitist friends of the anti-Christ (false Messiah) will have all that they need during this time. Also this is the natural result of socialism, and I believe the coming world government will be a mixing of Fabian Socialism and Crony Capitalism.

Revelation 6:7 – 8

> "And when he had opened the fourth seal, I heard the voice of the fourth beast say, Come and see.
> 8 And I looked, and behold a pale horse: and his name that sat on him was Death, and Hell followed with him. And power was given unto them over the fourth part of the earth, to kill with sword, and with hunger, and with death, and with the beasts of the earth."

The breaking of the fourth seal gives us the inevitable result of the breaking of the first three seals; namely disease and death, which of course is what Jesus Christ also makes reference to in Matthew 24:7c:

> "... and pestilences"

The Prophecy Puzzle

One might say that a spirit of murder comes upon desperate people. They are hungry, discontent and most of all helpless. To make matters worse the animals are also hungry and turn to attacking people to fill their stomachs. Rev. 6:8 continues on to say that a geographic area covering one-fourth of the earth will be devastated by these plagues. This could represent small areas around the world or it could be one large area.

I believe that the events of the first four seals are for the most part the result of the actions of mankind. I want to make it clear that I'm not trying to eliminate God's hand in these events, but I believe He will use mankind to judge mankind at this time, just as He used King Nebuchadnezzar in the seventh century B.C. (Jeremiah 27:1 – 22).

Revelation 6:9 – 11

> "And when he had opened the fifth seal, I saw under the altar the souls of them that were slain for the word of God, and for the testimony which they held:
> 10 And they cried with a loud voice, saying, How long, O Lord, holy and true, dost thou not judge and avenge our blood on them that dwell on the earth?
> 11 And white robes were given unto every one of them; and it was said unto them, that they should rest yet for a little season, until their fellowservants also and their brethren, that should be killed as they were, should be fulfilled."

The events that happen with the breaking of the fifth seal only happen in heaven and because they do not happen on the earth, Jesus Christ

The Prophecy Puzzle

doesn't mention them in Matthew 24. With the opening of the fifth seal we see the souls under the altar, but it should be noted that the souls are not physically under the altar. This is symbolic language to identify these people as martyrs. They were killed for their faith in Jesus Christ (YHWH). They ask YHWH how long it will be before He judges the world. YHWH's reply is that more people must still be martyred before the end comes (Remember the end is a reference to the end of this age, which comes with the events of the breaking of the sixth seal). We are also told that these souls receive white robes, which indicate the gift of Jesus Christ's righteousness by which they are saved (Rom. 3:21 – 26, Matthew 22:9–13, John 6:28, 29, Gal. 3:26 – 27, Eph 5:25–27).

There is one more point to be made from this passage, and it is that these souls are not asleep. Soul sleep is not Biblical. It is very clear from this passage that these people who were dead physically were very much alive and aware of their existence at this time, which is clearly before their resurrection.

Revelation 6:12 – 17

> "And I beheld when he had opened the sixth seal, and, lo, there was a great earthquake; and the sun became black as sackcloth of hair, and the moon became as blood;
> 13 And the stars of heaven fell unto the earth, even as a fig tree casteth her untimely figs, when she is shaken of a mighty wind.
> 14 And the heaven departed as a scroll when it is rolled together; and every mountain and island were moved out of their places.

The Prophecy Puzzle

> 15 And the kings of the earth, and the great men, and the rich men, and the chief captains, and the mighty men, and every bondman, and every free man, hid themselves in the dens and in the rocks of the mountains;
> 16 And said to the mountains and rocks, Fall on us, and hide us from the face of him that sitteth on the throne, and from the wrath of the Lamb:
> 17 For the great day of his wrath is come; and who shall be able to stand?"

Before we go through all of the events of the sixth seal I would like to stop and just note that the first thing that happens is a great earthquake and that is what Jesus Christ makes reference to in Matthew 24:7d:

> "... and earthquakes, in divers places."

Christ Jesus goes on from that point to make it clear that all those events are not the end, but only "the beginning of sorrows" (Mat. 24:8). In Matthew 24:9 – 13 He goes back over the "beginning of sorrows" He just discussed and fills in a little more detail about those times.

Matthew 24:9 – 13

> "Then shall they deliver you up to be afflicted, and shall kill you: and ye shall be hated of all nations for my name's sake.
> 10 And then shall many be offended, and shall betray one another, and shall hate one another.
> 11 And many false prophets shall rise, and shall deceive many.

The Prophecy Puzzle

> 12 And because iniquity shall abound, the love of many shall wax cold.
> 13 But he that shall endure unto the end, the same shall be saved."

In verse 9, "Then" is speaking of the first half of the seven-year tribulation. I need to emphasize that. Jesus Christ is going over the time just discussed, which is the first half of the seven-year tribulation (the seals we just discussed in Revelation 6:1 – 11).

Remembering that the time being referred to is the first three and half years of the seven-year tribulation and understanding who the "you" and "those" are referring to in this passage are of utmost importance.

In this passage Jesus Christ is speaking to Christians. It is the Christian who will be persecuted during the first half of the seven-year tribulation. The Jews are for the most part living peaceably in Israel during this time (Ezekiel 38:8 – 16).

Ezekiel 38:11 – 12

> "And thou shalt say, I will go up to the land of unwalled villages; I will go to them that are at rest, that dwell safely, all of them dwelling without walls, and having neither bars nor gates,
> 12 To take a spoil, and to take a prey; to turn thine hand upon the desolate places that are now inhabited, and upon the people that are gathered out of the nations, which have gotten cattle and goods, that dwell in the midst of the land."

The Prophecy Puzzle

Because of the peace treaty they had signed with the false Messiah, they have rebuilt the temple and even started the sacrifices again, but that brings us to where we are in the progression of the breaking of seals. We are at the breaking of the sixth seal, and it is at this time the false Messiah (anti-Christ) has a change of heart and attacks Israel.

Further evidence of this being the case is the prophecy in Daniel 11:24 – 35. There we are given more details about the actions of the false Messiah during the first half of the seven-year tribulation period.

Daniel 11:24 – 35

> "He shall enter peaceably even upon the fattest places of the province; and he shall do that which his fathers have not done, nor his fathers' fathers; he shall scatter among them the prey, and spoil, and riches: yea, and he shall forecast his devices against the strong holds, even for a time.
> 25 And he shall stir up his power and his courage against the king of the south with a great army; and the king of the south shall be stirred up to battle with a very great and mighty army; but he shall not stand: for they shall forecast devices against him.
> 26 Yea, they that feed of the portion of his meat shall destroy him, and his army shall overflow: and many shall fall down slain.
> 27 And both these kings' hearts shall be to do mischief, and they shall speak lies at one table; but it shall not prosper: for yet the end shall be at the time appointed.

The Prophecy Puzzle

28 Then shall he return into his land with great riches; and his heart shall be against the holy covenant; and he shall do exploits, and return to his own land.
29 At the time appointed he shall return, and come toward the south; but it shall not be as the former, or as the latter.
30 For the ships of Chittim shall come against him: therefore he shall be grieved, and return, and have indignation against the holy covenant: so shall he do; he shall even return, and have intelligence with them that forsake the holy covenant.
31 And arms shall stand on his part, and they shall pollute the sanctuary of strength, and shall take away the daily sacrifice, and they shall place the abomination that maketh desolate.
32 And such as do wickedly against the covenant shall he corrupt by flatteries: but the people that do know their God shall be strong, and do exploits.
33 And they that understand among the people shall instruct many: yet they shall fall by the sword, and by flame, by captivity, and by spoil, many days.
34 Now when they shall fall, they shall be holpen with a little help: but many shall cleave to them with flatteries.
35 And some of them of understanding shall fall, to try them, and to purge, and to make them white, even to the time of the end: because it is yet for a time appointed."

In the verses just before this passage (vv. 21 – 23) we see how the false Messiah came to power, just as described in the opening of the first seal

The Prophecy Puzzle

(Rev. 6:1 – 2). Then we see how in the time of peace that immediately follows the signing of the peace treaty with Israel we have wars and rumors of war just as they are mentioned in the second seal (Revelation 6:3 – 4) and Matthew 24:6 – 7. We even see in Dan. 11:24 how the false Messiah uses his position to make sure his friends are well off when the masses go hungry, just as described in the third seal (Rev. 6:5 – 6) and Matthew 24:7).

What happens in verses 30 and 31 is what is of most importance here. The regular sacrifices that the Jews had been making to God in their temple are stopped and the abomination of desolation is set up. This occurs at the middle of the seven-year tribulation (Dan. 9:27). The actions taken by the false Messiah at the time of the abomination of desolation are described for us in the following two verses in Daniel.

Daniel 11:36 – 37

> "And the king shall do according to his will; and he shall exalt himself, and magnify himself above every god, and shall speak marvellous things against the God of gods, and shall prosper till the indignation be accomplished: for that that is determined shall be done.
> 37 Neither shall he regard the God of his fathers, nor the desire of women, nor regard any god: for he shall magnify himself above all."

There is confusion regarding v. 37 where it states that he (the false Messiah) will not regard the desire of women, and there is more than one possibility. What is clear is that the verse is dealing with his not recognizing any other gods (2Thes. 2:4). The controversy is over the meaning of "the desire of women." If the false Messiah is Jewish "the God of his fathers," would refer to YHWH, the God of the Bible and then the most logical meaning for the "desire of women" would be the Messiah (Christ Jesus). This is because from the time of the prophecies of the Messiah, Jewish women had hoped they would be the one chosen to be the mother of the Messiah. It was **their desire** to be the mother of the Messiah.

Some object to this understanding, because it implies that the false Messiah (anti-Christ) is Jewish and they do not believe that is the case. That is a good point and we will discuss the identity of the false Messiah later, but for now I would suggest it truly doesn't matter. If some of his ancestors were Christian, then the "God of his fathers," would still be YHHW. Even if his ancestors worshipped a false god, it doesn't mandate that "the desire for women" could not refer to the Messiah. The point of the verse is that the false Messiah will not worship the god of his ancestors nor the Messiah, or any god at all; and that will be the case no matter what ethnicity he might be.

The understanding that the "desire of women" is a reference to the Messiah is the simplest, and in the immediate context the most logical way to understand it. I do acknowledge that there are many other theories out there that might be correct, but it would be too much to look at all of them; but we will look at one. It is the one that is probably the most often stated, that it means he is homosexual. He might be, but that is not the subject matter of this verse, so I don't think that is the correct understanding.

Getting back to our timeline, we're now near the middle of the seven-year tribulation and looking at Revelation 6:12 – 17:

The Prophecy Puzzle

"And I beheld when he had opened the sixth seal, and, lo, there was a great earthquake; and the sun became black as sackcloth of hair, and the moon became as blood;

13 And the stars of heaven fell unto the earth, even as a fig tree casteth her untimely figs, when she is shaken of a mighty wind.

14 And the heaven departed as a scroll when it is rolled together; and every mountain and island were moved out of their places.

15 And the kings of the earth, and the great men, and the rich men, and the chief captains, and the mighty men, and every bondman, and every free man, hid themselves in the dens and in the rocks of the mountains;

16 And said to the mountains and rocks, Fall on us, and hide us from the face of him that sitteth on the throne, and from the wrath of the Lamb:

17 For the great day of his wrath is come; and who shall be able to stand?"

There was a huge earthquake, but this earthquake is different from others, because it is much larger and timed with the breaking of the sixth seal. Every mountain and island moves (feels) this earthquake. As far as recorded history goes, that happened for the first time on 12/25/04. I think that was nothing in comparison to the earthquake that will happen with the breaking of the sixth seal. Also at this time the sun becomes black (dark) and the moon becomes like blood (red?). This is probably a direct result of the earthquake. There will be huge amounts of smoke from fires and debris filling the air and blocking out and tainting the light from the sun and moon.

The Prophecy Puzzle

I live in Southern California and I believe we experienced a small hint of what is being referred to here. There were times during bad forest fires that the sun and moon took on a very eerie deep orange-red appearance.

The stars falling from the sky would also add to the debris in the air. And of course these are not literal stars, for that is impossible. A star is much larger than the earth and just one star would totally demolish the earth. As far as it is referring to physical stars, it is referring to the earth being hit by meteors. Meteors that burn up as they enter the earth's atmosphere are often referred to as falling or shooting **stars**.

I believe this reference of stars falling to the earth is <u>also</u> a reference to Satan and his angels being cast out of heaven to the earth. If we recall the outline in chapter seven, it was explained how the same events are to be told several times in the book of Revelation, each with a slightly different focus. So as we look at different recordings of these same events we will get a better understanding of them. Let's look at a couple other passages in Revelation, which give us a fuller understanding of what is happening at this time.

Revelation 9:1

> "And the fifth angel sounded, and I saw a star fall from heaven unto the earth: and to him was given the key of the bottomless pit."

I bring this verse up at this time because it makes it clear that a star can refer to something other than a physical star. In this case and in others in the Bible, a star refers to an angel.

The Prophecy Puzzle

Revelation 12:7 – 17

"And there was war in heaven: Michael and his angels fought against the dragon; and the dragon fought and his angels,

8 And prevailed not; neither was their place found any more in heaven.

9 And the great dragon was cast out, that old serpent, called the Devil, and Satan, which deceiveth the whole world: he was cast out into the earth, and his angels were cast out with him.

10 And I heard a loud voice saying in heaven, Now is come salvation, and strength, and the kingdom of our God, and the power of his Christ: for the accuser of our brethren is cast down, which accused them before our God day and night.

11 And they overcame him by the blood of the Lamb, and by the word of their testimony; and they loved not their lives unto the death.

12 Therefore rejoice, ye heavens, and ye that dwell in them. Woe to the inhabiters of the earth and of the sea! for the devil is come down unto you, having great wrath, because he knoweth that he hath but a short time.

13 And when the dragon saw that he was cast unto the earth, he persecuted the woman which brought forth the man child.

14 And to the woman were given two wings of a great eagle, that she might fly into the wilderness, into her

> place, where she is nourished for a time, and times, and half a time, from the face of the serpent.
> 15 And the serpent cast out of his mouth water as a flood after the woman, that he might cause her to be carried away of the flood.
> 16 And the earth helped the woman, and the earth opened her mouth, and swallowed up the flood which the dragon cast out of his mouth.
> 17 And the dragon was wroth with the woman, and went to make war with the remnant of her seed, which keep the commandments of God, and have the testimony of Jesus Christ."

Before this time Satan had lost his position in heaven (Ez. 28:13 – 16), but still had limited access to it (Job 1:7; 1 Peter 5:8; Rev. 12:10). At this time he is cast down to the earth, **never again being able to return to heaven**.

We will make reference to the above passage again, but at this time we will be using Revelation 6:12 – 17 as our main point of reference.

We see at this time (Rev. 6:14) the sky is split apart like a scroll. This is probably a dimensional split allowing the glory of heaven to flash into the earth's atmosphere for a moment. We see something similar, but at a much smaller scale in Acts 9:3 – 5, when Jesus Christ introduced himself to Paul. I believe what we see happening here with the opening of the sixth seal is the heavens being opened in order for Christ Jesus to return in the clouds, which is exactly what is depicted in the remainder of this passage (vv. 15 – 16). In other words, what is being described, are the events that surround the **rapture.** We see the result of the rapture in the next chapter (Revelation 7:9 – 17).

The Prophecy Puzzle

I do not think it is possible to nail down the exact timing of these events, but perhaps by looking at a few more passages we can bring things into better focus. The passages we will be primarily looking at are Ezekiel 38, Hosea 5:15, Joel 2:28 – 32, Mat. 24:9 – 31 and Revelation 6:12 – 7:17, 12:6 – 17, 14:1 – 20.

One of the clearest markers of time in these events is the moon turning to blood. So let's use that as a marker and see what we find.

Joel 2:28 – 32

> "And it shall come to pass afterward, that I will pour out my spirit upon all flesh; and your sons and your daughters shall prophesy, your old men shall dream dreams, your young men shall see visions:
> 29 And also upon the servants and upon the handmaids in those days will I pour out my spirit.
> 30 And I will shew wonders in the heavens and in the earth, blood, and fire, and pillars of smoke.
> 31 The sun shall be turned into darkness, and the moon into blood, before the great and the terrible day of the LORD come.
> 32 And it shall come to pass, that whosoever shall call on the name of the LORD shall be delivered: for in mount Zion and in Jerusalem shall be deliverance, as the LORD hath said, and in the remnant whom the LORD shall call."

The Prophecy Puzzle

Acts 2:17 – 21

"And it shall come to pass in the last days, saith God, I will pour out of my Spirit upon all flesh: and your sons and your daughters shall prophesy, and your young men shall see visions, and your old men shall dream dreams:
18 And on my servants and on my handmaidens I will pour out in those days of my Spirit; and they shall prophesy:
19 And I will shew wonders in heaven above, and signs in the earth beneath; blood, and fire, and vapour of smoke:
20 The sun shall be turned into darkness, and the moon into blood, before that great and notable day of the Lord come:
21 And it shall come to pass, that whosoever shall call on the name of the Lord shall be saved."

When we look at these two passages together we see that the first half of this prophecy was fulfilled on Pentecost Sunday, but the rest of it was not. I would suggest that the signs and wonders in the heavens and earth, blood, fire, vapor and the sun being darkened and the moon turning to blood are the same events, which occur with the breaking of the sixth seal. Note also that verse 20 states that the sun and moon going dark will happen **before** the Day of the LORD, which begins with the wrath of the Lamb being poured out upon the earth through the seven trumpets and seven vials of wrath (Rev. 8:6 – 11:19, 16:1 – 16:21). I need to emphasize that point. The Day of the LORD begins with <u>His</u> wrath, which begins after the sealing of the 144,000 Jewish believers and the rapture.

The Prophecy Puzzle

In Matthew 24:13 – 31 we see a similar description of the events just discussed, including the sun and moon being darkened. I believe it is referring to the same event described in the breaking of the sixth seal. To clarify that, we will need to take a closer look at Matthew 24:13 – 31. Remember Mat. 24:13 had brought us up to the "great tribulation" (the second half of the seven-year tribulation).

Matthew 24:13 – 31

> "But he that shall endure unto the end, the same shall be saved.
> 14 And this gospel of the kingdom shall be preached in all the world for a witness unto all nations; and then shall the end come.
> 15 When ye therefore shall see the abomination of desolation, spoken of by Daniel the prophet, stand in the holy place, (whoso readeth, let him understand:)
> 16 Then let them which be in Judaea flee into the mountains:
> 17 Let him which is on the housetop not come down to take any thing out of his house:
> 18 Neither let him which is in the field return back to take his clothes.
> 19 And woe unto them that are with child, and to them that give suck in those days!
> 20 But pray ye that your flight be not in the winter, neither on the sabbath day:
> 21 For then shall be great tribulation, such as was not since the beginning of the world to this time, no, nor ever shall be.

The Prophecy Puzzle

22 And except those days should be shortened, there should no flesh be saved: but for the elect's sake those days shall be shortened.
23 Then if any man shall say unto you, Lo, here is Christ, or there; believe it not.
24 For there shall arise false Christs, and false prophets, and shall shew great signs and wonders; insomuch that, if it were possible, they shall deceive the very elect.
25 Behold, I have told you before.
26 Wherefore if they shall say unto you, Behold, he is in the desert; go not forth: behold, he is in the secret chambers; believe it not.
27 For as the lightning cometh out of the east, and shineth even unto the west; so shall also the coming of the Son of man be.
28 For wheresoever the carcase is, there will the eagles be gathered together.
29 Immediately after the tribulation of those days shall the sun be darkened, and the moon shall not give her light, and the stars shall fall from heaven, and the powers of the heavens shall be shaken:
30 And then shall appear the sign of the Son of man in heaven: and then shall all the tribes of the earth mourn, and they shall see the Son of man coming in the clouds of heaven with power and great glory.
31 And he shall send his angels with a great sound of a trumpet, and they shall gather together his elect from the four winds, from one end of heaven to the other."

The Prophecy Puzzle

I believe the reference to the sun and moon going dark in verse 29 is the same event described in the breaking of the sixth seal. Notice the same events in the same order. Also the sixth seal is another description of Zechariah 14:3, and Zechariah 14:2 is the tribulation being spoken of in Matthew 24:29. Of course these do not happen in a moment, but over a period of time.

Zechariah 14:2 – 3

> For I will gather all nations against Jerusalem to battle; and the city shall be taken, and the houses rifled, and the women ravished; and half of the city shall go forth into captivity, and the residue of the people shall not be cut off from the city. 3 Then shall the LORD go forth, and fight against those nations, as when he fought in the day of battle.

Matthew 24:14 is simply stating that before the **end**, that is before the "**Day of the LORD**" comes, the gospel will be preached throughout the world. We learn in Revelation 14:6 – 7 that is accomplished by an angel. After this worldwide proclamation of the gospel, the wrath of God will come. The wrath of God is the **beginning** of the Day of the LORD. Remember, the Jewish day begins with the evening (darkness, "choshek" in Hebrew and it figuratively means chaos, misery and destruction) and then moves into the day (light, figuratively happiness) (Genesis 1:5).

Matthew 24:15 – 22 is Jesus Christ warning the Jews who are alive at the time of the Abomination of Desolation, and He goes into detail on what they should do on the day the false Messiah attacks.

The Prophecy Puzzle

Matthew 24:23 – 28 is a warning to not be fooled by people claiming the Messiah is here or there. Jesus Christ explains that when He returns everyone in the world will see Him (Rev. 6:15 – 17). Also when He returns He will bring judgment with Him, which He does at the opening of the sixth seal (Rev. 6:12 – 17) and will end with the battle of Armageddon, hence the reference to the birds eating the corpses (Mat. 24:28, Rev. 19:17 – 18).

Matthew 24:29 – 31 is another description of what happens at the opening of the sixth seal. It is set up by the false Messiah's attack on Israel at the middle of the seven-year tribulation (Ezekiel 38:8 – 16), the Israelites cry out to the LORD (Hosea 5:15 KJV, Mat. 23:37 – 39), which sets in motion the Great Tribulation:
- The sun and moon is darkened (Rev. 6:12).
- The stars of heaven fall to the earth (Rev. 6:13).
- The powers of heaven are shaken.
    - The stars also represent angels and they fall at this time because of the battle they just lost in heaven (Revelation 12:7 – 9).
    - While it is not stated here I believe it is at this time that Satan inhabits the image that was made for him and placed in the temple (Rev. 13:15).
- Christ Jesus appears in the clouds in glory and the people on earth cower (Rev. 6:14 – 16).
    - Somewhere among these events is when the rapture happens.
        - While the rapture is not specifically stated here in Revelation six, we do see the results of it in Rev. 7:9 – 17.
    - Note that in Mat. 24:31 it describes the sound of the trumpet that accompanies the rapture.

The Prophecy Puzzle

- 1Cor. 15:51 – 52: Behold, I shew you a mystery; We shall not all sleep, but we shall all be changed, 52 In a moment, in the twinkling of an eye, at the last trump: for the trumpet shall sound, and the dead shall be raised incorruptible, and we shall be changed.
- 1Thes. 4:16 – 17: For the Lord himself shall descend from heaven with a shout, with the voice of the archangel, and with the trump of God: and the dead in Christ shall rise first: 17 Then we which are alive and remain shall be caught up together with them in the clouds, to meet the Lord in the air: and so shall we ever be with the Lord.
- As another interesting fact, the trumpet had two purposes for Israel. It was used as a call to worship and a call to battle.
  - At this time Christ returns to battle for the Jews and provide them a way of escape (Zechariah 14:1 – 6).
  - Also at this time, Christians will be gathered (raptured) to be in the presence of the LORD to forever worship Him.

Because most Evangelicals I know; believe the rapture will happen before or at the beginning of the seven-year tribulation, I would like to take this time to answer some of their concerns before we move on in the text in Revelation. There are too many for me to address all of them, but I will look at two of the most valid.

The Prophecy Puzzle

The first one I will look at is the doctrine of the imminent return of Jesus Christ. People hold to this doctrine, because many times we are told to be ready, because we do not know the time of Jesus Christ's return (rapture). What we are actually told is that we do not know the day or the hour, but we should know the season (1 Thes. 5:1 – 4). This means that Jesus Christ's return should be marked by events associated with His return. If there are no signs associated with the rapture, how could anyone know the season in which it will occur? In other words Jesus Christ cannot return until those specific signs associated with His return happen. Those signs are the very ones we have been studying in Matthew 24 and Revelation 6.

Another point to be made about this issue is that Jesus Christ could **not** return at anytime in the past, because some specific things had to happen; because they were foretold by YHWH that they **must** happen.

First of all in John 21:19 Jesus Christ tells Peter that he will die. Therefore the rapture could not happen until Peter died. In Acts 27:23 – 25 Jesus Christ told Paul that he would testify of Him in Rome. Therefore the rapture could not happen until Paul had reached Rome. The most significant of these is found in Acts Chapter 3.

Acts 3:20 – 21

> "And he shall send Jesus Christ, which before was preached unto you: 21 Whom the heaven must receive until the times of restitution of all things, which God hath spoken by the mouth of all his holy prophets since the world began."

The Prophecy Puzzle

The times of restitution begin with the wrath of the Lamb, which we saw arrive in Rev. 6:16 – 17, which is near the middle of the seven-year tribulation. Some might argue that the time of restoration doesn't start until the setting up of the Millennium Kingdom. That is true, but what is the first step of setting up the Millennium Kingdom? It is to judge this world through the great tribulation.

When I was young my best friend's father owned a body shop. He was well known for restoring vintage automobiles. Before he could ever start painting the car he had to strip it down to its frame and sandblast it. It will be similar with the restoration of the earth. YHWH-God starts the restoration process with the cleansing (judging) of the world.

Hosea 5:15 (KJV), also supports this view:

Hosea 5:15

> "I will go and return to my place, till they acknowledge their offence, and seek my face: in their affliction they will seek me early."

In this verse Christ Jesus is speaking and states that He must stay in heaven **until** Israel as a nation admits their sin and seeks Him as their Messiah. It also states that they will call out to Him very early in their affliction, which means soon after the false Messiah begins his attack upon Israel (Ez. 38:8 – 16).

If you desire to do more study on the subject of Jesus' imminent return I would recommend a CD by Dr. Robert Morey, "The Imminent return of Christ".

The Prophecy Puzzle

As far as watching for the LORD goes, believe me, after three plus years of worldwide persecution, Christians will be watching for Christ Jesus.

Also, I believe YHWH reveals His truth as it is needed (Dan. 12:4). The truth that the rapture would not happen until the middle of the seven-year tribulation was not needed until the generation that will be raptured is alive. Before then it was beneficial for people not to understand that truth, because it heightened the urgency for salvation. I would also point out that none of us knows the time of Christ Jesus' return for us individually. Death could happen at any moment, so we absolutely should always be ready for His return.

The second one I'll look at is the fact that the church will not experience the wrath of God. That statement is true, but I believe the Bible is clear that YHWH's wrath does not start until the second half of the seven-year tribulation.

Revelation 6:16 – 17

> "And said to the mountains and rocks, Fall on us, and hide us from the face of him that sitteth on the throne, and from the wrath of the Lamb: 17 For the great day of his wrath is come; and who shall be able to stand?"

Revelation 6:16 is the first mention of God's wrath in the book of Revelation. As I stated earlier, the events of the first six seals are all the doing of mankind. I don't believe anything else needs to be added to that, so let's return to where we left off in the book of Revelation, chapter seven. Here we will see the two primary results of the rapture. Many take this as something out of chronological order, but as we will

The Prophecy Puzzle

see there is no reason to do that, in fact it is perfectly logical for them to be where they are in the text.

Revelation 7:1 – 17

"And after these things I saw four angels standing on the four corners of the earth, holding the four winds of the earth, that the wind should not blow on the earth, nor on the sea, nor on any tree.
2 And I saw another angel ascending from the east, having the seal of the living God: and he cried with a loud voice to the four angels, to whom it was given to hurt the earth and the sea,
3 Saying, Hurt not the earth, neither the sea, nor the trees, till we have sealed the servants of our God in their foreheads.
4 And I heard the number of them which were sealed: and there were sealed an hundred and forty and four thousand of all the tribes of the children of Israel.
5 Of the tribe of Juda were sealed twelve thousand. Of the tribe of Reuben were sealed twelve thousand. Of the tribe of Gad were sealed twelve thousand.
6 Of the tribe of Aser were sealed twelve thousand. Of the tribe of Nepthali were sealed twelve thousand. Of the tribe of Manasses were sealed twelve thousand.
7 Of the tribe of Simeon were sealed twelve thousand. Of the tribe of Levi were sealed twelve thousand. Of the tribe of Issachar were sealed twelve thousand.
8 Of the tribe of Zabulon were sealed twelve thousand. Of the tribe of Joseph were sealed twelve thousand. Of the tribe of Benjamin were sealed twelve thousand.

The Prophecy Puzzle

9 After this I beheld, and, lo, a great multitude, which no man could number, of all nations, and kindreds, and people, and tongues, stood before the throne, and before the Lamb, clothed with white robes, and palms in their hands;
10 And cried with a loud voice, saying, Salvation to our God which sitteth upon the throne, and unto the Lamb.
11 And all the angels stood round about the throne, and about the elders and the four beasts, and fell before the throne on their faces, and worshipped God,
12 Saying, Amen: Blessing, and glory, and wisdom, and thanksgiving, and honour, and power, and might, be unto our God for ever and ever. Amen.
13 And one of the elders answered, saying unto me, What are these which are arrayed in white robes? and whence came they?
14 And I said unto him, Sir, thou knowest. And he said to me, These are they which came out of great tribulation, and have washed their robes, and made them white in the blood of the Lamb.
15 Therefore are they before the throne of God, and serve him day and night in his temple: and he that sitteth on the throne shall dwell among them.
16 They shall hunger no more, neither thirst any more; neither shall the sun light on them, nor any heat.
17 For the Lamb which is in the midst of the throne shall feed them, and shall lead them unto living fountains of waters: and God shall wipe away all tears from their eyes."

The Prophecy Puzzle

The 144,000 Jews must be sealed and protected, before YHWH's wrath can be carried out on the earth. But what do these 144,000 Jews have to do with the rapture? Well, they are the "firstfruits" of Israel for the Messiah. I believe that is what Christ Jesus meant when He said the last would be first (Mat. 19:30). The last Jews to receive Christ Jesus as their Savior and LORD would be the first ones in His **earthly** kingdom.

At the time of the rapture all the Jews who are Christians will **not** be raptured to heaven, but will be sealed by these angels and be protected as they go through the great tribulation here on earth **in Jerusalem**. Incidentally there are roughly 14 million Jews alive today and it is estimated that about 1% of them are born-again Christians. That means there are about 140,000 Jewish born-again Christians alive today. That is getting pretty close to the 144,000 spoken of here.

After our introduction to the 144,000 Jews on earth we see in verse 9 that we are taken to heaven where we see the countless millions who have been raptured.

There is nothing in the passage that indicates that they were martyred as some suggest. They are there because of the blood of the Lamb, not because of their blood. Also it doesn't make any sense to present those who were martyred throughout the seven-year tribulation at this point. It would be completely out of chronological order and doesn't fit the flow of events being presented at this time.

The argument that they cannot be "the church" because John doesn't know them (vv. 13 – 14) is baseless. In John's time the church consisted of maybe 100,000 people. There is no reason to expect John to know that this group of millions and millions of people is the church.

The Prophecy Puzzle

To further support this view that the sealing of the 144,000 and the rapture happen somewhere among the events of the breaking of the sixth seal let's look at some other prophecies such as:

Hosea 5:15 (KJV)

"I (Jesus Christ) will go and return to my place (heaven), till they acknowledge their offence, and seek my face: in their affliction they will seek me early."

Yes, we have just looked at this verse a short time ago, but this time I would like to connect it to Matthew 24:15 – 20 where we saw Jesus Christ tell the Jews in Jerusalem that when they see the abomination of desolation they should flee and pray. It is obvious to me that it is at this time that the Jews cry out to Jesus Christ as their Messiah and God (YHWH). As we were told in Hosea 5:15, they would cry out to Him early in their affliction. Also if we return to Zechariah 14:1 – 5 and understand that this is taking place at the abomination of desolation we see clearly that Jesus Christ does return to provide a way of escape for the Jews in Jerusalem at that time.

Zechariah 14:1 – 5

"Behold, the day of the LORD cometh, and thy spoil shall be divided in the midst of thee.
2 For I will gather all nations against Jerusalem to battle; and the city shall be taken, and the houses rifled, and the women ravished; and half of the city shall go forth into captivity, and the residue of the people shall not be cut off from the city.

The Prophecy Puzzle

> 3 Then shall the LORD go forth, and fight against those nations, as when he fought in the day of battle.
> 4 And his feet shall stand in that day upon the mount of Olives, which is before Jerusalem on the east, and the mount of Olives shall cleave in the midst thereof toward the east and toward the west, and there shall be a very great valley; and half of the mountain shall remove toward the north, and half of it toward the south.
> 5 And ye shall flee to the valley of the mountains; for the valley of the mountains shall reach unto Azal: yea, ye shall flee, like as ye fled from before the earthquake in the days of Uzziah king of Judah: and the LORD my God shall come, and all the saints with thee."

Some suggest that this is another description of the battle of Armageddon, but answer these two questions:

1. Why would Jesus Christ be providing the Jews an escape from Jerusalem at the battle of Armageddon (v. 5)? At the battle of Armageddon He is coming to destroy the armies that have surrounded the Jews. This is clearly Christ Jesus providing a way of escape for the Jews who are in Jerusalem so they can flee to safety, which they probably find in Petra.
2. Does the Day of the LORD start with the pouring out of His wrath introduced in the opening of the sixth seal and carried out with the seven trumpets and bowls (vials), or with Armageddon? It clearly starts with His wrath (Isaiah 13:6, Joel 2:31 – 32, Rev. 6:14 – 17, 8:6 – 11:19, 16:1 - 21). And Zechariah 14:1 states this is the coming of the Day of the LORD.

The Prophecy Puzzle

The last passage I would like to look at to prove this point is Ezekiel 38:1 – 16.

Ezekiel 38:1 – 16

"And the word of the LORD came unto me, saying,
2 Son of man, set thy face against Gog, the land of Magog, the chief prince of Meshech and Tubal, and prophesy against him,
3 And say, Thus saith the Lord GOD; Behold I am against thee, O Gog, the chief prince of Meshech and Tubal:
4 And I will turn thee back, and put hooks into thy jaws, and I will bring thee forth, and all thine army, horses and horsemen, all of them clothed with all sorts of armour, even a great company with bucklers and shields, all of them handling swords:
5 Persia, Ethiopia, and Libya with them; all of them with shield and helmet:
6 Gomer, and all his bands; the house of Togarmah of the north quarters, and all his bands: and many people with thee.
7 Be thou prepared, and prepare for thyself, thou, and all thy company that are assembled unto thee, and be thou a guard unto them.
8 After many days thou shalt be visited: in the latter years thou shalt come into the land that is brought back from the sword, and is gathered out of many people, against the mountains of Israel, which have been always waste: but it is brought forth out of the nations, and they shall dwell safely all of them.

The Prophecy Puzzle

9 Thou shalt ascend and come like a storm, thou shalt be like a cloud to cover the land, thou, and all thy bands, and many people with thee.
10 Thus saith the Lord GOD; It shall also come to pass, that at the same time shall things come into thy mind, and thou shalt think an evil thought:
11 And thou shalt say, I will go up to the land of unwalled villages; I will go to them that are at rest, that dwell safely, all of them dwelling without walls, and having neither bars nor gates,
12 To take a spoil, and to take a prey; to turn thine hand upon the desolate places that are now inhabited, and upon the people that are gathered out of the nations, which have gotten cattle and goods, that dwell in the midst of the land.
13 Sheba, and Dedan, and the merchants of Tarshish, with all the young lions thereof, shall say unto thee, Art thou come to take a spoil? hast thou gathered thy company to take a prey? to carry away silver and gold, to take away cattle and goods, to take a great spoil?
14 Therefore, son of man, prophesy and say unto Gog, Thus saith the Lord GOD; In that day when my people of Israel dwelleth safely, shalt thou not know it?
15 And thou shalt come from thy place out of the north parts, thou, and many people with thee, all of them riding upon horses, a great company, and a mighty army:
16 And thou shalt come up against my people of Israel, as a cloud to cover the land; it shall be in the latter days, and I will bring thee against my land, that the

The Prophecy Puzzle

heathen may know me, when I shall be sanctified in thee, O Gog, before their eyes."

This is another passage, which has a great misunderstanding surrounding it. There has been a longstanding debate over when this battle occurs. There are two main positions held. Some believe it is a battle that could happen at any time before the seven-year tribulation begins, and others believe it is just another description of the battle of Armageddon.

Well, they are both wrong, at least in part. The first sixteen verses describe what will happen at the **middle** of the seven-year tribulation. They tell how the false-Messiah approaches Jerusalem to stop the daily sacrifices and sets himself up as God in the Holy of Holies (Dan. 9:27). You don't think he just walks up and says, "Hi, I'm here to perform the abomination that leads to desolation. Would you please let me in?" No, he comes ready for battle. That is why Christ Jesus tells the people to flee for their lives when they see it happening (Matthew 24:15 – 16). Now, the remainder of Ezekiel 38 describes the battle of Armageddon. The period "." at the end of Ezekiel 38:16 represents about 3 ½ years, just as the comma in Isaiah 61:2 between "LORD" and "And" has represented about 2000 years. It is also very likely that this battle doesn't truly end during this 3 ½ year period. Here in Ezekiel 38 we are given the details of the beginning and the end, but there is probably some military presence and activity around Israel the whole 3 ½ years. One clue to this is that the two witnesses in Rev. 11:5 who are at the temple mount during this 3 ½ year period have the power to protect themselves by destroying their attackers with fire.

Some might not yet be convinced that this is describing what happens in the middle of the seven-year tribulation, but note what it says in verse 11. The anti-Christ comes against a city (Jerusalem), which is

The Prophecy Puzzle

"**unwalled**" where the people are living in **peace** and **feeling safe**. That is not the case in Jerusalem today and it will not be the case **until** the time the false Messiah forms a peace treaty with Israel and gives them permission to start building the temple. The only time these conditions will be known is during the **first half** of the seven-year tribulation.

As we will see in the following chapters, the other biblical accounts of these events agree with what is recorded here. Remember, beginning with chapter six we have the same story presented to us three times, each having a slightly different emphasis.

Let's return to our text that we are focusing on, Revelation 6:1 – 11:19. We left off at 8:1 and I would like to look at Revelation 8:1 – 13 more closely now.

Revelation 8:1 – 13

> "And when he had opened the seventh seal, there was silence in heaven about the space of half an hour.
> 2 And I saw the seven angels which stood before God; and to them were given seven trumpets.
> 3 And another angel came and stood at the altar, having a golden censer; and there was given unto him much incense, that he should offer it with the prayers of all saints upon the golden altar which was before the throne.
> 4 And the smoke of the incense, which came with the prayers of the saints, ascended up before God out of the angel's hand.

The Prophecy Puzzle

5 And the angel took the censer, and filled it with fire of the altar, and cast it into the earth: and there were voices, and thunderings, and lightnings, and an earthquake.

6 And the seven angels which had the seven trumpets prepared themselves to sound.

7 The first angel sounded, and there followed hail and fire mingled with blood, and they were cast upon the earth: and the third part of trees was burnt up, and all green grass was burnt up.

8 And the second angel sounded, and as it were a great mountain burning with fire was cast into the sea: and the third part of the sea became blood;

9 And the third part of the creatures which were in the sea, and had life, died; and the third part of the ships were destroyed.

10 And the third angel sounded, and there fell a great star from heaven, burning as it were a lamp, and it fell upon the third part of the rivers, and upon the fountains of waters;

11 And the name of the star is called Wormwood: and the third part of the waters became wormwood; and many men died of the waters, because they were made bitter.

12 And the fourth angel sounded, and the third part of the sun was smitten, and the third part of the moon, and the third part of the stars; so as the third part of them was darkened, and the day shone not for a third part of it, and the night likewise.

13 And I beheld, and heard an angel flying through the midst of heaven, saying with a loud voice, Woe, woe,

The Prophecy Puzzle

woe, to the inhabiters of the earth by reason of the other voices of the trumpet of the three angels, which are yet to sound!"

After the 144,000 have been sealed and the Gentile Christians have been raptured, we have a period of silence of 30 minutes in heaven (8:1). This introduces the whole subject of time in heaven, but that would be for another book. For our purposes here let's just recognize that for a period of 30 minutes "earth-time" there was silence. We are not told the purpose of these 30 minutes, so we can only speculate, but I think it is for all to contemplate the severity of the judgments, which are now to begin to come upon the earth.

We are not told the content of these prayers being poured out upon the altar in verse 3, but could it be; "Thy kingdom come"? That is in essence what the saints under the altar asked for in Rev. 6:10. Also it fits what follows, because we see that the breaking of the seventh seal is the preparation for the beginning of YHWH's reign on the earth. The seven trumpets are handed out (v. 2). The prayers of the saints are replaced with fire (judgment), which will be soon cast down to the earth (v. 3).

Before we read about the blowing of the seven trumpets we need to decide if we are to take them literally or symbolically. Are we to see them as direct judgments from the hand of YHWH or does He use the armies of mankind to carry them out as we see He did many times in the Old Testament (2Chr. 28:6)?
I'm not ruling out the supernatural work of God, but for the most part I believe the first four trumpets describe the results of the anti-Christ's actions against Egypt and other countries, but especially Egypt. I base this primarily on two passages, Daniel 11:36 – 45 and Ezekiel 32:1 – 32.

The Prophecy Puzzle

Daniel 11:36 – 45 gives a relatively detailed description of the false-Messiah's actions after he declares himself to be God. We will quickly study these two passages.

Dan 11:36 – 45

"And the king shall do according to his will; and he shall exalt himself, and magnify himself above every god, and shall speak marvellous things against the God of gods, and shall prosper till the indignation be accomplished: for that that is determined shall be done.
37 Neither shall he regard the God of his fathers, nor the desire of women, nor regard any god: for he shall magnify himself above all.
38 But in his estate shall he honour the God of forces: and a god whom his fathers knew not shall he honour with gold, and silver, and with precious stones, and pleasant things.
39 Thus shall he do in the most strong holds with a strange god, whom he shall acknowledge and increase with glory: and he shall cause them to rule over many, and shall divide the land for gain.
40 And at the time of the end shall the king of the south push at him: and the king of the north shall come against him like a whirlwind, with chariots, and with horsemen, and with many ships; and he shall enter into the countries, and shall overflow and pass over.

The Prophecy Puzzle

41 He shall enter also into the glorious land, and many countries shall be overthrown: but these shall escape out of his hand, even Edom, and Moab, and the chief of the children of Ammon.
42 He shall stretch forth his hand also upon the countries: and the land of Egypt shall not escape.
43 But he shall have power over the treasures of gold and of silver, and over all the precious things of Egypt: and the Libyans and the Ethiopians shall be at his steps.
44 But tidings out of the east and out of the north shall trouble him: therefore he shall go forth with great fury to destroy, and utterly to make away many.
45 And he shall plant the tabernacles of his palace between the seas in the glorious holy mountain; yet he shall come to his end, and none shall help him."

- Daniel 11:36: This is a description of his turning on Israel. Putting a stop to their sacrifices and setting up the image in the Holy of Holies (Dan. 9:27).
- Daniel 11:37: He declares all other religions to be false and all must worship him alone. He even declares the world religious system, which he used to gain power, to be false and has it destroyed (Rev. 17).
- 11:38 – 43: Describe the events that accompany the blowing of the first four trumpets (Rev. 8:6 – 12).
- 11:44: Describe the events, which occur with the blowing of the sixth trumpet (Rev. 9:13 – 21).
    - The fifth trumpet isn't mentioned here, because it occurs in heaven.
- 11:45: Sets the stage for the battle of Armageddon.

The Prophecy Puzzle

Just as a note of clarification Daniel 12:1 – 3 points back to 11:36. It is at that time, the time of the rapture, near the middle of the seven-year tribulation that these events will occur. This is made clear in 12:1 where it refers to the time of trouble that's worse than any other. It begins with the anti-Christ coming to set up the Abomination of Desolation.

Ok, now let's look at each of the first four trumpets. The first trumpet brings hail and fire mixed with blood upon the earth (Rev. 8:7). They result in one-third of the earth and the trees being burned up, with all the grass being burned up.

As I stated earlier there is debate over what exactly these things are. What is clear is that they are judgments from YHWH. Possibly what we see is YHWH using mankind to carry out these judgments on mankind. He has used armies to judge nations many times throughout the Old Testament. Today we do have weapons that destroy vegetation without harming buildings, but it could have some kind of "natural" cause.

There is special emphasis placed on the blood. Does literal blood fall from the sky? YHWH is capable of having that happen and that could be exactly what happens, but others believe it should be understood that blood would be shed with the coming of this judgment. Still others believe it should be understood that the rain would be red in color as if it were blood. There have been many documented cases of red snow throughout history, but I am not saying that is the situation here, only that some believe it is a possibility.

Another point to take note of is that there is no mention of the number of animals or people killed in this judgment. That suggests that there were no deaths or at least very few directly related to this judgment.

The Prophecy Puzzle

The blowing of the second trumpet records something like a huge mountain falling into the sea (Rev. 8:8 – 9). The result is one-third of the sea is turned into blood, which in turn causes one-third of the sea life to die and one-third of the ships on the sea to be destroyed.

Again is this a literal mountain? Does the water truly become blood or is it red tide? I don't know. What I do find interesting is that the Atlantic Ocean contains roughly one-third of the earth's seawater. I don't know if that means the Atlantic Ocean is the victim of this judgment or not, but it is the right size. One last point I would like to make is that this must have been either physically a very violent event or a nuclear explosion to result in the destruction of one-third of the ships on the sea. Another interesting fact is that red tide could be a natural result of a nuclear explosion within the ocean.

The blowing of the third trumpet results in a star falling from heaven onto one-third of the rivers and springs. It results in those rivers and springs becoming wormwood (bitter/poison) and many people dying from drinking the water. Perhaps it is just a coincidence, but I've heard the Russian word for "wormwood" is Chernobyl. Chernobyl if you recall was the sight of a severe nuclear accident. Could it be a hint that this wormwood has something to do with nuclear contamination, like fallout from a nuclear bomb? Again that largely depends on one's view on if these judgments are directly from YHWH or if He is using mankind to bring them about.

The blowing of the fourth trumpet results in one-third of the sun, moon and stars being darkened. We are not told how that happens. Some believe that one-third of the sun, moon and stars themselves are literally darkened. Others believe it means that <u>from the earth</u> one-

The Prophecy Puzzle

third of them are hidden from view. So in other words if someone is in the affected area, he will not be able to see anything of the sun, moon or stars. If this is the case, it seems to fit what is described for us in Ezekiel 32:7 – 8, and would indicate that Egypt is within the area being affected by this judgment. Another interesting theory is that the rotation of the earth is sped up so that from this time forward there will only be sixteen hours per day. That would result in the sun, moon and stars being visible one-third less of the time than they currently are visible. I suppose it is possible, but this would have many other effects upon the earth as well.

After the blowing of the fourth trumpet we have the <u>announcement</u> of the three woes, which are about to come upon the earth with the blowing of the last three trumpets. Make a mental note that **the three woes are contained in the last three trumpets**. It will help clarify the timing of some things later.

This brings us to the next passage that we will look at in depth, Revelation 9:1 – 12, which contains the blowing of the fifth trumpet.

> Revelation 9:1 – 12
>
> "And the fifth angel sounded, and I saw a star fall from heaven unto the earth: and to him was given the key of the bottomless pit.
> 2 And he opened the bottomless pit; and there arose a smoke out of the pit, as the smoke of a great furnace; and the sun and the air were darkened by reason of the smoke of the pit.
> 3 And there came out of the smoke locusts upon the earth: and unto them was given power, as the scorpions of the earth have power.

The Prophecy Puzzle

4 And it was commanded them that they should not hurt the grass of the earth, neither any green thing, neither any tree; but only those men which have not the seal of God in their foreheads.

5 And to them it was given that they should not kill them, but that they should be tormented five months: and their torment was as the torment of a scorpion, when he striketh a man.

6 And in those days shall men seek death, and shall not find it; and shall desire to die, and death shall flee from them.

7 And the shapes of the locusts were like unto horses prepared unto battle; and on their heads were as it were crowns like gold, and their faces were as the faces of men.

8 And they had hair as the hair of women, and their teeth were as the teeth of lions.

9 And they had breastplates, as it were breastplates of iron; and the sound of their wings was as the sound of chariots of many horses running to battle.

10 And they had tails like unto scorpions, and there were stings in their tails: and their power was to hurt men five months.

11 And they had a king over them, which is the angel of the bottomless pit, whose name in the Hebrew tongue is Abaddon, but in the Greek tongue hath his name Apollyon.

12 One woe is past; and, behold, there come two woes more hereafter."

The Prophecy Puzzle

Some believe we are to take this passage symbolically, but I believe these are literal "demonic locust" and not a description of modern instruments of war or anything like that. I believe this for three reasons: One, because of their description; two, because of the limited duration of their attack; and thirdly, because of their leader – the angel of the bottomless pit.

When the fifth trumpet is blown, the first thing we are told of is an angel which **had** fallen from heaven. The word "fall" is in the "perfect participle active" and refers to something that happened in the past and continued on from that point in time. John now sees the star, which had fallen to the earth in the past and has remained on the earth since then. I emphasize that it had fallen sometime earlier, because I believe this is a reference to Satan when he fell from heaven near the middle of the seven-year tribulation (Rev. 12:7 – 9). It is also at this time that Satan is given the key to open the bottomless pit.

Even though Satan had fallen earlier, he isn't given the key to the bottomless pit until the blowing of the fifth trumpet. He also at this time opens the abyss (bottomless pit) and large amounts of smoke and demonic locusts come out (v. 3). For five months these demon locusts torment anyone on the earth who does not have the seal of God. Their sting is like the sting of a scorpion, but worse. It creates so much pain that those who are stung by them wish they could die, but are unable to do so. Some believe that the people literally cannot die after being stung, but others, as I do, believe what is being communicated is that the result of the sting is so painful people want to die, but the sting in not lethal. I think this language is used just to emphasize the severity of the pain, but I suppose I could be wrong about that.

The Prophecy Puzzle

I find the king they have over them very interesting, because his name is Abaddon. It means "destruction" and it is appropriate, because he is "the destroyer". He is Satan, the star that had fallen to the earth in v. 1. Another very interesting point is that supposedly "Abaddon" is the secret password Freemasons are told to use to escape the coming judgment.

Just as a point of interest, there are many books written on Freemasonry, one that gives a nicely balanced history on Freemasonry is "The Origins and Teachings of Freemasonry" by Dr. Robert Morey. If you would like a resource that gives a more esoteric view of Freemasonry, I would recommend the DVD, "Secret Mysteries of America's Beginnings" produced by Chris Pinto.

The five months of torment brought about by these demon locust, represent the **first woe**, which was announced with the blowing of the fourth trumpet. The reader is also reminded that two more woes are still to come. We are given a detailed description of the second woe in the sixth trumpet, but the third is somewhat veiled in the seventh trumpet; nonetheless as we will see, it is there.

Revelation 9:13 – 11:14

> "And the sixth angel sounded, and I heard a voice from the four horns of the golden altar which is before God,
> 14 Saying to the sixth angel which had the trumpet, Loose the four angels which are bound in the great river Euphrates.
> 15 And the four angels were loosed, which were prepared for an hour, and a day, and a month, and a year, for to slay the third part of men.

The Prophecy Puzzle

16 And the number of the army of the horsemen were two hundred thousand thousand: and I heard the number of them.

17 And thus I saw the horses in the vision, and them that sat on them, having breastplates of fire, and of jacinth, and brimstone: and the heads of the horses were as the heads of lions; and out of their mouths issued fire and smoke and brimstone.

18 By these three was the third part of men killed, by the fire, and by the smoke, and by the brimstone, which issued out of their mouths.

19 For their power is in their mouth, and in their tails: for their tails were like unto serpents, and had heads, and with them they do hurt.

20 And the rest of the men which were not killed by these plagues yet repented not of the works of their hands, that they should not worship devils, and idols of gold, and silver, and brass, and stone, and of wood: which neither can see, nor hear, nor walk:

21 Neither repented they of their murders, nor of their sorceries, nor of their fornication, nor of their thefts.

10:1 And I saw another mighty angel come down from heaven, clothed with a cloud: and a rainbow was upon his head, and his face was as it were the sun, and his feet as pillars of fire:

2 And he had in his hand a little book open: and he set his right foot upon the sea, and his left foot on the earth,

3 And cried with a loud voice, as when a lion roareth: and when he had cried, seven thunders uttered their voices.

The Prophecy Puzzle

4 And when the seven thunders had uttered their voices, I was about to write: and I heard a voice from heaven saying unto me, Seal up those things which the seven thunders uttered, and write them not.
5 And the angel which I saw stand upon the sea and upon the earth lifted up his hand to heaven,
6 And sware by him that liveth for ever and ever, who created heaven, and the things that therein are, and the earth, and the things that therein are, and the sea, and the things which are therein, that there should be time no longer:
7 But in the days of the voice of the seventh angel, when he shall begin to sound, the mystery of God should be finished, as he hath declared to his servants the prophets.
8 And the voice which I heard from heaven spake unto me again, and said, Go and take the little book which is open in the hand of the angel which standeth upon the sea and upon the earth.
9 And I went unto the angel, and said unto him, Give me the little book. And he said unto me, Take it, and eat it up; and it shall make thy belly bitter, but it shall be in thy mouth sweet as honey.
10 And I took the little book out of the angel's hand, and ate it up; and it was in my mouth sweet as honey: and as soon as I had eaten it, my belly was bitter.
11 And he said unto me, Thou must prophesy again before many peoples, and nations, and tongues, and kings.

The Prophecy Puzzle

11:1 And there was given me a reed like unto a rod: and the angel stood, saying, Rise, and measure the temple of God, and the altar, and them that worship therein.
2 But the court which is without the temple leave out, and measure it not; for it is given unto the Gentiles: and the holy city shall they tread under foot forty and two months.
3 And I will give power unto my two witnesses, and they shall prophesy a thousand two hundred and threescore days, clothed in sackcloth.
4 These are the two olive trees, and the two candlesticks standing before the God of the earth.
5 And if any man will hurt them, fire proceedeth out of their mouth, and devoureth their enemies: and if any man will hurt them, he must in this manner be killed.
6 These have power to shut heaven, that it rain not in the days of their prophecy: and have power over waters to turn them to blood, and to smite the earth with all plagues, as often as they will.
7 And when they shall have finished their testimony, the beast that ascendeth out of the bottomless pit shall make war against them, and shall overcome them, and kill them.
8 And their dead bodies shall lie in the street of the great city, which spiritually is called Sodom and Egypt, where also our Lord was crucified.
9 And they of the people and kindreds and tongues and nations shall see their dead bodies three days and an half, and shall not suffer their dead bodies to be put in graves.

The Prophecy Puzzle

> 10 And they that dwell upon the earth shall rejoice over them, and make merry, and shall send gifts one to another; because these two prophets tormented them that dwelt on the earth.
> 11 And after three days and an half the Spirit of life from God entered into them, and they stood upon their feet; and great fear fell upon them which saw them.
> 12 And they heard a great voice from heaven saying unto them, Come up hither. And they ascended up to heaven in a cloud; and their enemies beheld them.
> 13 And the same hour was there a great earthquake, and the tenth part of the city fell, and in the earthquake were slain of men seven thousand: and the remnant were affrighted, and gave glory to the God of heaven.
> 14 The second woe is past; and, behold, the third woe cometh quickly."

One might be asking why I included chapters ten and eleven with chapter nine, the blowing of the sixth trumpet. Well, it is because they are all part of the sixth trumpet and the second woe. Hopefully you will see that clearly at the end of this section.

Going forward on the premise that chapters ten and eleven are part of the sixth trumpet, let's look at the description of the sixth trumpet itself in chapter nine. When the sixth trumpet is blown an angel is instructed to release the four (fallen) angels that were being held at the base of the Euphrates River.

These fallen angels bring about the death of one-third of the people on earth (vv. 16, 18); but it should be noted that they don't do the killing, they only lead this army of two hundred million (Rev. 16:14).

The Prophecy Puzzle

Before we go any further we should examine this army. There are three views regarding who or what are the soldiers in this army. Some believe that they are actual demons. Some believe this is the army the false Messiah puts together from the unified resources of the western world. Still others, as I do, believe it is the Chinese army. I believe that for the following reasons:

1. If we look at Dan. 11:39 - 45 we find several armies. I believe the above-mentioned army is the one, which causes the rumors from the East (v. 44).
2. It has been reported in recent years that China at this time has an available army of two hundred million men.
3. In Vv. 18 – 19 the description of the weaponry could sound lot like modern war machinery.
4. The Chinese colors are bright red and gold, and in Rev. 9:17 John says the breastplates of the riders were bright red, dark blue and bright yellow (gold).
5. If one adds-up the population of the countries between China and the Euphrates River (Israel), it comes out to be about one-third of the population of the world today (2008).

Using the numbers from the U.S. Census Bureau website I found that the estimated populations for the following countries in 2008, which either boarder China or are found between China and the Euphrates River are (rounded off to the nearest one hundred thousand):

>Afghanistan - 32,700,000, Bangladesh - 153,500,000, Cambodia - 14,000,000, India – 1,100,00,000, Indonesia - 237,500,000, Iran - 65,000,000; Iraq - 28,000,000, Japan – 127,000,000; Laos - 6,700,000,

The Prophecy Puzzle

>Malaysia - 25,000,000, Mongolia - 3,000,000, Burma - 47,800,000, Pakistan - 167,000,000, Philippines - 92,700,000, Nepal - 29,500,000, North Korea - 23,500,000, South Korea - 49,000,000, Thailand - 65,500,000, Vietnam - 86,000,000.

That gives us a total population for that area of 2,353,400,000. The estimated population for the whole earth is right around 7,000,000,000. If we do the math, 2,353,400,000, is 33.62% of the earth's population of 7,000,000,000. That is about three tenths of one percent of being exactly one-third. Perhaps it is just coincidence, and I admit that this is not proof that this army is from China, but I believe it gives strong evidence that it is. Be that true or not, what is clear is that even after all this death and chaos the rest of mankind does not repent. That is something to stop and think about because by this point in time over half of the world's population has been killed.

The next point of controversy we must address is the meaning of verse 15. Some view this as meaning nothing more than it expressing the exact moment or hour prepared by God. Others believe what is being said is that this army will have one year, one month, one day and one hour to carry out this killing. I believe that is point. This army will have 391 days and one hour to carry out their killing. Based upon my previous argument, I believe it will take China's army 391 days to work their way across the land between them and Israel, arriving there just in time for the battle of Armageddon.

This makes perfect sense; because later on we see that the Euphrates River is dried up to allow this army to pass through (Rev. 16:12). It takes them a little over a year to reach the Euphrates River from China. This means the army would travel about ten miles a day and that seems

The Prophecy Puzzle

reasonable to me. They arrive there just in time for the sixth bowl of wrath to be poured out, drying up the river (Rev. 16:12) so they may cross it.

Moving onto another interesting point, in Rev. 9:20 it makes mention of people worshiping idols and I know that is part of many religions, but I was struck how "mainstream" it has become when I saw a news report recently. On March 3, 2008, ABC's "Good Morning America" program featured a story that reported that people were burying statues of St. Joseph in their front yards in order to promote the sale of their house. Then the new owners were to dig up these statues and put them in their homes for good luck. The reporter went on to say that these statues are selling at a rate of 10,000 a month. If that is not a sign of the times, I don't know what is.

In Rev. 9:21 it states that one of the evils the people refuse to repent of is sorcery. The power of the imagination or our thoughts is so much a part of our culture today. It is being pushed upon us everywhere. Every day and night it is subtly and sometimes not so subtly fed to us in TV shows and movies. We have plenty of overt "New Age" books filling the bookshelves of our bookstores, but worse than that one can find some of them like "A course in Miracles" or "The Secret" in "Christian bookstores" and even being taught in some churches. What they truly do is push sorcery upon us. And yes, it is sorcery. It can all be traced back to Gnostic and other pagan beliefs. Along with this we see a rise in popularity of Wicca or witchcraft as well. We can certainly thank the "Harry Potter" books and movies for that, at least in part. I believe without a doubt that Witchcraft, which is a religion that focuses on "**mother earth**" (Anyone tell you to "think green" lately?) and sexual immorality, will hold a central part in the coming world religion. The environmental aspect of it will be in the spotlight, but its sexual

The Prophecy Puzzle

immorality portion might only be practiced behind closed doors. Or I suppose, they could just change the definition of what is immoral. Nothing would surprise me.

Two books that deal with the dangers of new age thought are "The Light that was Dark" and "Deceived on Purpose" both by Warren Smith.

Ok, I think we need to read chapter ten of the book of Revelation again at this point, because this can be misunderstood and it is essential to understand how chapters ten and eleven are part of the blowing of the sixth trumpet.

Revelation 10:1 – 11

> "And I saw another mighty angel come down from heaven, clothed with a cloud: and a rainbow was upon his head, and his face was as it were the sun, and his feet as pillars of fire:
> 2 And he had in his hand a little book open: and he set his right foot upon the sea, and his left foot on the earth,
> 3 And cried with a loud voice, as when a lion roareth: and when he had cried, seven thunders uttered their voices.
> 4 And when the seven thunders had uttered their voices, I was about to write: and I heard a voice from heaven saying unto me, Seal up those things which the seven thunders uttered, and write them not.
> 5 And the angel which I saw stand upon the sea and upon the earth lifted up his hand to heaven,

The Prophecy Puzzle

6 And sware by him that liveth for ever and ever, who created heaven, and the things that therein are, and the earth, and the things that therein are, and the sea, and the things which are therein, that there should be time no longer:
7 But in the days of the voice of the seventh angel, when he shall begin to sound, the mystery of God should be finished, as he hath declared to his servants the prophets.
8 And the voice which I heard from heaven spake unto me again, and said, Go and take the little book which is open in the hand of the angel which standeth upon the sea and upon the earth.
9 And I went unto the angel, and said unto him, Give me the little book. And he said unto me, Take it, and eat it up; and it shall make thy belly bitter, but it shall be in thy mouth sweet as honey.
10 And I took the little book out of the angel's hand, and ate it up; and it was in my mouth sweet as honey: and as soon as I had eaten it, my belly was bitter.
11 And he said unto me, Thou must prophesy again before many peoples, and nations, and tongues, and kings."

There has been much discussion about the identity of this angel and what the seven thunders said, but we are not told and I don't think either is the focus of the passage. What is important is the angel's message at the end of verse six, that the end is coming now and there would be no more delay. In other words the blowing of the seventh trumpet contains the end of YHWH's wrath and it will follow very

The Prophecy Puzzle

quickly after this two hundred million-man army crosses the Euphrates River (10:7).

Verses 8 through 11 in chapter ten have John taking and eating the little book, which is sweet in his mouth, but bitter in his stomach. He is also told that he must once again prophesy to the nations. All of this is to communicate to us that the vision, which John is about to receive takes him back to the middle of the seven-year tribulation. The book is sweet in his mouth, because it is the Word of God; but then is bitter because it is about the judgments (wrath) of YHWH.

Once again I think it would be good to read chapter 11 of the book of Revelation at this time.

Revelation 11:1 – 14

> "And there was given me a reed like unto a rod: and the angel stood, saying, Rise, and measure the temple of God, and the altar, and them that worship therein.
> 2 But the court which is without the temple leave out, and measure it not; for it is given unto the Gentiles: and the holy city shall they tread under foot forty and two months.
> 3 And I will give power unto my two witnesses, and they shall prophesy a thousand two hundred and threescore days, clothed in sackcloth.
> 4 These are the two olive trees, and the two candlesticks standing before the God of the earth.
> 5 And if any man will hurt them, fire proceedeth out of their mouth, and devoureth their enemies: and if any man will hurt them, he must in this manner be killed.

The Prophecy Puzzle

6 These have power to shut heaven, that it rain not in the days of their prophecy: and have power over waters to turn them to blood, and to smite the earth with all plagues, as often as they will.

7 And when they shall have finished their testimony, the beast that ascendeth out of the bottomless pit shall make war against them, and shall overcome them, and kill them.

8 And their dead bodies shall lie in the street of the great city, which spiritually is called Sodom and Egypt, where also our Lord was crucified.

9 And they of the people and kindreds and tongues and nations shall see their dead bodies three days and an half, and shall not suffer their dead bodies to be put in graves.

10 And they that dwell upon the earth shall rejoice over them, and make merry, and shall send gifts one to another; because these two prophets tormented them that dwelt on the earth.

11 And after three days and an half the Spirit of life from God entered into them, and they stood upon their feet; and great fear fell upon them which saw them.

12 And they heard a great voice from heaven saying unto them, Come up hither. And they ascended up to heaven in a cloud; and their enemies beheld them.

13 And the same hour was there a great earthquake, and the tenth part of the city fell, and in the earthquake were slain of men seven thousand: and the remnant were affrighted, and gave glory to the God of heaven.

14 The second woe is past; and, behold, the third woe cometh quickly."

The Prophecy Puzzle

Chapter eleven also gives us an understanding of where we are in time. In 11:2 it makes reference to the building of the temple. For 42 months, the last half of the seven-year tribulation, the Gentiles will have access to the outer court of the temple; but the inner court will be occupied by the two witnesses and the 144,000 Jews who were sealed and placed there at the time of the rapture. In 11:3 – 6 we see the two witnesses are in complete control of that area.

I also wanted to point out what it says in 11:14, that the second woe is past. That is why YHWH takes John and us, back to the middle of the seven-year tribulation. **We must have the context of the two witnesses and their ministry in order to understand the passing of the second woe**. The second woe comes with the completion of the ministry of the two witnesses.

There are some very important points that must be made in 11:1, but who these two witnesses are is not one of them, but for what it is worth, Moses and Elijah would be my guess.

The first point to make is that the temple is described as the "temple of God". It is not the temple of the anti-Christ or Satan. Also there is mention of those who worship YHWH within the temple. If this is at the middle of the seven-year tribulation, how could this be? I thought that at the opening of the sixth seal we saw the anti-Christ, putting up and bringing to life an image in the very Holy of Holies! Yes we did see that and yes it is speaking of the temple in Jerusalem, but note that the passage says nothing about how long the false Messiah and his image are allowed to stay there. Please stay with me as I try to walk us though these events. Yes, we have the abomination of desolation spoken of just now, but look at what it says in Zechariah.

The Prophecy Puzzle

Zechariah 5:5 – 11

"Then the angel that talked with me went forth, and said unto me, Lift up now thine eyes, and see what is this that goeth forth.
6 And I said, What is it? And he said, This is an ephah that goeth forth. He said moreover, This is their resemblance through all the earth.
7 And, behold, there was lifted up a talent of lead: and this is a woman that sitteth in the midst of the ephah.
8 And he said, This is wickedness. And he cast it into the midst of the ephah; and he cast the weight of lead upon the mouth thereof.
9 Then lifted I up mine eyes, and looked, and, behold, there came out two women, and the wind was in their wings; for they had wings like the wings of a stork: and they lifted up the ephah between the earth and the heaven.
10 Then said I to the angel that talked with me, Whither do these bear the ephah?
11 And he said unto me, To build it an house in the land of Shinar: and it shall be established, and set there upon her own base."

I believe this is speaking of the image, which represented the religion of Satan (Babylon) from the beginning. The anti-Christ and his image are forced to flee the Holy of Holies shortly after his abomination of it. How can that be you ask? Didn't the Jew's have to flee Jerusalem when the anti-Christ and his army came to desecrate the temple? Yes they did, but what happens after that? We have the sealing of the 144,000

The Prophecy Puzzle

Jews. And where do we find them shortly after their sealing? On Mount Zion! See it for yourself in Revelation 14:1:

> "And I looked, and, lo, a Lamb stood on the Mount Sion, and with him an hundred forty and four thousand...."

More importantly, notice that Jesus Christ is with them! We will explain the timing of these events further in the next chapter, but for now understand that this is shortly after the abomination of desolation.

Let's look at Revelation 11:3 – 6 again. We now have the two witnesses, those who stand before the God of the earth (Josh. 2:11). If Jesus Christ and the 144,000 Jews are there at this time, this is literally true. In 11:5 and 6 we see that everyone there is perfectly safe, because of the ability YHWH gives the two witnesses and of course, because YHWH (Jesus Christ) is there.

Revelation 11:7 brings us back to the events of 9:21, which was when the two hundred million-man army reached the Euphrates River. It would seem that the two witnesses are being killed at about the same time this two million man army reaches the Euphrates River.

So the point about the **second woe** is that it didn't consist of just the death and resurrection of the two witnesses, but also the 391 days of killing of one-third of the people on the face of the earth by this army of two hundred million (9:18).

With the completion of the second woe, we are told again that the third woe is coming quickly, and so it is. We see the events of the third woe given to us in a broad way in the very next passage.

The Prophecy Puzzle

Revelation 11:15 – 19

> "And the seventh angel sounded; and there were great voices in heaven, saying, The kingdoms of this world are become the kingdoms of our Lord, and of his Christ; and he shall reign for ever and ever.
> 16 And the four and twenty elders, which sat before God on their seats, fell upon their faces, and worshipped God,
> 17 Saying, We give thee thanks, O Lord God Almighty, which art, and wast, and art to come; because thou hast taken to thee thy great power, and hast reigned.
> 18 And the nations were angry, and thy wrath is come, and the time of the dead, that they should be judged, and that thou shouldest give reward unto thy servants the prophets, and to the saints, and them that fear thy name, small and great; and shouldest destroy them which destroy the earth.
> 19 And the temple of God was opened in heaven, and there was seen in his temple the ark of his testament: and there were lightnings, and voices, and thunderings, and an earthquake, and great hail."

This passage describes <u>ALL</u> that will happen with the blowing of the seventh trumpet, including the pouring out of the seven bowls of God's wrath. It must be noted that the **twenty-four elders <u>in heaven</u>** say all of these things (v. 15).

The Prophecy Puzzle

The twenty-four elders in heaven say:
- God is now ruling on the earth, the kingdom is now Christ Jesus' to rule forever.
  - One of His first acts is to judge those who dwell on the earth.
    - He does this through the pouring out of the seven bowls of wrath.
- The nations <u>were</u> angry (past tense) and God's wrath <u>has come</u> (present/ready).
  - This brings them to present time. The seven bowls of God's wrath are **ready** to be poured out upon the earth, but they have not yet been so.
- After that, the time for the saints to be rewarded has come (18b).
  - The wedding supper of the Lamb (also seen in Revelation 19:7 – 10).
- After that, the time <u>has come</u> to destroy those who destroy the earth (18c).
  - This is carried out by the actual pouring of the seven bowls of God's wrath upon the earth.
  - Included in this is the battle of Armageddon (Revelation 19:11 – 21).

In order to make sense of the previous and Rev. 11:19 we need to understand that verse 19 is no longer what he <u>hears</u>, but what he <u>sees</u>. What he sees is the temple being opened, which is what we are also shown in Revelation 15:5, which is the preparation for the bowls of wrath to be poured out upon the earth. The lighting, noises, thunder, earthquake and heavy hail in the second half of verse 19 is the description of the seventh and last bowl of YHWH's wrath (Rev. 16:21), which sums up the third woe.

The Prophecy Puzzle

That brings us to the end of this prophecy. Revelation 12:1 starts the story over again.

The Prophecy Puzzle

CHAPTER NINE

The Timing of Events According to Revelation 12:1 – 16:21

****

As stated at the end of the last chapter, Revelation 12:1 starts a new prophecy, but it is largely the same prophecy we just studied. The main differences are that it starts at an earlier point in time than the previous and it emphasizes events that are occurring in heaven during this time, as well as the role and person of the false Messiah (anti-Christ). It also puts an emphasis on God's wrath by giving a detailed description of the final and most severe judgments of YHWH, the seven bowls (vials) of wrath. Let's start by looking at the first portion of the text.

The Prophecy Puzzle

Revelation 12:1 – 12

"And there appeared a great wonder in heaven; a woman clothed with the sun, and the moon under her feet, and upon her head a crown of twelve stars:
2 And she being with child cried, travailing in birth, and pained to be delivered.
3 And there appeared another wonder in heaven; and behold a great red dragon, having seven heads and ten horns, and seven crowns upon his heads.
4 And his tail drew the third part of the stars of heaven, and did cast them to the earth: and the dragon stood before the woman which was ready to be delivered, for to devour her child as soon as it was born.
5 And she brought forth a man child, who was to rule all nations with a rod of iron: and her child was caught up unto God, and to his throne.
6 And the woman fled into the wilderness, where she hath a place prepared of God, that they should feed her there a thousand two hundred and threescore days.
7 And there was war in heaven: Michael and his angels fought against the dragon; and the dragon fought and his angels,
8 And prevailed not; neither was their place found any more in heaven.
9 And the great dragon was cast out, that old serpent, called the Devil, and Satan, which deceiveth the whole world: he was cast out into the earth, and his angels were cast out with him.
10 And I heard a loud voice saying in heaven, Now is come salvation, and strength, and the kingdom of our

The Prophecy Puzzle

God, and the power of his Christ: for the accuser of our brethren is cast down, which accused them before our God day and night.
11 And they overcame him by the blood of the Lamb, and by the word of their testimony; and they loved not their lives unto the death.
12 Therefore rejoice, ye heavens, and ye that dwell in them. Woe to the inhabiters of the earth and of the sea! for the devil is come down unto you, having great wrath, because he knoweth that he hath but a short time."

The first and most important question to answer is found in verse 1. Who is this woman? There have been many suggestions over the years, but all but one is easily disproved.

The first view I would like to look at is that she is the "Virgin Mary". This is believed, because she gave physical birth to Jesus Christ and soon after His birth Herod did try to kill Him by having all the children in Bethlehem under the age of two killed (Mat. 2:16). It is also suggested that she fled into Egypt for 3 ½ years after His birth (Mat. 2:14 – 15). The argument is concluded by stating that Jesus Christ was taken up to heaven after His death and resurrection (Acts 1:9 – 11) and then kicked Satan out of heaven to the earth (Rev. 12:7– 8).

At first glance it sounds pretty good, but there are some problems with this view. For starters nowhere in Scripture is Mary described as a woman with twelve stars, etc. Then there is the fact that the child was caught up to heaven **before** the woman fled into the wilderness (Rev. 12:5 – 6). The final point is the timing of the war in heaven. Their scenario would suggest that the war takes place when Jesus Christ

The Prophecy Puzzle

returns to heaven, when that is not the case. This is still a future event and will occur near the middle of the seven-year tribulation.

Incidentally, the EU holds to this view. It has said that the twelve stars on its flag is a tribute to her; her being the Virgin Mary, aka, the Queen of Heaven, Queen of Nations, etc. I think you get my point. An interesting book about this "queen" is "Queen of All" by Jim Tetlow, Roger Oakland and Brad Myers.

The next view I will look at is that this woman is actually the Church, the bride of Christ. Those who hold this view believe that the church is the mother of the saints and that her being clothed with the sun, represents the imputed righteousness of the Lord Jesus Christ. They go on to suggest that the moon under her feet represents the world as she stands upon it, but lives above it. The crown on her head with the twelve stars represents the doctrine of the gospel preached by the twelve apostles. They conclude their argument by suggesting that she has brought forth this holy progeny to Christ, through great suffering.

The number one problem with this view is that there is no Scripture to support any of it! On the contrary the Church is always represented as the <u>virgin</u> bride of Christ. There is no biblical reason to make the moon represent the world. In my opinion this view is very imaginative, but has no biblical basis.

The last view we'll look at is the correct view and it is that this woman represents Israel, the chosen vessel to bring the Messiah into the world. We know this because **Scripture interprets Scripture!** In Gen. 37:9 – 10 Jacob (Israel) knew whom the sun, moon and the other eleven stars were representing. It was his wife, eleven other sons and himself. The rest is fairly self-evident. Jesus Christ was born of Israel.

The Prophecy Puzzle

He is the Lion of the tribe of Judah. He was caught up to heaven forty days after His resurrection.

Before moving on I must point out a problem that some have stumbled onto at this point. They assume that Rev. 12:3 – 4 are referring to the same events of Rev. 12:7 – 10. They are very different events. Verses 3 and 4, are speaking of Satan's rebellion against YHWH, where he loses his **position** in heaven. He still has access to heaven as we plainly see in Job 1:6, 2:1. It was at the time of his losing his position (vv. 3 and 4) that he persuaded one-third of the angels to follow him in his rebellion against YHWH. What we see in verses 7 through 10 is the battle, which takes place in heaven near the middle of the seven-year tribulation where Satan and the angels who followed him lose **all access** to heaven. We see from Dan. 12:1 that it corresponds with the rapture (His people / believers being rescued, and the first resurrection (Dan. 12:2).

Getting back to the subject on hand in Revelation 12, verse 6 jumps forward in time to the point Israel needs to flee from their homes into the wilderness. This happens as we pointed out earlier, at the middle of the seven-year tribulation when the anti-Christ puts a stop to their sacrifices and sets up the abomination of desolation (Dan. 9:27). She will be protected in the wilderness for 1260 days. Exactly where this wilderness is, we are not told; but many, as do I, believe it is Petra.

Now moving onto the "war in heaven" (Rev. 12:7 – 10), it happens at or very near the time of the false Messiah's attack on Israel to set up the abomination of desolation. We have that confirmed in 12:14, where we are told that Israel would be protected from Satan for three and a half years.

The Prophecy Puzzle

The result of this war in heaven is that Satan is cast out of heaven and never has any access to it again (v. 10). Up until this point in time he did have access and he used that access to accuse the saints, but the saints overcame his accusations by claiming the blood of the Lamb and their testimony of faith in Christ Jesus (Revelation 12:11, Romans 10:10).

Ezekiel 28 gives us a more detailed description of Satan's fall, so let's take a closer look at it there.

Ezekiel 28:14 – 17

> "Thou art the anointed cherub that covereth; and I have set thee so: thou wast upon the holy mountain of God; thou hast walked up and down in the midst of the stones of fire.
> 15 Thou wast perfect in thy ways from the day that thou wast created, till iniquity was found in thee.
> 16 By the multitude of thy merchandise they have filled the midst of thee with violence, and thou hast sinned: therefore I will cast thee as profane out of the mountain of God: and I will destroy thee, O covering cherub, from the midst of the stones of fire.
> 17 Thine heart was lifted up because of thy beauty, thou hast corrupted thy wisdom by reason of thy brightness: I will cast thee to the ground, I will lay thee before kings, that they may behold thee."

Note where Satan was in verse 14; he is on the holy mountain of God in the midst of the stones of fire. In verse 16 we see Satan being cast out of those places. In other words he is losing his position in heaven. Now

The Prophecy Puzzle

look at verse 17. There he is cast down to the **ground**. This is what is being referred to in Revelation 12:7 – 9, Satan's banishment from heaven all together.

Revelation 12:12 is the recording of the celebration in heaven, because Satan is forever banished. The second half of v. 12 **announces** the **coming** of the first woe, which is also announced **after** the fourth trumpet (Rev. 8:13) and then carried out with the blowing of the fifth trumpet (Rev. 9:1 – 12).

Revelation 12:13 – 17

> "And when the dragon saw that he was cast unto the earth, he persecuted the woman which brought forth the man child.
> 14 And to the woman were given two wings of a great eagle, that she might fly into the wilderness, into her place, where she is nourished for a time, and times, and half a time, from the face of the serpent.
> 15 And the serpent cast out of his mouth water as a flood after the woman, that he might cause her to be carried away of the flood.
> 16 And the earth helped the woman, and the earth opened her mouth, and swallowed up the flood which the dragon cast out of his mouth.
> 17 And the dragon was wroth with the woman, and went to make war with the remnant of her seed, which keep the commandments of God, and have the testimony of Jesus Christ."

The Prophecy Puzzle

This passage gives an account of the events happening on the earth after Satan and his fallen angels have been banished from heaven. Just as we saw in the previous passage, Satan, through the hand of the anti-Christ and his army attack Israel. Some of Israel with the help of Christ Jesus, flees into the wilderness (again probably Petra) and she is given protection and provision for 1260 days (3 ½ years) (Rev. 12:6), but most are slaughtered in this attack (Zechariah 13:8 – 9).

We are not told the specifics of how Satan attacks Israel or how Israel is able to flee his presence in this passage. But I believe we are given a more detailed description of how Christ Jesus provides an escape for Israel in Zechariah 14.

Zechariah 14:4 – 5a

> "And his feet shall stand in that day upon the mount of Olives, which is before Jerusalem on the east, and the mount of Olives shall cleave in the midst thereof toward the east and toward the west, and there shall be a very great valley; and half of the mountain shall remove toward the north, and half of it toward the south.
> 5 And ye shall flee to the valley of the mountains; for the valley of the mountains shall reach unto Azal: yea, ye shall flee, like as ye fled from before the earthquake in the days of Uzziah king of Judah:"

From this passage we see that Jesus Christ returns to the Mount of Olives and provides a way of escape for the Jews fleeing Jerusalem. While there is some debate if this is a literal flood or symbolic of the army the false Messiah sends after the people fleeing, the ultimate point is that YHWH provides a way of escape for Israel by having the Mount of Olives split in two, or as it is put in Revelation 12, the earth opened her mouth.

The passage in Revelation 12 ends with verse 17 stating that some time after Satan's attack on Israel fails, he turns his hateful attention toward "the remnant of her seed, which keep the commandments of God, and have the testimony of Jesus Christ." There is no denying that those being referred to in v. 17 are Christians, but note that it also states that they are part of her offspring, meaning they are Jewish (Revelation 12:1); so as I discussed earlier in chapter 8, this is a reference to the 144,000 Jewish Christians who are taken to the temple and sealed at the time of the rapture (Rev. 7:1 – 8).

Let's return to where we left off, Revelation 13. It gives detailed information about the "kingdom beast" and the "man beast" (the false Messiah / anti-Christ). To aid in the proper understanding of this passage, let me ask you a question. If I were to ask you to tell me about Israel, your response to me might be to ask, "The man or the nation?" And that would be a good question, because in the Bible, "Israel" is used to refer to both. This also happens in regards to the "beast" here in the book of Revelation. It refers to a man as well as a kingdom.

Revelation 13:1 – 10

> "And I stood upon the sand of the sea, and saw a beast rise up out of the sea, having seven heads and ten horns, and upon his horns ten crowns, and upon his heads the name of blasphemy.
> 2 And the beast which I saw was like unto a leopard, and his feet were as the feet of a bear, and his mouth as

The Prophecy Puzzle

the mouth of a lion: and the dragon gave him his power, and his seat, and great authority.
3 And I saw one of his heads as it were wounded to death; and his deadly wound was healed: and all the world wondered after the beast.
4 And they worshipped the dragon which gave power unto the beast: and they worshipped the beast, saying, Who is like unto the beast? who is able to make war with him?
5 And there was given unto him a mouth speaking great things and blasphemies; and power was given unto him to continue forty and two months.
6 And he opened his mouth in blasphemy against God, to blaspheme his name, and his tabernacle, and them that dwell in heaven.
7 And it was given unto him to make war with the saints, and to overcome them: and power was given him over all kindreds, and tongues, and nations.
8 And all that dwell upon the earth shall worship him, whose names are not written in the book of life of the Lamb slain from the foundation of the world.
9 If any man have an ear, let him hear.
10 He that leadeth into captivity shall go into captivity: he that killeth with the sword must be killed with the sword. Here is the patience and the faith of the saints."

Before we go into the details of the chapter I would like to give a brief timeline of the events within it. I believe 13:1 – 10 records what happens in the first half of the seven-year tribulation and brings us up to the point in time when the false Messiah stands in the temple of God and declares that he is God (the abomination of desolation).

The Prophecy Puzzle

First we see the revival of the Roman/Ottoman Empire. In verse 5 we are introduced to the false Messiah (anti-Christ) who comes to power and is given three and half years to rule. During his reign he will severely persecute Christians. Note verse 8 is in the future tense. This is after he has declared himself to be God; during the second half of the seven-year tribulation it will be the law, that one must worship the beast. It is likely that the only people who will not worship him will be those who have turned to Christ Jesus as their Savior and LORD after the rapture (v. 8).

As we look into the details of this passage we will be doing so from the two different viewpoints mentioned earlier. First we will look at it from the point of view that the beast is a kingdom, and then as if it is a person.

First of all let's identify this first beast that John sees. It comes out of the sea. This is significant, because the sea in the Bible can refer to the governments of the world. That is exactly the point in this passage, to verify this let's look at Daniel 7:23 – 25.

Daniel 7:23 – 25

> "Thus he said, The fourth beast shall be the fourth kingdom upon earth, which shall be diverse from all kingdoms, and shall devour the whole earth, and shall tread it down, and break it in pieces.
> 24 And the ten horns out of this kingdom are ten kings that shall arise: and another shall rise after them; and he shall be diverse from the first, and he shall subdue three kings.

The Prophecy Puzzle

> 25 And he shall speak great words against the most High, and shall wear out the saints of the most High, and think to change times and laws: and they shall be given into his hand until a time and times and the dividing of time."

Here in Daniel it is very clear that the fourth kingdom (the kingdom-beast) is in existence and the anti-Christ is a horn. The point being that in our passage in Revelation, the beast that comes out of the sea is a reference to the fourth kingdom or the kingdom-beast as I like to refer to it.

We had covered this back in chapter eight with the opening of the sixth seal, but because it is essential for the proper understanding of Revelation 13, I wanted to mention it again. We need to understand that all of the ten horns are on one of the seven heads. The ten horns are on the last head, just as with the beast in Daniel 7, or even the toes in Nebuchadnezzar's dream in Daniel 2.

Oh, now I did it. I mentioned the toes in Nebuchadnezzar's dream. I probably should ignore this; because some of you might think I am nuts at this point and close this book to never read it again, but I hope that will not be the case. Yes I know this might sound totally ridiculous to some of you, but I believe it is in accordance with the teaching of the Bible.

Daniel 2:42 – 43

> "And as the toes of the feet were part of iron, and part of clay, so the kingdom shall be partly strong, and partly broken.

> 43 And whereas thou sawest iron mixed with miry clay, they shall mingle themselves with the seed of men: but they shall not cleave one to another, even as iron is not mixed with clay."

Clay or land is a reference to humanity, for from the dust we were created (Gen. 2:7). Notice in verse 43 that the iron, which is mixed with the clay, is referred to as "they" and that "they" shall mingle with the seed of men. This can only mean that "they" are something other than human (the seed of men). These "end-time leaders", these toes or horns (at least some of them) could either be more fallen angels who left their natural domain (the spiritual realm) and somehow took upon themselves physical form as the ones recorded in Genesis 6:1 – 4, or demons like those that lead the two million man army (Rev. 9:14 – 15). I don't know if the anti-Christ is one of them, or as most believe, a human possessed by a demon. I suppose that could be the case with the toes as well, but to be honest I think it is more than that. For a detailed look at this issue please read my book, *Unmasking the Sons of GOD*. In any case I wanted to raise the issue, because we are hearing more and more about UFO's and if they turn out to be "real", I what to warn everyone that these "other than human" entities are not aliens from another planet; but are either fallen angels or their offspring who are somehow able to travel between the physical and spiritual realm/dimension, and their purpose is to deceive and lead people away from YHWH. Chuck Missler has a very good study on the subject titled, *"Mischievous Angels or Sethites?"*

Another point to be made here in Daniel 2 is that there are two legs. Some have made the case that this represents the splitting of the Roman Empire into two, the Roman Catholic Church and the Eastern Orthodox Church, but that is not the split that is being referred to here.

The Prophecy Puzzle

The two legs, which make up this end-time world government is that of the <u>Western</u> Roman Empire and the <u>Eastern</u> Roman Empire, which became the Byzantine Empire and later the **Ottoman Empire**. The East and the West will be brought together. The two primary players in a religious sense are the Roman Catholic Church and Islam. Both religions have a history of combining religion with politics, just as the final "kingdom-beast" will do.

The Roman Catholic Church has been for years trying to bring Islam and all the other religions and faiths of the world under its umbrella. Islam too has the goal of a one-world religion, namely, Islam; but I believe there is a segment within Islam that wants to accomplish this by compromise. As I write this I have a Quran in front of me, which was translated by Rashad Khalifa, Ph.D. (Revised Edition III). If you open to the first page this is what you will read, "Anyone who submits to God and devotes the worship to God ALONE is a "Submitter." Thus, one may be a Jewish Submitter, a Christian Submitter, a Buddhist Submitter, a Hindu Submitter, or a Muslim Submitter." And this is in part what is written on the back cover, "PROCLAIMING One unifying religion for all the people… This book consolidates all the messages delivered by all of God's messengers into one global message…"

Another point to consider is that Islam needs to separate itself from the Muslim terrorists and one way they can do this is to agree to entering into a union with the Roman Catholic Church (at least on the surface). If this does happen, time will reveal that it would be more accurate to say that Islam will be taking control of the Roman Catholic Church, not just forming a union with it.

This is where the "Virgin Mary" comes into play. "She" is the one major entity the Roman Catholics and the Muslims both venerate. In her

The Prophecy Puzzle

visions "she" has stated that one of her goals is to unite the peoples of the world. As I stated earlier "she" <u>under different names</u> is venerated in cultures and religions around the world.

There are many signs that the EU has already incorporated this "goddess" into their government and just as described for us in Revelation 17, they use each other to accomplish their goals. Two good books on this subject are "The EU and the Supra-Religion" by Robert Congdon, and "Queen of All" by Jim Tetlow, Roger Oakland and Brad Myers.

Ok, be that as it may, the point of Revelation 13 is that the beast out of the sea is the kingdom-beast and not the anti-Christ. It is the kingdom-beast, the new and improved Roman Empire united with the Ottoman Empire or vise versa, which is wounded and revived. It would appear that both of these Empires have long vanished from the face of the earth, but now before our eyes we see the revival of both those kingdoms and one day they will unite.

The EU is gaining economic and military strength with each passing day. In May of 2004 it passed the United States to be the largest economic power in the world. The Islamic world has enormous wealth due to its oil reserves. Together they will take its place as the world's only super power. How the United States will lose that status I do not know, but it seems that it will sometime in the future. Some believe it will be hit by a nuclear attack, but to be honest all we need to do is continue to hold to the economic and environmental policies of socialism we have embraced today for our decrease to occur. There is another possibility, that we just become so passive that we simply choose not to be involved in world affairs. That too seems to be the way we as a nation are moving.

The Prophecy Puzzle

Having already passed the United States, the EU has taken note of its most serious competition in the future, China and India. In order to combat their great potential, the EU has plans to expand its membership, from the current 27 countries to 109. They plan to begin by reaching out to the Middle East and then to the Americas. That could also explain why there is no mention of the United States in prophecy; it simply becomes part of the New Roman Empire.

I find it interesting that in the Bible, this end-times "kingdom-beast" incorporates most of Europe and portions of the Middle East, but not Russia and China (the kings of North and the East, Dan. 11:44). All the pieces seem to be falling into place.

Back to our text in Revelation 13:5, which once again makes the point I made a few paragraphs ago, that from the pre-existing empire the anti-Christ – the mouth here in verse 5 comes to the forefront. We are once again told that from the time that he declares himself to be God he has 42 months to continue.

Revelation 13:6 – 8 describe the reign of the false Messiah, but verses 9 and 10 remind and encourage the reader that YHWH will in the end make sure justice is carried out.

Looking at Revelation 13:1 – 10, from the view of the "man-beast" instead of the "kingdom-beast" we see the following. The head, which is wounded in verse 3, is that of the anti-Christ. He is wounded to the point of death and from Zechariah 11:17 it appears that this "man-beast" will lose the use of his right arm and eye, or it may be a reference to the corruption of his power and vision. In any case, he is revived and a "mouth" is given him, which in this view is referring to a person

The Prophecy Puzzle

(Revelation 13:11 – 13). This person persuades people to worship the beast (false Messiah). This mouth is later on referred to as the "false prophet" (Rev. 19:20).

Revelation 13:11 – 18

"And I beheld another beast coming up out of the earth; and he had two horns like a lamb, and he spake as a dragon.
12 And he exerciseth all the power of the first beast before him, and causeth the earth and them which dwell therein to worship the first beast, whose deadly wound was healed.
13 And he doeth great wonders, so that he maketh fire come down from heaven on the earth in the sight of men,
14 And deceiveth them that dwell on the earth by the means of those miracles which he had power to do in the sight of the beast; saying to them that dwell on the earth, that they should make an image to the beast, which had the wound by a sword, and did live.
15 And he had power to give life unto the image of the beast, that the image of the beast should both speak, and cause that as many as would not worship the image of the beast should be killed.
16 And he causeth all, both small and great, rich and poor, free and bond, to receive a mark in their right hand, or in their foreheads:
17 And that no man might buy or sell, save he that had the mark, or the name of the beast, or the number of his name.

The Prophecy Puzzle

> 18 Here is wisdom. Let him that hath understanding count the number of the beast: for it is the number of a man; and his number is Six hundred threescore and six."

As with 13:1 – 10 I would like to give a brief timeline of the events covered in Revelation 13:11 – 18. These events happen at the middle of the seven-year tribulation. The false Messiah/prophet sets up an idol in the Jewish temple and brings it to life. He forces all to worship it under the penalty of death. In addition to that he makes a law declaring that everyone must have the "mark of the beast" in order to buy or sell anything.

Again as we look at the details of this passage we will do so from the two viewpoints just described in the previous passage, the kingdom-beast and the man-beast. First we will look at it from the kingdom-beast view. In which case we are not actually being introduced to a completely new beast here in this passage, but it is an explanation of the mouth (the anti-Christ) introduced in 13:5. So then the reference of the beast coming out of the earth would be indicating that it is a human being. The word "earth," "ge" in the Greek, comes from the root word meaning, "soil" and therefore it could be alluding to this beast being human, because YHWH made man out of "ge" (Gen. 2:7, 1Cor. 15:47). What we see here in this passage is a more detailed description of the false Messiah. Don't forget our rule of parallelism, which we have already seen used in the book of Revelation. He has two horns, because he overtook three of the original ten horns (Daniel 7:24). Now he represents one of the three horns and has these two extra horns to represent the remaining two positions of power, which he overtook.

The Prophecy Puzzle

Some believe the two horns symbolize that he has both military and religious authority. If this is the case perhaps one of the horns (powers) he dethrones is the head of the false world religion, because we see in Revelation 17:15 – 16 this world religion destroyed by the false Messiah. In any case the false Messiah has all the authority of the first beast (the kingdom-beast). In other words he is the ruler of this revived Roman Empire, which everyone had thought was dead (v. 12).

If we look at it from the man-beast view, this as a description of the false **prophet**, the anti-Christ's right-hand man. The head that is killed and brought to life is the anti-Christ. The false prophet is described as a lamb with two horns, because he exercises all the power of the anti-Christ (the first beast). Because of that he is able to deceive the world and persuade them to worship the anti-Christ and the anti-Christ's image, which had been brought to life.

In either view the false Messiah or the false prophet does many impressive things to deceive the world, but his greatest achievement is to bring this image of the beast to life (v. 14).

Much speculation has been made over what this image is exactly. All I can do is speculate as well for we are not given details about it. I believe that this image that is brought to life is probably a clone or a biomechanical creation, that is given a spirit – an evil spirit, and not just any evil spirit, but I believe that the evil spirit that indwells this image is probably that evil spirit/goddess masquerading as the "Queen of Heaven", "the Virgin Mary", "the Queen of Nations", etc.; who I believe is none other than **Satan himself**. We are told in 2Cor. 11:14, that, "Satan himself is transformed into an angel of light." One of the main characteristics of these sightings people have of this "goddess" is a shining forth of a great light. Coincidentally this image is brought to

The Prophecy Puzzle

life for the abomination of desolation, which as we stated several times already occurs in the middle of the seven-year tribulation, which also coincides with Satan being banished from heaven (Revelation 12:7 – 9).

Another passage to consider is Ezekiel 28:17. I know we looked at it before, but let's take just one more look at it. It says, "… I will lay thee before kings, that they may behold thee." What I understand YHWH to be saying in this verse is that when Satan is banished from heaven, He will make him visible to the people on the earth. Satan, by indwelling this image will be visible to all mankind and he will for a short time receive the worship he has desired for ages.

The last thing we are told of the false Messiah's/prophet's activities at this time is that he makes it law that all must have the mark of the beast in order to buy or sell anything. This could mean several things and there have been many suggestions over the years. First of all let's acknowledge that it is a literal mark on the hand or forehead. The Greek word translated mark is "charagma" which literally means an etching in the skin, something like a brand or a tattoo.

One of the most common beliefs at this time is that it will be a microchip that is implanted under the skin. We have the technology to do that today and it would make financial transactions simple and identity theft very difficult. I believe that is part of it, but because of the literal meaning of "charagma" being "an etching in the skin", I believe the literal marking the skin is part of it as well.

That leaves us with one final discussion from this passage. That is, what is the meaning of the number of the beast being 666? Over the years, there have been numerous explanations of what this means, but I think it is safe to say that at this time no one knows <u>for sure</u> what it means.

The Prophecy Puzzle

One possibility is that the number of the kingdom-beast is that of the man-beast. To quote F.F. Bruce, "The [kingdom] beast is embodied in the emperor [man-beast], and it is one of the emperors whose 'number' is to be reckoned." In other words the letters of the false Messiah's name in Greek would add up to 666.

Another suggestion has been that it represents a satanic trinity. Each of the 6's representing one of the **imperfect** members of this trinity. I don't think this is a valid possibility, because it is clear in the text that it is a number of a man (13:18), not that of three men or a man and two demons, etc.

One of the oldest suggestions is that it represents the Pope. There are some coincidences that could lend creditability to this view. For instance the official language of the Roman Catholic Church is Latin and in Latin the Pope is often referred to as the **"Vicarius Filii Dei"** (The Vicar of the Son of God). In Latin as in Greek and Hebrew each letter has a value. Here are values of the letters used in the title:

- V = 5, I = 1, C = 100, A = 0, R = 0, I = 1, U = 5, S = 0
- F = 0, I = 1, L = 50, I = 1, I = 1
- D = 500, E = 0, I = 1
- 5+1+100+0+0+1+5+0+0+1+50+1+1+500+0+1= **<u>666</u>**.

Now, I've been around long enough to know that one can make numbers say anything one wants to make them say, so I would not put too much merit to the phrase "Vicarius Filii Dei" adding up to 666. But along with this coincidence, some of the doctrines of the Roman Catholic Church would seem to be pleasing to a false Messiah. For example, one could interpret the following quote from the Council of

The Prophecy Puzzle

Trent to be stating that anyone who claims a man can be justified by faith alone is damned to hell (anathema). Here is the quote:

> "If anyone saith that justifying faith is nothing else but confidence in the divine mercy which remits sin for Christ's sake alone; or, that this confidence alone is that whereby we are justified, let him be anathema" (forever cursed) (Sess. VI, Can. 12).

Many would say that is the heart of the gospel for a born-again evangelical Christian and because of that, it **could** be said that according to the Roman Catholic Church all born-again Christians are condemned to hell. This is not the only problematic teaching of the Roman Catholic Church. One that is not official doctrine of the church, but is proclaimed verbally and understood to be true by most Roman Catholics is that virtually no one actually goes to hell; Buddhists, Muslims, JW's, Mormons, Hindus, even evangelical Christians and all others as long as they are sincere in their faith will eventually enter into heaven. This is a false teaching and therefore against (anti) Christ Jesus (Acts 4:12, Eph 2:8 – 9).

Another suggestion has been that it represents the number of a bill in the European Union. I have read that there is a bill numbered 666 and that it deals with a man named Javier Solana, the Foreign Minister of the EU. Again, I think this is a stretch, because it is the number of a man (Rev. 13:18), not a bill. But I have to confess, if, and I emphasize if, everything I've read about Javier Solana is true, he certainly could be the false Messiah. But again, I doubt very much that all those things I've heard are true.

The Prophecy Puzzle

The most recent view I've seen comes from Walid Shoebat's book, "Why I Left Jihad". On page 320, He explains that the "666" in the Greek is not actually a number, but a symbol, the Muslim symbol of two crossed swords followed by the Arabic word for "Allah" or "Bism Allah" (in the name of Allah). Walid goes on to say on page 322 that this "Islamic Shahadatan is actually a declaration of allegiance and servitude to Allah and Muhammad. Right now this inscription of this declaration is worn by millions of Muslims on the forehead or right arm."

Walid suggests that those who copied John's original writing didn't know it wasn't Greek so they wrote the Greek letters that most resembled what they saw. As I pointed out earlier, I do see the coming together of the Middle East with the West in the Revived Roman Empire, so it could be plausible. Perhaps it is this with the electronic chip under the skin.

That does bring up the subject of the identity of the false Messiah and there are countless suggestions about who he is or will be, but at this point I don't think anyone knows for sure. In jest I warn if Javier Solana becomes the next Pope, well, watch out! In all seriousness, what I do know is that the wise person will keep their eye on Israel and realize that it will be the false Messiah who brings peace to Israel through a peace treaty **that includes** giving the Jews the right to rebuild their **temple** and start making offerings again.

So at the time of my writing this we cannot know who the false Messiah will be, but we are given clues about the anti-Christ in the Bible. He is referred to as the Gog of Magog (Ez. 38:2) and the Assyrian (Is. 10:5). If we look on a modern map we see that the countries of Turkey, Syria and Iraq would primarily cover the area that was Magog and Assyria. I

The Prophecy Puzzle

believe the anti-Christ will come from one of these countries or possibly one of the countries that border them.

Moving on to chapter 14, I have to point out the timing of these events. The end of chapter 13 left us near the middle of the seven-year tribulation. It was at that time Satan was banished from heaven and it was at that time the false Messiah is revealed for whom he truly is and it was at that time the image to the beast is placed in the Holy of Holies and is brought to life (possessed by Satan). So as we go into chapter 14 we are still near the middle of the seven-year tribulation.

Revelation 14:1 – 5

> "And I looked, and, lo, a Lamb stood on the mount Sion, and with him an hundred forty and four thousand, having his Father's name written in their foreheads.
> 2 And I heard a voice from heaven, as the voice of many waters, and as the voice of a great thunder: and I heard the voice of harpers harping with their harps:
> 3 And they sung as it were a new song before the throne, and before the four beasts, and the elders: and no man could learn that song but the hundred and forty and four thousand, which were redeemed from the earth.
> 4 These are they which were not defiled with women; for they are virgins. These are they which follow the Lamb whithersoever he goeth. These were redeemed from among men, being the firstfruits unto God and to the Lamb.

The Prophecy Puzzle

> 5 And in their mouth was found no guile: for they are without fault before the throne of God."

As I stated in chapter 8, at the time of the rapture the Jewish Christians are not raptured to heaven, but are taken to Jerusalem, where they are sealed (Rev. 7:4) and recognized as the firstfruits unto God and members of His Millennium Kingdom on earth (Revelation 14:4). I also had pointed out that today there are about 14 million Jews alive in the world and that about 1 % of them are born-again Christians. That means there are about 140,000 Jews who are born-again Christians today. That is pretty close to the 144,000 seen here. That might mean the time is getting close.

Another thing we learn about these 144,000 is that they were the only ones **on earth** that could **learn** the new song, which was being sung in heaven before the throne of God (Rev. 14:2 – 3). We also learn they are virgins and that there is no guile in their mouths and are without fault. This is not speaking of physical realities. It means that they were true born-again followers of Christ Jesus. They had not committed spiritual adultery. They are found to be without guile or fault because they have been cleansed in the blood of the Lamb and therefore are not condemned (Romans 8:1, Hebrews 10:14). They will from that time forward follow Jesus Christ. Incidentally, there is nothing, absolutely nothing, in this passage to indicate that they witness to anyone.

Revelation 14:6 – 13

> "And I saw another angel fly in the midst of heaven, having the everlasting gospel to preach unto them that dwell on the earth, and to every nation, and kindred, and tongue, and people,

The Prophecy Puzzle

7 Saying with a loud voice, Fear God, and give glory to him; for the hour of his judgment is come: and worship him that made heaven, and earth, and the sea, and the fountains of waters.

8 And there followed another angel, saying, Babylon is fallen, is fallen, that great city, because she made all nations drink of the wine of the wrath of her fornication.

9 And the third angel followed them, saying with a loud voice, If any man worship the beast and his image, and receive his mark in his forehead, or in his hand,

10 The same shall drink of the wine of the wrath of God, which is poured out without mixture into the cup of his indignation; and he shall be tormented with fire and brimstone in the presence of the holy angels, and in the presence of the Lamb:

11 And the smoke of their torment ascendeth up for ever and ever: and they have no rest day nor night, who worship the beast and his image, and whosoever receiveth the mark of his name.

12 Here is the patience of the saints: here are they that keep the commandments of God, and the faith of Jesus.

13 And I heard a voice from heaven saying unto me, Write, Blessed are the dead which die in the Lord from henceforth: Yea, saith the Spirit, that they may rest from their labours; and their works do follow them."

After all the chaos of the anti-Christ and his army attacking Jerusalem (Ezek. 38:8 – 16) and some of the Jews with YHWH's help escaping from the anti-Christ (Zech. 14:1 – 5a), we have an angel go out

The Prophecy Puzzle

throughout the world to proclaim the everlasting gospel. This is what Jesus Christ meant in Matthew 24:14:

> "And this gospel of the kingdom shall be preached in all the world for a witness unto all nations; and then shall the end come."

I believe that this happens somewhere among the events of the sixth seal and definitely before the breaking of the seventh seal, because the seventh seal contains the events of the seven trumpets, which mark the beginning of the pouring out of God's wrath upon the earth (Revelation 6:12 – 17, 8:5).

After the first angel proclaims the gospel throughout the world, another angel announcing that Mystery Babylon is fallen (Rev. 14:8) goes out. This declaration is the same spoken of in Revelation 18:1 – 4:

> "And after these things I saw another angel come down from heaven, having great power; and the earth was lightened with his glory.
> 2 And he cried mightily with a strong voice, saying, Babylon the great is fallen, is fallen, and is become the habitation of devils, and the hold of every foul spirit, and a cage of every unclean and hateful bird.
> 3 For all nations have drunk of the wine of the wrath of her fornication, and the kings of the earth have committed fornication with her, and the merchants of the earth are waxed rich through the abundance of her delicacies."

The Prophecy Puzzle

> 4 And I heard another voice from heaven, saying, Come out of her, my people, that ye be not partakers of her sins, and that ye receive not of her plagues."

After the announcement of the fall of Babylon, a third angel goes throughout the world proclaiming that if anyone worships the beast or his image or takes the mark of the beast they will be judged by the true God, YHWH. So no one can claim they took the mark of beast in ignorance. This could be understood to be the meaning of Rev. 18:4 as well. In any case this angel's flight obviously takes place before the anti-Christ **enforces** his new law, Rev. 13:15 – 17:

> 15 And he had power to give life unto the image of the beast, that the image of the beast should both speak, and cause that as many as would not worship the image of the beast should be killed.
> 16 And he causeth all, both small and great, rich and poor, free and bond, to receive a mark in their right hand, or in their foreheads:
> 17 And that no man might buy or sell, save he that had the mark, or the name of the beast, or the number of his name.

Along with this warning, an encouragement to all who would trust the true God, YHWH goes out.

As an additional encouragement to those who read his letter John is instructed to write down that those who die, because of their faith in and allegiance to Christ Jesus from that time forward will be greatly rewarded. I believe this is a constant truth, but it will obviously be even more necessary during the last half of the seven-year tribulation (the great tribulation), because the Gentiles who trust in Christ Jesus after the rapture will live underground in poverty or be killed.

Revelation 14:14 – 20

> "And I looked, and behold a white cloud, and upon the cloud one sat like unto the Son of man, having on his head a golden crown, and in his hand a sharp sickle.
> 15 And another angel came out of the temple, crying with a loud voice to him that sat on the cloud, Thrust in thy sickle, and reap: for the time is come for thee to reap; for the harvest of the earth is ripe.
> 16 And he that sat on the cloud thrust in his sickle on the earth; and the earth was reaped.
> 17 And another angel came out of the temple which is in heaven, he also having a sharp sickle.
> 18 And another angel came out from the altar, which had power over fire; and cried with a loud cry to him that had the sharp sickle, saying, Thrust in thy sharp sickle, and gather the clusters of the vine of the earth; for her grapes are fully ripe.
> 19 And the angel thrust in his sickle into the earth, and gathered the vine of the earth, and cast it into the great winepress of the wrath of God.
> 20 And the winepress was trodden without the city, and blood came out of the winepress, even unto the horse bridles, by the space of a thousand and six hundred furlongs [200 miles]."

There have been many "understandings" of this passage over the years, but we are only going to look at two of them. The first being that after

The Prophecy Puzzle

the messages of the three angels have been delivered YHWH-God's wrath is carried out on the earth. The first sickle represents the seven trumpets and the second sickle represents the seven bowls of God's wrath, ending with the battle of Armageddon. This fits perfectly with chapter fifteen if we understand that once again John is using parallelism. The events that are represented by the swinging of the two sickles are given to us in detail in chapters fifteen and sixteen (the preparation of and sounding/pouring out of the seven trumpets and bowls of wrath).

The second view is that the first swing of the sickle represented the rapture. This is based upon the fact that the first angel swings his sickle <u>on</u> the earth. Some translators believe "on" should be translated "above" or "over". The Greek word used here is "epi" and is translated "above" five times in the New Testament and is translated "over" fifty-five times in the New Testament. Because of this and because of the context, it is possible that the first sickle actually describes the rapture and the second sickle which is flung **into** (ĕis) the earth represents God's wrath, ending with the battle of Armageddon. This last part isn't debated much. It is clearly a reference to the gathering of the armies of the world to the valley of Megiddo for the battle of Armageddon, where there is to be so much bloodshed that it flows for 200 miles.

Either understanding could be correct. The main point to come away with from this passage is that at this time which is after the sixth seal is broken, but before the seventh one is broken; the rapture has happened and after that the wrath of God is poured out upon the earth (Revelation 7:9 – 8:1).

The Prophecy Puzzle

As I stated earlier, in the style of parallelism, the events described in a very broad manner at the end of chapter fourteen (verses 19 – 20) are now given to us in great detail in chapters fifteen and sixteen.

Revelation 15:1 – 8

"And I saw another sign in heaven, great and marvellous, seven angels having the seven last plagues; for in them is filled up the wrath of God.
2 And I saw as it were a sea of glass mingled with fire: and them that had gotten the victory over the beast, and over his image, and over his mark, and over the number of his name, stand on the sea of glass, having the harps of God.
3 And they sing the song of Moses the servant of God, and the song of the Lamb, saying, Great and marvellous are thy works, Lord God Almighty; just and true are thy ways, thou King of saints.
4 Who shall not fear thee, O Lord, and glorify thy name? for thou only art holy: for all nations shall come and worship before thee; for thy judgments are made manifest.
5 And after that I looked, and, behold, the temple of the tabernacle of the testimony in heaven was opened:
6 And the seven angels came out of the temple, having the seven plagues, clothed in pure and white linen, and having their breasts girded with golden girdles.
7 And one of the four beasts gave unto the seven angels seven golden vials full of the wrath of God, who liveth for ever and ever.

The Prophecy Puzzle

> 8 And the temple was filled with smoke from the glory of God, and from his power; and no man was able to enter into the temple, till the seven plagues of the seven angels were fulfilled."

What we see in here are the preparations that are being made in heaven for the wrath of God to be poured out upon the earth. I think it is important to notice that at this time we find that those who died for their faith during the great tribulation are in heaven and they are singing the song of Moses. Yes, those who die during the last half of the seven-year tribulation do go to heaven upon their death, just as we do. But they will have to wait to receive their new physical glorified bodies (Rev. 20:4), but until then they are alive in heaven with God in spiritual bodies.

One sad conclusion I come to from this passage is that it seems that no one comes to faith in Christ Jesus once the bowls of wrath begin to be poured upon the earth. I believe this is confirmed in Rev. 16:9, 11 and 21, where it states that the people refused to repent and continued to blaspheme God. This brings us to chapter 16.

Revelation 16:1 – 21

> "And I heard a great voice out of the temple saying to the seven angels, Go your ways, and pour out the vials of the wrath of God upon the earth.
> 2 And the first went, and poured out his vial upon the earth; and there fell a noisome and grievous sore upon the men which had the mark of the beast, and upon them which worshipped his image.

The Prophecy Puzzle

3 And the second angel poured out his vial upon the sea; and it became as the blood of a dead man: and every living soul died in the sea.

4 And the third angel poured out his vial upon the rivers and fountains of waters; and they became blood.

5 And I heard the angel of the waters say, Thou art righteous, O Lord, which art, and wast, and shalt be, because thou hast judged thus.

6 For they have shed the blood of saints and prophets, and thou hast given them blood to drink; for they are worthy.

7 And I heard another out of the altar say, Even so, Lord God Almighty, true and righteous are thy judgments.

8 And the fourth angel poured out his vial upon the sun; and power was given unto him to scorch men with fire.

9 And men were scorched with great heat, and blasphemed the name of God, which hath power over these plagues: and they repented not to give him glory.

10 And the fifth angel poured out his vial upon the seat of the beast; and his kingdom was full of darkness; and they gnawed their tongues for pain,

11 And blasphemed the God of heaven because of their pains and their sores, and repented not of their deeds.

12 And the sixth angel poured out his vial upon the great river Euphrates; and the water thereof was dried up, that the way of the kings of the east might be prepared.

The Prophecy Puzzle

13 And I saw three unclean spirits like frogs come out of the mouth of the dragon, and out of the mouth of the beast, and out of the mouth of the false prophet.

14 For they are the spirits of devils, working miracles, which go forth unto the kings of the earth and of the whole world, to gather them to the battle of that great day of God Almighty.

15 Behold, I come as a thief. Blessed is he that watcheth, and keepeth his garments, lest he walk naked, and they see his shame.

16 And he gathered them together into a place called in the Hebrew tongue Armageddon.

17 And the seventh angel poured out his vial into the air; and there came a great voice out of the temple of heaven, from the throne, saying, It is done.

18 And there were voices, and thunders, and lightnings; and there was a great earthquake, such as was not since men were upon the earth, so mighty an earthquake, and so great.

19 And the great city was divided into three parts, and the cities of the nations fell: and great Babylon came in remembrance before God, to give unto her the cup of the wine of the fierceness of his wrath.

20 And every island fled away, and the mountains were not found.

21 And there fell upon men a great hail out of heaven, every stone about the weight of a talent: and men blasphemed God because of the plague of the hail; for the plague thereof was exceeding great."

The Prophecy Puzzle

We are not told exactly when these bowls of wrath are poured out, so at this time I will ignore that issue; but I will provide a suggestion when I present my timeline.

The first bowl of YHWH's wrath is poured out, which results in everyone who had received the mark of the beast or worshiped his image getting "loathsome and malignant sores" all over their bodies.

The second bowl of YHWH's wrath results in all the seas of the world becoming blood (poisonous) and the death of **all** life within them. I see no reason that this cannot be literal blood; but at this point in time I don't think its composition really matters. What is important is that it is deadly.

With the pouring out of the third bowl of YHWH's wrath all the rivers and springs (fresh water) become blood (poisonous) and an angel proclaims that YHWH's judgments are right. Verse six states that they deserve the judgment they are receiving. This is a true statement, but we should step back and realize that we too, **in our own righteousness** deserve God's judgment. We are saved completely by God's grace. Our own righteous can only condemn us (Gal. 5:2 – 5). The fourth bowl of YHWH's wrath is actually poured out upon the sun. I believe the result of this is solar flares. These unusually violent explosions produce more heat than normal and scorch the earth. We have observed and experienced these for some years now, but thankfully, nothing like the ones that will happen at this time.

As I pointed out earlier the people do not repent because of these plagues and continue to blaspheme God's name. In so doing they are acknowledging that they know that YHWH, the God of the Bible is responsible for the plagues.

The Prophecy Puzzle

The fifth bowl of God's wrath is poured out specifically on the "throne of the beast," which is the actual physical city of Babylon in Iraq. Some believe that the actual location will be Dubai, because of its great wealth today and the fact that it is situated as the original city of Babylon was; near the mouth of the Euphrates River. Over the years the mouth of the river has gradually moved further into the sea, leaving the original Babylon further inland than it originally had been located. They could be right, but with all that is happening in Iraq these days, I would not rule out the original site of ancient Babylon. In any case we see a detailed account of its destruction being carried out in chapter eighteen (Revelation 18:1 – 24), which we will discuss more when we get there.

The sixth bowl of YHWH's wrath results in the Euphrates River being dried up, making it easy for the kings of the East (the two hundred million-man army mentioned back in Rev. 9:13 – 21) to cross over to Israel, so they can be included in the battle of Armageddon, which is part of the seventh bowl of God's wrath.

Some would think that Rev. 16:15 seems to be out of place, but stop and think about how the Jews in Israel and perhaps those hiding in the rocks of Petra might feel at this time. They find themselves surrounded by all the armies of the world and if that is not bad enough, the two witnesses who have been protecting them, have just been killed (Rev. 11:7 – 14). This is a real point of testing their faith. YHWH, here in verse 15 is encouraging them to hang in there. He will come against their enemies like a thief in the night. Meaning when they least expect it. In fact we should look at Luke 12:35 – 40 to give us further insight into this situation.

The Prophecy Puzzle

Luke 12:35 – 40

> "Let your loins be girded about, and your lights burning;
> 36 And ye yourselves like unto men that wait for their lord, when he will return from the wedding; that when he cometh and knocketh, they may open unto him immediately.
> 37 Blessed are those servants, whom the lord when he cometh shall find watching: verily I say unto you, that he shall gird himself, and make them to sit down to meat, and will come forth and serve them.
> 38 And if he shall come in the second watch, or come in the third watch, and find them so, blessed are those servants.
> 39 And this know, that if the goodman of the house had known what hour the thief would come, he would have watched, and not have suffered his house to be broken through.
> 40 Be ye therefore ready also: for the Son of man cometh at an hour when ye think not."

Notice in verse 36 that the Lord is returning from a wedding, just as Jesus Christ is returning from the marriage supper of the Lamb when He returns to save the Jews at the battle of Armageddon (Revelation 19:7 – 19). Also in verse 40 we have that same warning to stay ready, for the Son of man will come at a time they don't expect it.

We cannot leave this passage (Revelation 16:13 – 16) without pointing out the "satanic trinity." It is made up of the dragon (Satan), the beast

The Prophecy Puzzle

(the anti-Christ) and the false prophet. YHWH uses them to entice all the armies of the world to gather for the battle of Armageddon.

The seventh and final bowl of YHWH's wrath is poured out. What is given to us here in Rev. 16:17 – 21 is actually an overview. We get a more detailed description of these events in Revelation 19:11 – 21 and Ezekiel 38:17 – 39:8. But from this passage (Rev. 16:17 – 21) we see the results of God's wrath. It ends with the most severe hailstorm ever; but there are four other events that happen at this time, the first of which is the greatest and most severe earthquake in all of history. Secondly, the great city (Jerusalem – Rev. 11:8) will split in three. Thirdly, Babylon is remembered by YHWH. Fourthly, every island will disappear and every mountain except Mount Zion will fall (Zechariah 14:9 – 11). The whole surface of the earth is changed at this time and the "new earth" has Jerusalem elevated above the rest of the surface of the earth.

The Prophecy Puzzle

CHAPTER TEN

Timing of Events According to Revelation 17:1 – 19:21

****

In this section there are four major events described for us in detail. The first is the destruction of the Harlot – the world religious system, which happens near the middle of the seven-year tribulation. The second is the destruction of the city Babylon, which happens near the end of the seven-year tribulation, the third is the marriage supper of the Lamb, which happens before the seventh bowl of wrath is poured out upon the earth, which is the fourth major event described in detail, the battle of Armageddon.

The Prophecy Puzzle

Revelation 17:1 – 18

"And there came one of the seven angels which had the seven vials, and talked with me, saying unto me, Come hither; I will shew unto thee the judgment of the great whore that sitteth upon many waters:
2 With whom the kings of the earth have committed fornication, and the inhabitants of the earth have been made drunk with the wine of her fornication.
3 So he carried me away in the spirit into the wilderness: and I saw a woman sit upon a scarlet coloured beast, full of names of blasphemy, having seven heads and ten horns.
4 And the woman was arrayed in purple and scarlet colour, and decked with gold and precious stones and pearls, having a golden cup in her hand full of abominations and filthiness of her fornication:
5 And upon her forehead was a name written, MYSTERY, BABYLON THE GREAT, THE MOTHER OF HARLOTS AND ABOMINATIONS OF THE EARTH.
6 And I saw the woman drunken with the blood of the saints, and with the blood of the martyrs of Jesus: and when I saw her, I wondered with great admiration.
7 And the angel said unto me, Wherefore didst thou marvel? I will tell thee the mystery of the woman, and of the beast that carrieth her, which hath the seven heads and ten horns.
8 The beast that thou sawest was, and is not; and shall ascend out of the bottomless pit, and go into perdition: and they that dwell on the earth shall wonder, whose

The Prophecy Puzzle

names were not written in the book of life from the foundation of the world, when they behold the beast that was, and is not, and yet is.

9 And here is the mind which hath wisdom. The seven heads are seven mountains, on which the woman sitteth.

10 And there are seven kings: five are fallen, and one is, and the other is not yet come; and when he cometh, he must continue a short space.

11 And the beast that was, and is not, even he is the eighth, and is of the seven, and goeth into perdition.

12 And the ten horns which thou sawest are ten kings, which have received no kingdom as yet; but receive power as kings one hour with the beast.

13 These have one mind, and shall give their power and strength unto the beast.

14 These shall make war with the Lamb, and the Lamb shall overcome them: for he is Lord of lords, and King of kings: and they that are with him are called, and chosen, and faithful.

15 And he saith unto me, The waters which thou sawest, where the whore sitteth, are peoples, and multitudes, and nations, and tongues.

16 And the ten horns which thou sawest upon the beast, these shall hate the whore, and shall make her desolate and naked, and shall eat her flesh, and burn her with fire.

17 For God hath put in their hearts to fulfil his will, and to agree, and give their kingdom unto the beast, until the words of God shall be fulfilled.

The Prophecy Puzzle

> 18 And the woman which thou sawest is that great city, which reigneth over the kings of the earth."

Here the world religious system is referred to as the great harlot and in this passage we learn the following things about her:
- 17:1, 15: She has judgment coming to her in the end, but until then has influence over many nations and cultures.
- 17:2: She was united with the kings of this world and she has spread her immoral acts throughout the world.
- 17:3, 7: She was supported and promoted by the kingdom-beast.
- 17:4: She was wealthy, vane and audacious. She identified herself with the colors of purple and scarlet.
- 17:6: She killed the Saints (holy ones) and the witnesses of Jesus Christ.
    - These are two different groups of people. The Old Testament Saints and New Testament Christians.
- 17:9: At the time of her judgment she will be located on seven mountains.
- 17:16: She is destroyed by the anti-Christ and the kingdom-beast.
- 17:18: She is a "city" which has a kingdom, which is above the kings of the earth.

I have a few observations from this list that I would like to discuss further. First of all in reference to her identifying herself with purple and scarlet, I think we can get some clues to the identity of the world religious system from these colors. Perhaps it is just coincidence, but maybe it's not, that the royal color of the ancient Roman Empire was purple. Also the Emperor's robe was always purple. Later on the Roman Catholic Church adopted scarlet as the royal color. So we have

The Prophecy Puzzle

the bringing together of the royal colors of the Roman Empire and the Roman Catholic Church.

Is the Roman Catholic Church the harlot of Revelation 17? **No**. The evil spirit behind the harlot got its start long before the Roman Catholic Church was ever formed, but at the time of this spirits final judgment, it will be associated with Rome. This spirit goes all the way back to the tower of Babel. It has had many faces over the centuries: Ishtar, Diana, Venus, Hermes, etc., but it comes down to her being the **queen of heaven**, and the evil spirit masquerading as this "angel of light" is none other than Satan (2Cor. 11:14). Once again, I recommend the DVD, "Messages from Heaven" produced by "Eternal Productions" (www.eternal-productins.org) as well as the book, "Queen of All" by Jim Tetlow, Roger Oakland and Brad Myers.

This spirit is not just in one religion, but them all; especially the two largest in the world. Consider the following facts. At the present time the Pope is strongly pushing the ecumenical movement. He wants all the world religions to come under the umbrella of the Roman Catholic Church. They have also changed their view toward other religions. They now teach that any sincere, good person of any religion can eventually make it into heaven, but at the same time they haven't changed their written position stated in the Second Vatican, Council of Trent. Also of the utmost significance, they confess that Mohammad was a prophet of God. Look in any modern Roman Catholic catechism or encyclopedia.

It is taught in our public schools today that to be a Muslim one must do two things: Believe Allah is God and that Mohammad is his prophet. The Roman Catholic Church today agrees with those two statements, so I guess the Roman Catholic Church today is part of the Muslim faith. Remember in the previous chapter I made the point that the final world

The Prophecy Puzzle

empire would be the uniting of the revived Roman and Ottoman Empires. That is exactly what we see happening before our eyes today, both in the religious realm as well as in the political realm.

Today it is clear that this world religious system is certainly linked with the Roman Catholic Church. One clue to this is her location (v. 9). She sits on seven hills. If you have ever been to Rome you have heard it referred to as the city that sits on seven hills. Also in verse 18, this religious system is identified with/by a city. How much more identified with Rome can one get, than to have Rome included in your name?

I won't discuss verses 8 – 12 here, because we dealt with them in detail in previous chapters (9 and 10).

To summarize, the harlot is an ancient religious system, which started with Nimrod and the tower of Babel. It is guilty of killing the followers of the true God (YHWH) from its beginning and will be identified with the world religion which is identified with a city that sits on seven hills (Rome).

Ok, we discussed what the harlot is and who is behind it, but this chapter in the end describes its destruction. Yes, for a time it will have influence with the kings of the world, but at sometime near the middle of the seven-year tribulation it will be destroyed by the very ones it had been manipulating. After the false Messiah destroys the harlot in Rome, his headquarters is now solely Babylon, the actual city of Babylon in Iraq or perhaps Dubai (Zechariah 5:6 – 11). The spirit behind the religion isn't destroyed for it is Satan. He takes residence in the image that the anti-Christ had made for him and is worshiped by all under the penalty of death (Rev. 13:15).

The Prophecy Puzzle

So as we just stated, the anti-Christ's first order of business after he declares himself to be God is to destroy the harlot. He does this with the help of the "kings" of this world (Rev. 17:11 – 18), but along with that order, he wages war against the Lamb (Jesus Christ).

This brings us to chapter 18, where we see the destruction of the actual city of Babylon in Iraq. Again, some believe that this is actually the city of Dubai and not Babylon, and they could be right; but I would not rule out the possibility of it actually being the city of Babylon. In fact, I wouldn't be surprised if it is restored and built to be an amazing city that even outshines Dubai in the years to come.

Revelation 18:1 – 4

> "1 And after these things I saw another angel come down from heaven, having great power; and the earth was lightened with his glory.
> 2 And he cried mightily with a strong voice, saying, Babylon the great is fallen, is fallen, and is become the habitation of devils, and the hold of every foul spirit, and a cage of every unclean and hateful bird.
> 3 For all nations have drunk of the wine of the wrath of her fornication, and the kings of the earth have committed fornication with her, and the merchants of the earth are waxed rich through the abundance of her delicacies.
> 4 And I heard another voice from heaven, saying, Come out of her, my people, that ye be not partakers of her sins, and that ye receive not of her plagues."

We discussed these verses back in Chapter Nine, so I won't do so now.

The Prophecy Puzzle

Revelation 18:5 – 24

"For her sins have reached unto heaven, and God hath remembered her iniquities.
6 Reward her even as she rewarded you, and double unto her double according to her works: in the cup which she hath filled fill to her double.
7 How much she hath glorified herself, and lived deliciously, so much torment and sorrow give her: for she saith in her heart, I sit a queen, and am no widow, and shall see no sorrow.
8 Therefore shall her plagues come in one day, death, and mourning, and famine; and she shall be utterly burned with fire: for strong is the Lord God who judgeth her.
9 And the kings of the earth, who have committed fornication and lived deliciously with her, shall bewail her, and lament for her, when they shall see the smoke of her burning,
10 Standing afar off for the fear of her torment, saying, Alas, alas, that great city Babylon, that mighty city! for in one hour is thy judgment come.
11 And the merchants of the earth shall weep and mourn over her; for no man buyeth their merchandise any more:
12 The merchandise of gold, and silver, and precious stones, and of pearls, and fine linen, and purple, and silk, and scarlet, and all thyine wood, and all manner vessels of ivory, and all manner vessels of most precious wood, and of brass, and iron, and marble,

The Prophecy Puzzle

13 And cinnamon, and odours, and ointments, and frankincense, and wine, and oil, and fine flour, and wheat, and beasts, and sheep, and horses, and chariots, and slaves, and souls of men.

14 And the fruits that thy soul lusted after are departed from thee, and all things which were dainty and goodly are departed from thee, and thou shalt find them no more at all.

15 The merchants of these things, which were made rich by her, shall stand afar off for the fear of her torment, weeping and wailing,

16 And saying, Alas, alas, that great city, that was clothed in fine linen, and purple, and scarlet, and decked with gold, and precious stones, and pearls!

17 For in one hour so great riches is come to nought. And every shipmaster, and all the company in ships, and sailors, and as many as trade by sea, stood afar off,

18 And cried when they saw the smoke of her burning, saying, What city is like unto this great city!

19 And they cast dust on their heads, and cried, weeping and wailing, saying, Alas, alas, that great city, wherein were made rich all that had ships in the sea by reason of her costliness! for in one hour is she made desolate.

20 Rejoice over her, thou heaven, and ye holy apostles and prophets; for God hath avenged you on her.

21 And a mighty angel took up a stone like a great millstone, and cast it into the sea, saying, Thus with violence shall that great city Babylon be thrown down, and shall be found no more at all.

The Prophecy Puzzle

> 22 And the voice of harpers, and musicians, and of pipers, and trumpeters, shall be heard no more at all in thee; and no craftsman, of whatsoever craft he be, shall be found any more in thee; and the sound of a millstone shall be heard no more at all in thee;
> 23 And the light of a candle shall shine no more at all in thee; and the voice of the bridegroom and of the bride shall be heard no more at all in thee: for thy merchants were the great men of the earth; for by thy sorceries were all nations deceived.
> 24 And in her was found the blood of prophets, and of saints, and of all that were slain upon the earth."

While there are some similarities with the harlot of chapter 17, they are clearly different entities. For instance in chapter 17 the kings of the earth rejoiced over her destruction, but here they mourn (v. 9). Also the immorality of the city of Babylon is different. The city of Babylon is guilty of the sorcery of materialism. There are **ten** references to material goods and merchants (vv. 3, 11, 12, 13, 14, 15, 16, 17, 19, 23). And just as chapter 17 speaks of more than just the day of Mystery Babylon's destruction, so does chapter 18. The materialism of Babylon has always been with us and YHWH has been calling His people out of it from the beginning of time. Jesus Christ spoke more about money than any other subject. Scripture makes it clear that a person's true beliefs are revealed by how they make and use their money (Mat. 6:19 – 24, Acts 16:16 – 19, 19:24 – 29 and James 4:4). One way to check if our faith is real is to look at where our money is going.

Now notice the language in verse 5; it says "… God has remembered her iniquities." This same language is used in Rev. 16:19, "Babylon came in remembrance before God". In Rev. 18:8 we are told that Babylon will

The Prophecy Puzzle

be destroyed in one day and then in verses 10, 17 and 19 it even declares that she will be destroyed in just **one hour**. I believe this is a literal hour. It should also be noted that the city is completely destroyed (18:21), and it is destroyed shortly before the Euphrates River is dried up. If we look closely at the fifth bowl of God's wrath (Rev. 16:17 – 21) we see that it happens just before the battle of Armageddon. It is very possible that the destruction of Babylon is linked to the drying up of the Euphrates River (Sixth Bowl, Rev. 16:12), since Babylon (or Dubai) is located on the Euphrates River.

Revelation 19:1 – 6

> "And after these things I heard a great voice of much people in heaven, saying, Alleluia; Salvation, and glory, and honour, and power, unto the Lord our God:
> 2 For true and righteous are his judgments: for he hath judged the great whore, which did corrupt the earth with her fornication, and hath avenged the blood of his servants at her hand.
> 3 And again they said, Alleluia. And her smoke rose up for ever and ever.
> 4 And the four and twenty elders and the four beasts fell down and worshipped God that sat on the throne, saying, Amen; Alleluia.
> 5 And a voice came out of the throne, saying, Praise our God, all ye his servants, and ye that fear him, both small and great.
> 6 And I heard as it were the voice of a great multitude, and as the voice of many waters, and as the voice of mighty thunderings, saying, Alleluia: for the Lord God omnipotent reigneth."

The Prophecy Puzzle

Here we see that God is praised by all those in heaven, angels and saints, for His righteous judgments upon the earth. These judgments refer to everything through the sixth bowl of wrath.

Revelation 19:7 – 10

> "Let us be glad and rejoice, and give honour to him: for the marriage of the Lamb is come, and his wife hath made herself ready.
> 8 And to her was granted that she should be arrayed in fine linen, clean and white: for the fine linen is the righteousness of saints.
> 9 And he saith unto me, Write, Blessed are they which are called unto the marriage supper of the Lamb. And he saith unto me, These are the true sayings of God.
> 10 And I fell at his feet to worship him. And he said unto me, See thou do it not: I am thy fellowservant, and of thy brethren that have the testimony of Jesus: worship God: for the testimony of Jesus is the spirit of prophecy."

This is the consummation of the marriage supper of the Lamb. It could be argued that the marriage supper of the Lamb began in heaven with the rapture, but without any doubt its completion is here on the earth with the Jews in Jerusalem. Jesus Christ will return with all the saints with Him to save the Jews from the armies of the world. Just for fun, try reading Psalms 23 with this in mind.

I believe the "wife" referred to in verse 7 is not just the church, but it includes all of Israel. And it is granted to all saints (Old and New Testament) to be arrayed with the same fine linen that covers, that of

The Prophecy Puzzle

course being the righteousness of Jesus Christ (Isaiah 61:10, Gal. 3:27, Rev. 19:14).

The last point to be made from this passage is that the angel in verse 10 emphatically refuses worship and commands John to only worship God. Just for clarification the word, "worship" is "*proskuneo*" in the Greek. It is the same word used to describe Jesus Christ being worshiped (Mat. 28:9, 17, John 9:38, Heb. 1:6). Jesus Christ is God (YHWH)!

Revelation 19:11 – 18

> "And I saw heaven opened, and behold a white horse; and he that sat upon him was called Faithful and True, and in righteousness he doth judge and make war.
> 12 His eyes were as a flame of fire, and on his head were many crowns; and he had a name written, that no man knew, but he himself.
> 13 And he was clothed with a vesture dipped in blood: and his name is called The Word of God.
> 14 And the armies which were in heaven followed him upon white horses, clothed in fine linen, white and clean.
> 15 And out of his mouth goeth a sharp sword, that with it he should smite the nations: and he shall rule them with a rod of iron: and he treadeth the winepress of the fierceness and wrath of Almighty God.
> 16 And he hath on his vesture and on his thigh a name written, KING OF KINGS, AND LORD OF LORDS.
> 17 And I saw an angel standing in the sun; and he cried with a loud voice, saying to all the fowls that fly in the

midst of heaven, Come and gather yourselves together
unto the supper of the great God;
18 That ye may eat the flesh of kings, and the flesh of
captains, and the flesh of mighty men, and the flesh of
horses, and of them that sit on them, and the flesh of
all men, both free and bond, both small and great."

This is a description of the battle of Armageddon. This time Jesus Christ is the one on the white horse and He is coming to make war. It says in verse 15 that He uses a sword, which comes out of His mouth to smite the armies. I think we get a clearer understanding of what that means if we look at the account of this battle in Ezekiel.

Ezekiel 38:21 – 22

"And I (Jesus Christ) will call for a sword against him
throughout all my mountains, saith the Lord GOD:
every man's sword shall be against his brother.
22 And I will plead against him with pestilence and
with blood; and I will rain upon him, and upon his
bands, and upon the many people that are with him, an
overflowing rain, and great hailstones, fire, and
brimstone."

Jesus Christ evidently confuses the armies so that they kill each other instead of the Jews. The Bible records this happening several times (Judges 7:22, 1Sam. 14:20). I'm not saying that is all that Jesus Christ does, but it is part of what He does.

It would be easy to just focus on the battle here, but there are so many more bits of gold in this passage. For instance, the name, which Jesus

The Prophecy Puzzle

Christ has written upon Him that no one knows, is the name of God, YHWH (Yahweh). No one really knows the true name of God. He has given us descriptions of Himself, but not His Name. In Isaiah 9:6 we are told that His name is "Wonderful" (not wonderful Counselor). Wonderful means it is beyond understanding. Since names are descriptive, it is impossible to give God one name, for He is infinite, and indeed, wonderful!

To evidence that Jesus Christ's name written upon Him is YHWH can be found by looking at Psalm 148:13 and Phil. 2:9.

> Psalm 148:13
>
> "Let them praise the name of the LORD: for his name alone is excellent; his glory is above the earth and heaven."

The word translated here as "LORD" is YHWH and it says very clearly that His name **alone** is excellent."

> Philippians 2:9
>
> "Wherefore God also hath highly exalted him, and given him a name which is above every name:"

The word translated "a" in this verse is "ho" in the Greek. It can be and often is translated "the" and in this case it should be. Some translators have translated it "the" in this verse. Jesus Christ was given **the** name, which is above every name. That means the name He was given is YHWH. There can only be one name that is above every name. That name is YHWH.

The Prophecy Puzzle

In the very next verse, Revelation 19:13; we are told that Jesus Christ's name is "The Word of God." As I just stated, in the Bible, names are often descriptive, as this one is here. It's not the only name Jesus Christ has, that is obvious, because He has many names throughout the Bible; which is clear from verse 16 where He is given another name, "King of Kings and Lord of Lords." "The Word of God" is only one of them. Jesus Christ having these names given to Him only adds to the name which is above every name, YHWH.

After the great slaughter, the beasts of the field and the birds are called together to get ready to eat the flesh of people killed (Ez. 39:17 – 20).

> Revelation 19:19 – 21
>
> "And I saw the beast, and the kings of the earth, and their armies, gathered together to make war against him that sat on the horse, and against his army.
> 20 And the beast was taken, and with him the false prophet that wrought miracles before him, with which he deceived them that had received the mark of the beast, and them that worshipped his image. These both were cast alive into a lake of fire burning with brimstone.
> 21 And the remnant were slain with the sword of him that sat upon the horse, which sword proceeded out of his mouth: and all the fowls were filled with their flesh."

Finally, the beast (anti-Christ) and the false prophet are captured and thrown alive into the lake of fire. The beast and false prophet stay alive

The Prophecy Puzzle

in the lake of fire and brimstone **forever** (Dan. 12:2, Mat. 25:46). I believe the reference to "all men" in 19:18 and "the remnant" in verse 21 refer to all those throughout the world that had received the mark of the beast. If they are not literally killed by Christ Jesus at this time, they are judged (Matthew 25:31 – 46). Some believe that this takes place during the extra 30 days or 15 days beyond those days mentioned in Daniel 12:11 – 12. I would not be dogmatic about it, but it makes sense to me.

The other timelines stopped with the battle of Armageddon, but this one continues in time covering the Millennium Kingdom and eternity. We will look at those events in the next chapter.

The Prophecy Puzzle

The Prophecy Puzzle

CHAPTER ELEVEN

The Judgment and the Millennium Kingdom – Revelation 20:1 – 15

****

Revelation 20:1 – 6

"And I saw an angel come down from heaven, having the key of the bottomless pit and a great chain in his hand.
2 And he laid hold on the dragon, that old serpent, which is the Devil, and Satan, and bound him a thousand years,
3 And cast him into the bottomless pit, and shut him up, and set a seal upon him, that he should deceive the

The Prophecy Puzzle

> nations no more, till the thousand years should be fulfilled: and after that he must be loosed a little season.
> 4 And I saw thrones, and they sat upon them, and judgment was given unto them: and I saw the souls of them that were beheaded for the witness of Jesus, and for the word of God, and which had not worshipped the beast, neither his image, neither had received his mark upon their foreheads, or in their hands; and they lived and reigned with Christ a thousand years.
> 5 But the rest of the dead lived not again until the thousand years were finished. This is the first resurrection.
> 6 Blessed and holy is he that hath part in the first resurrection: on such the second death hath no power, but they shall be priests of God and of Christ, and shall reign with him a thousand years."

Finally we see that Satan is thrown into the bottomless pit where he will be held captive for 1,000 years. And yes it is a literal thousand years, which we will discuss shortly, but first we must look at verses 4 – 6. I do find it interesting that Satan isn't thrown into the lake of fire right away, but has to wait until the thousand-year Millennium Kingdom is completed. I believe this is because once someone enters the lake of fire there is no exiting it. One is there for eternity, so please don't go there. If you haven't received Christ Jesus as your Savor and LORD, do so now. He has promised all who call out to Him for salvation will be saved (Rom. 10:13).

Blessed and holy are those who have part in the **first** resurrection! Yes indeed! While there is some debate over who is included in this group, I believe it is made up of <u>all believers</u>. It starts with Adam and Eve and ends with the last person to enter the Kingdom of God to this point in time. The last people to be saved are those who were martyred for their faith during the last half of the seven-year tribulation. The Old Testament saints must be included in this group and are part of those seen on thrones, for if they are not; they do not have part in the first resurrection. If that is the case they are not saved, for only those who are included in the first resurrection escape judgment for their sins and an eternity in the lake of fire.

One other thing happens at this time according to verse 4 and I believe what is being communicated here is that at this time all of these saints are judged (rewarded) for how they lived their lives as believers. This is a reference to the "bema seat" judgment.

At this point I would like to interject Psalms 98 – 100, because I believe this is the time for which they were written and will probably be sung at this time.

Psalms 98

> "O sing unto the LORD a new song; for he hath done marvellous things: his right hand, and his holy arm, hath gotten him the victory.
> 2 The LORD hath made known his salvation: his righteousness hath he openly shewed in the sight of the heathen.
> 3 He hath remembered his mercy and his truth toward the house of Israel: all the ends of the earth have seen the salvation of our God.

The Prophecy Puzzle

4 Make a joyful noise unto the LORD, all the earth: make a loud noise, and rejoice, and sing praise.
5 Sing unto the LORD with the harp; with the harp, and the voice of a psalm.
6 With trumpets and sound of cornet make a joyful noise before the LORD, the King.
7 Let the sea roar, and the fulness thereof; the world, and they that dwell therein.
8 Let the floods clap their hands: let the hills be joyful together
9 Before the LORD; for he cometh to judge the earth: with righteousness shall he judge the world, and the people with equity."

Psalms 99

"The LORD reigneth; let the people tremble: he sitteth between the cherubims; let the earth be moved.
2 The LORD is great in Zion; and he is high above all the people.
3 Let them praise thy great and terrible name; for it is holy.
4 The king's strength also loveth judgment; thou dost establish equity, thou executest judgment and righteousness in Jacob.
5 Exalt ye the LORD our God, and worship at his footstool; for he is holy.
6 Moses and Aaron among his priests, and Samuel among them that call upon his name; they called upon the LORD, and he answered them.

The Prophecy Puzzle

7 He spake unto them in the cloudy pillar: they kept his testimonies, and the ordinance that he gave them.
8 Thou answeredst them, O LORD our God: thou wast a God that forgavest them, though thou tookest vengeance of their inventions.
9 Exalt the LORD our God, and worship at his holy hill; for the LORD our God is holy."

Psalms 100

"Make a joyful noise unto the LORD, all ye lands.
2 Serve the LORD with gladness: come before his presence with singing.
3 Know ye that the LORD he is God: it is he that hath made us, and not we ourselves; we are his people, and the sheep of his pasture.
4 Enter into his gates with thanksgiving, and into his courts with praise: be thankful unto him, and bless his name.
5 For the LORD is good; his mercy is everlasting; and his truth endureth to all generations."

I wanted to bring attention to just a couple of things. Psalm 98 speaks to Israel and begins by making reference to the victory and salvation Jesus Christ brought at the battle of Armageddon. Psalm 99 speaks to the Gentiles who survived the seven-year tribulation and had not received the mark of the beast. It instructs them to come to Zion where Jesus Christ will be sitting in the Holy of Holies, between the cherubim, and worship Him there (Zech 14:16). Psalm 100 continues these instructions on how to worship YHWH.

The Prophecy Puzzle

I don't want to spend too much time on the Millennium Kingdom, because for us, getting there is what is important, and hopefully each of us will find out what it is like firsthand. But I would like to briefly give the descriptions of life during that time according to what YHWH has told us in the Bible.

From Zechariah 14:8 – 21: This is a very broad description of the Millennium Kingdom.
- 14:8: There will be:
    - A fresh water supply going out from the temple throughout the land.
    - There will be seasons.
- 14:9: Jesus Christ will reign over all the earth!
- 14:10: The earth will be made flat, except for Jerusalem, which will be raised on a mountain.
- 14:11: There will no longer be any effects of the curse **in Jerusalem**, and the people there will live in security.
- 14:16: Every year everyone will have to travel to Jerusalem to celebrate the Feast of Booths.
    - Some highlights about the Feast of Booths. It was a time:
        - To celebrate.
        - To reflect on God's provision through difficult times.
            - Just as the Israelites would have perished in the desert with Moses, without God's help, so would have those who survived the great tribulation.
            - For that matter, we all would have perished in our sins without God's help.

The Prophecy Puzzle

- To acknowledge mankind's complete dependence on God.
- 14:17: There will be judgments and punishments.
- 14:20: Everything **in Jerusalem** will be holy onto the Lord.
- 14:21b: There will be no Canaanite in the house of the Lord.
    - Mat. 21:12 – 13: Canaanites here is a reference to the merchants who made excessive profits. They did this by:
        - Demanding people use temple money to purchase what they needed to make sacrifices and then giving an unfair exchange rate.
        - Claiming that an offering wasn't good enough to offer to the Lord, so the person would have to purchase a lamb or a dove, etc. from them. Again they would overcharge for that animal.
    - From this verse we see that there will be the offering of animal sacrifices to God in the temple during the Millennium Kingdom.

From Isaiah 65:19 – 25 we see that in the Millennium Kingdom there will be:
- 65:19: No more crying **in Jerusalem**.
- 65:20, 23: There will be babies born.
- 65:20: There will be people who die.
    - Most everyone will live at least to the age of one hundred.
    - It would seem **only** the **wicked** would die during the Millennium Kingdom.
- 65:24: Christ Jesus will forever be present and have an intimate relationship with the Israelites.

The Prophecy Puzzle

- 65:25: There will be no wild beasts **in** the **holy mountain** (Jerusalem, perhaps all of Israel).

From Ezekiel 39:7 – 48:35 we learn that:
- 39:29: God's Spirit is on Israel.
- 40: - 42: The Temple will be there.
- 43:5: God's Spirit will fill the house (Temple).
  - Dan. 8:13 – 14: About a year and half after the beginning of the millennium kingdom the Shekinah Glory will return to the Holy of Holies.
    - Evidently it will take that long to cleanse it.
- 44:9: There will be "unbelievers" there.
  - Circumcision will be enforced with the rest of the Law (I believe).
- 44:29 (45:17): There will be sin.
- 44:30: There will be "taxes" (firstfruits offerings).
- 44:31: There will be death for animals.
- 45:10 – 12: There will be commerce.
- 45:21: People will observe the Passover.
- 46:1 (Is. 65:22 – 23): People will have jobs and observe the Sabbath.
- 46:16 – 18 (Is. 65:21): People will have private property.
- 46:17: There will be servants.
- 47:1 – 10: There will be an endless fresh water supply.
- 47:11: There will be salt water there as well.
- 47:12: There will be an abundance of food.
- 47:23: There will be a distinction between Jews and Gentiles.
  - This of course is speaking of the people who are not part of the "first resurrection". We are in our glorified bodies, helping the LORD Jesus govern.

The Prophecy Puzzle

People are usually surprised that during the Millennium Kingdom, animal sacrifices and other aspects of the Old Testament Law are in force. I believe there are some good reasons for this.

First of all, the Millennium Kingdom corresponds with the Feast of Booths, which is being lived out at this time. The whole Torah was completely read at the celebration of the Feast of Booths and the reading of the Torah symbolized the living of life according to it. The Temple sacrifices are part of following the Torah.

Another reason for the sacrifices is because the church age, the age of grace, is past. These people living under Jesus Christ's reign, not reigning with Him, are now under the same rules the "Old Testament saints" had been. The Old Testament saints looked forward to the coming of the Messiah and believed in Him (YHWH) to save them. They were saved by grace through faith just as we are, but their faith had to be expressed in the offering of the sacrifices to cover their sins, etc. In the same way those in the Millennium Kingdom who do truly trust YHWH are ultimately saved by grace, being covered by Jesus Christ's blood; but they profess that faith by the looking back to Christ Jesus' sacrifice and obeying the Law.

Well, that is all I have for the Millennium Kingdom. Like I said, getting there is the important part. I hope I'll see you there, but for now let's continue on in the book of Revelation.

Revelation 20:7 – 10

> "And when the thousand years are expired, Satan shall be loosed out of his prison,

The Prophecy Puzzle

> 8 And shall go out to deceive the nations which are in the four quarters of the earth, Gog and Magog, to gather them together to battle: the number of whom is as the sand of the sea.
> 9 And they went up on the breadth of the earth, and compassed the camp of the saints about, and the beloved city: and fire came down from God out of heaven, and devoured them.
> 10 And the devil that deceived them was cast into the lake of fire and brimstone, where the beast and the false prophet are, and shall be tormented day and night for ever and ever."

At the end of the thousand-year reign of Jesus Christ on the earth, Satan is released. He goes to the nations to convince them to rebel against YHWH and to attack Him. It seems from this description that the large majority of people on the earth at that time ("the number of them is like the sand of the seashore") join with Satan to attack YHWH-God and His Saints. It could even be all the people outside of Israel join him. This goes to show the wickedness of mankind's heart (Jer. 17:9). Even after living in the perfect environment for one thousand years the first chance they get mankind rebels against YHWH-God. Their rebellion doesn't last too long, for all those who follow Satan are devoured by fire from heaven.

After this last attempt to remove YHWH from His throne, Satan is thrown into the lake of fire and brimstone to spend eternity with his previous cohorts, the false prophet and the anti-Christ, who are already there.

The Prophecy Puzzle

Revelation 20:11 – 15

> "And I saw a great white throne, and him that sat on it, from whose face the earth and the heaven fled away; and there was found no place for them.
> 12 And I saw the dead, small and great, stand before God; and the books were opened: and another book was opened, which is the book of life: and the dead were judged out of those things which were written in the books, according to their works.
> 13 And the sea gave up the dead which were in it; and death and hell delivered up the dead which were in them: and they were judged every man according to their works.
> 14 And death and hell were cast into the lake of fire. This is the second death.
> 15 And whosoever was not found written in the book of life was cast into the lake of fire."

As God the Father approaches the world, His holiness causes the heavens and the earth to flee (disappear, fall apart). This is just as it is described for us in 2Peter 3:7, 10. I believe this means they literally disintegrate. They literally fly apart at the atomic level. For after that we see that YHWH had to create an all new heavens and earth (Revelation 21:1).

The judgment in this passage is the great white throne judgment. At this time we see all those who ever lived and did not receive salvation by grace through faith in Jesus Christ (YHWH) being raised for judgment. These are the "rest of the dead" from Revelation 20:5 and Dan. 12:2. They are the **spiritually** dead. These people, who had not

The Prophecy Puzzle

received the righteousness of Jesus Christ as a gift through faith in YHWH, are now judged according to **what they did** during their lives. The books contain the recorded history of every last thing "good" or bad these people did. There clearly are different levels of judgment/pain in the lake of fire depending upon the light one received in this life and what kind of life one lived (Matthew 11:23 – 24, Mark 12:38 – 40, 2 Peter 2:20 – 22).

I believe the language in verses 13 and 14 have two purposes. The first is to make a distinction between the physical body and the spirit. The sea and death is a reference to the resting places of the physical bodies of these people. Hell (Hades) is a reference to the spiritual place these people's souls/spirits have been in torment since their physical death. This is important to note, because it is stating that there will be a physical resurrection for the unsaved, just as there is for the saved (Dan. 12:2).

I also believe this language is used to emphasize that everyone will be judged. No one will escape God's final judgment. The only way to escape the lake of fire is to have your name written in the book of life. There is only one way to have your name found in the book of life and that is to have trusted in YHWH, calling out to Him and believing in His provision to be saved. Today that faith is expressed by receiving Christ Jesus as one's Savior and LORD (Acts 4:12). This is true because:

- We have all sinned and therefore are under God's righteous judgment (Exodus 32:32 – 33, Romans 3:23).
- Anyone who overcomes will be found in the book of life (Rev. 3:5).
- The only way to overcome is to be born of God, to be "born again" (John 3:5 – 7, 1 John 5:4 - 5).

The Prophecy Puzzle

- The only way to be born again is to receive Jesus Christ, for who He is, Savior and LORD (YHWH, God, Master) (John 20:28, 2Cor. 5:19 – 21, 1 John 5:11 – 12).

There is a group of people not discussed here. What happens to the people who live through the Millennium kingdom? There are only two groups of people here, those who survived it and those who did not. Those who survived are those who were in the camp of the saints (Rev. 20:9) or did not attack the camp of the saints with Satan. Those who sided with Satan were destroyed. Also in the section about life in the Millennium Kingdom, I suggested that only the wicked (non-believer) would die. So, anyone who died during the Millennium Kingdom would have been included in the white throne judgment. Those who survived the Millennium Kingdom would only be those who are numbered with the saints (believers) and they too, like the rest of us would be saved by grace through faith. They would be the ones who names are in the book of life in Revelation 20:15.

The Prophecy Puzzle

The Prophecy Puzzle

CHAPTER TWELVE

The New Heavens and the New Earth – Revelation 21:1 – 22:21

****

Revelation 21:1 – 22:5

"And I saw a new heaven and a new earth: for the first heaven and the first earth were passed away; and there was no more sea.
2 And I John saw the holy city, new Jerusalem, coming down from God out of heaven, prepared as a bride adorned for her husband.
3 And I heard a great voice out of heaven saying, Behold, the tabernacle of God is with men, and he will

The Prophecy Puzzle

dwell with them, and they shall be his people, and God himself shall be with them, and be their God.

4 And God shall wipe away all tears from their eyes; and there shall be no more death, neither sorrow, nor crying, neither shall there be any more pain: for the former things are passed away.

5 And he that sat upon the throne said, Behold, I make all things new. And he said unto me, Write: for these words are true and faithful.

6 And he said unto me, It is done. I am Alpha and Omega, the beginning and the end. I will give unto him that is athirst of the fountain of the water of life freely.

7 He that overcometh shall inherit all things; and I will be his God, and he shall be my son.

8 But the fearful, and unbelieving, and the abominable, and murderers, and whoremongers, and sorcerers, and idolaters, and all liars, shall have their part in the lake which burneth with fire and brimstone: which is the second death.

9 And there came unto me one of the seven angels which had the seven vials full of the seven last plagues, and talked with me, saying, Come hither, I will shew thee the bride, the Lamb's wife.

10 And he carried me away in the spirit to a great and high mountain, and shewed me that great city, the holy Jerusalem, descending out of heaven from God,

11 Having the glory of God: and her light was like unto a stone most precious, even like a jasper stone, clear as crystal;

12 And had a wall great and high, and had twelve gates, and at the gates twelve angels, and names written

The Prophecy Puzzle

thereon, which are the names of the twelve tribes of the children of Israel:

13 On the east three gates; on the north three gates; on the south three gates; and on the west three gates.

14 And the wall of the city had twelve foundations, and in them the names of the twelve apostles of the Lamb.

15 And he that talked with me had a golden reed to measure the city, and the gates thereof, and the wall thereof.

16 And the city lieth foursquare, and the length is as large as the breadth: and he measured the city with the reed, twelve thousand furlongs. The length and the breadth and the height of it are equal.

17 And he measured the wall thereof, an hundred and forty and four cubits, according to the measure of a man, that is, of the angel.

18 And the building of the wall of it was of jasper: and the city was pure gold, like unto clear glass.

19 And the foundations of the wall of the city were garnished with all manner of precious stones. The first foundation was jasper; the second, sapphire; the third, a chalcedony; the fourth, an emerald;

20 The fifth, sardonyx; the sixth, sardius; the seventh, chrysolite; the eighth, beryl; the ninth, a topaz; the tenth, a chrysoprasus; the eleventh, a jacinth; the twelfth, an amethyst.

21 And the twelve gates were twelve pearls; every several gate was of one pearl: and the street of the city was pure gold, as it were transparent glass.

22 And I saw no temple therein: for the Lord God Almighty and the Lamb are the temple of it.

The Prophecy Puzzle

23 And the city had no need of the sun, neither of the moon, to shine in it: for the glory of God did lighten it, and the Lamb is the light thereof.
24 And the nations of them which are saved shall walk in the light of it: and the kings of the earth do bring their glory and honour into it.
25 And the gates of it shall not be shut at all by day: for there shall be no night there.
26 And they shall bring the glory and honour of the nations into it.
27 And there shall in no wise enter into it any thing that defileth, neither whatsoever worketh abomination, or maketh a lie: but they which are written in the Lamb's book of life.
22:1 And he shewed me a pure river of water of life, clear as crystal, proceeding out of the throne of God and of the Lamb.
2 In the midst of the street of it, and on either side of the river, was there the tree of life, which bare twelve manner of fruits, and yielded her fruit every month: and the leaves of the tree were for the healing of the nations.
3 And there shall be no more curse: but the throne of God and of the Lamb shall be in it; and his servants shall serve him:
4 And they shall see his face; and his name shall be in their foreheads.
5 And there shall be no night there; and they need no candle, neither light of the sun; for the Lord God giveth them light: and they shall reign for ever and ever."

The Prophecy Puzzle

What I said about the Millennium Kingdom goes double for the new heavens and the new earth, as well as the New Jerusalem. So I'm not going to comment on it at all, other than to say, Praise YHWH! He is a merciful, gracious and loving God! Hallelujah!

There is one verse in this passage that could have an impact on people today, so I would like to take a moment to look at it. The verse is 21:8. It gives us a list of characteristics possessed by the people who are not allowed to enter the New Jerusalem. Some of these make perfect sense, such as the unbelieving and idolaters; I mean of course someone who doesn't believe in YHWH or worships a false god would not be allowed into the New Jerusalem. Also, it is not necessarily the committing of these sins that keep people out of heaven, it is the continual embracing of these sins and refusal to repent. I say this because in 1Cor. 6:9 – 11 some of those who became Christians **were** guilty of these sins and others, but had been washed by the blood of Jesus Christ. In other words, all those who are not allowed into heaven are those who did not turn to YHWH or Jesus Christ as their Savior and LORD. This is clarified by the specific mention of all liars. I believe this is in reference to a specific lie made mention of in First John.

1 John 2:22 – 23

> "Who is a liar but he that denieth that Jesus is the Christ? He is antichrist, that denieth the Father and the Son.
> 23 Whosoever denieth the Son, the same hath not the Father: (but) he that acknowledgeth the Son hath the Father also."

The Prophecy Puzzle

The point is the liar is the one who denies that Jesus Christ is YHWH and rejects Him as their Savior and LORD. Because of this they cannot enter the New Jerusalem. Today the only way to be saved is to confess and receive Jesus Christ as one's Savior and LORD (Rom. 10:9).

There is a characteristic included in this list that seems out of place, so I want to look at it. This attribute is fear. Why should someone be kept out of heaven, simply because they were fearful? Well, in one sense fear can be evidence of unbelief and disobedience (Philippians 4:6 – 7). Others believe what this is speaking of is what Jesus Christ spoke of in Matthew 13:20 – 21:

> "20 But he that received the seed into stony places, the same is he that heareth the word, and anon with joy receiveth it;
> 21 Yet hath he not root in himself, but dureth for a while: for when tribulation or persecution ariseth because of the word, by and by he is offended."

Those who are fearful are those who deny their faith in Jesus Christ to preserve their current life in this world. Jesus Christ also said the following in Matthew 10:33, "But whosoever shall deny me before men, him will I also deny before my Father which is in heaven." Also in 2 Timothy 2:12 the Holy Spirit through Paul warns us that, ".... If we deny him, he also will deny us:" I believe this could be what is being referred to here, in Rev. 21:7, which brings us to 2Cor. 13:5:

> "Examine yourselves, whether ye be in the faith; prove your own selves. Know ye not your own selves, how that Jesus Christ is in you, except ye be reprobates?"

The Prophecy Puzzle

I believe YHWH tests our faith to validate it. He does this not to reveal the truth to Himself, but to us. One way is with the threat of our lives, but there are many others. The wise will validate their faith in their heart before he or she is face to face with YHWH, for it would be tragic to find out then one's faith isn't a true saving faith (Mat. 7:21 – 23).

Also as we approach a time of which I believe will be one of great persecution for all who truly follow Christ Jesus; I want to encourage all to hold fast to your faith, even in the threat of death. Jesus Christ is faithful and true!

This last passage brings us back to the first century A.D. when John received this revelation. Here we find the closing thoughts of John and Christ Jesus.

> Revelation 22:6 – 21

> "And he said unto me, These sayings are faithful and true: and the Lord God of the holy prophets sent his angel to shew unto his servants the things which must shortly be done.
> 7 Behold, I come quickly: blessed is he that keepeth the sayings of the prophecy of this book.
> 8 And I John saw these things, and heard them. And when I had heard and seen, I fell down to worship before the feet of the angel which shewed me these things.
> 9 Then saith he unto me, See thou do it not: for I am thy fellowservant, and of thy brethren the prophets, and of them which keep the sayings of this book: worship God.

The Prophecy Puzzle

10 And he saith unto me, Seal not the sayings of the prophecy of this book: for the time is at hand.
11 He that is unjust, let him be unjust still: and he which is filthy, let him be filthy still: and he that is righteous, let him be righteous still: and he that is holy, let him be holy still.
12 And, behold, I come quickly; and my reward is with me, to give every man according as his work shall be.
13 I am Alpha and Omega, the beginning and the end, the first and the last.
14 Blessed are they that do his commandments, that they may have right to the tree of life, and may enter in through the gates into the city.
15 For without are dogs, and sorcerers, and whoremongers, and murderers, and idolaters, and whosoever loveth and maketh a lie.
16 I Jesus have sent mine angel to testify unto you these things in the churches. I am the root and the offspring of David, and the bright and morning star.
17 And the Spirit and the bride say, Come. And let him that heareth say, Come. And let him that is athirst come. And whosoever will, let him take the water of life freely.
18 For I testify unto every man that heareth the words of the prophecy of this book, If any man shall add unto these things, God shall add unto him the plagues that are written in this book:
19 And if any man shall take away from the words of the book of this prophecy, God shall take away his part out of the book of life, and out of the holy city, and from the things which are written in this book.

The Prophecy Puzzle

> 20 He which testifieth these things saith, Surely I come quickly. Amen. Even so, come, Lord Jesus.
> 21 The grace of our Lord Jesus Christ be with you all. Amen."

The first thing we learn from this passage is that God gave John this revelation so he could give it to all of Jesus Christ's bond-servants, so that they may know what will come in the future and be blessed by heeding the words of these prophecies.

So what are the blessings in the book of Revelation? There are actually seven beatitudes in the book of Revelation. They are: 1:3, 14:13, 16:15, 19:8 – 9, 20:6, 22:7, 14. The general teaching of all these verses is that in order to be blessed one must come to Jesus Christ for life and then have steadfastness, alertness and obedience, and that they who persevere in their faith will be eternally rewarded.

Jesus Christ again states that He is coming quickly. As I stated in the beginning of this book, to YHWH a thousand years is like a day. So indeed He is coming quickly. I believe it is very likely that His coming will be in my lifetime. If this turns out to be true or not, I believe the reason Christ Jesus tells us that He is coming soon and that He is bringing His reward with Him is to encourage us to continue on in our faith, no matter where we might find ourselves at this time. No matter where we are in life, this time will pass, but we will have an eternal reward waiting for us if we persevere.

Jesus Christ follows this encouragement with another statement of His deity in verse 13. He is the same "first and the last" spoken of as YHWH in the O.T. (Isaiah 44:6, 48:12). I believe this is to guarantee that He

The Prophecy Puzzle

can and will deliver on these promises. He is God and cannot lie (Titus 1:2).

In the midst of Christ's statements we have verses 11 and 12, which have caused some confusion. I believe this is here to set the urgency of repentance. For Jesus Christ's coming will happen quickly when it happens and at that time it will be too late to change one's fate. If one is found in a state of rejecting Jesus Christ when the end comes, that person will spend eternity in his unjustified condition. At the same time it is to encourage those who are walking with the LORD to continue to do so.

In His closing statements Christ Jesus once again declares that He is the Messiah (v. 16). That statement is followed by another statement informing everyone that the Holy Spirit is in the world, and is through the church and the Bible, calling all people to receive Christ Jesus as their Savior and LORD (v. 17).

The second to last point made in the book of Revelation is the importance of not taking away or adding to the prophecies of the book of Revelation (as well as the whole Bible) (vv. 18 – 19).

Then Jesus Christ gives one last warning, or statement of fact, that He is coming quickly, which John follows up with, "Amen. Even so, come, Lord Jesus!" I think this is added to emphasize the point that even though Jesus Christ's coming includes a lot of suffering, we want Him to return. Amen? Amen!

It would be easy to overlook the very last verse in the book of Revelation, but I would urge us all not to do that. I know I am in constant need of grace. May the LORD's grace be with us all, amen!

The Prophecy Puzzle

CHAPTER THIRTEEN

The Historic View of the Seven Churches

****

As mentioned earlier in the book, there is debate over if this view is true. That is one reason I placed it at the end of the book. So keep that in mind as you read through it. I personally believe as our Jewish friends have been known to say, "Coincidence is not a kosher word." In the letter to the seven churches we find many accurate descriptions of the church over the centuries. I believe they are there by God's design, but please prayerfully make up your own mind.

The first of these coincidences is that just as there are seven letters to the seven churches there are also seven "kingdom parables" in the gospel of Matthew, chapter 13. I believe the "kingdom parables" and the

The Prophecy Puzzle

letter to the seven churches in Revelation work together to give us a picture of the church age from its beginning to its end. Here we go!

Matthew 13:18 – 23

"Hear ye therefore the parable of the sower.
19 When any one heareth the word of the kingdom, and understandeth it not, then cometh the wicked one, and catcheth away that which was sown in his heart. This is he which received seed by the way side.
20 But he that received the seed into stony places, the same is he that heareth the word, and anon with joy receiveth it;
21 Yet hath he not root in himself, but dureth for a while: for when tribulation or persecution ariseth because of the word, by and by he is offended.
22 He also that received seed among the thorns is he that heareth the word; and the care of this world, and the deceitfulness of riches, choke the word, and he becometh unfruitful.
23 But he that received seed into the good ground is he that heareth the word, and understandeth it; which also beareth fruit, and bringeth forth, some an hundredfold, some sixty, some thirty."

Revelation 2:1 – 7

"Unto the angel of the church of Ephesus write; These things saith he that holdeth the seven stars in his right hand, who walketh in the midst of the seven golden candlesticks;

The Prophecy Puzzle

> 2 I know thy works, and thy labour, and thy patience, and how thou canst not bear them which are evil: and thou hast tried them which say they are apostles, and are not, and hast found them liars:
> 3 And hast borne, and hast patience, and for my name's sake hast laboured, and hast not fainted.
> 4 Nevertheless I have somewhat against thee, because thou hast left thy first love.
> 5 Remember therefore from whence thou art fallen, and repent, and do the first works; or else I will come unto thee quickly, and will remove thy candlestick out of his place, except thou repent.
> 6 But this thou hast, that thou hatest the deeds of the Nicolaitans, which I also hate.
> 7 He that hath an ear, let him hear what the Spirit saith unto the churches; To him that overcometh will I give to eat of the tree of life, which is in the midst of the paradise of God."

These passages describe the church from its beginning on Pentecost to about 100 A.D. As seen in the passage from Revelation they were pure in doctrine, even fighting against false teachers to protect the true faith. They were hard working and evangelical. Perhaps too hard working toward the end of the century, because it seems they got caught up in activity for Jesus Christ instead of loving Him through worship and prayer (a danger for all of us as well).

We see how this church fits into "The Parable of the Sower" fairly easily. They were the first church; the instrument God used to spread the gospel and as they did, it fell on all types of soil (people). Some never believed the gospel. Some said they believed, but when their faith

The Prophecy Puzzle

was tested they walked away. Some believed, but because of the pursuit of earthly riches, never produced any fruit. Finally and thankfully there were those who believed with their whole hearts and were used by God to share the gospel with others.

I believe we also gain some insight from the name of the first church in the book of Revelation, "Ephesus," because it means "Maiden of Choice" or "Darling". I believe it expresses the love God has for His bride, the church.

Next we have "The Parable of the Tares" and the church at Smyrna:

> Matthew 13:24 – 30, 36 – 39

> "24 Another parable put he forth unto them, saying, The kingdom of heaven is likened unto a man which sowed good seed in his field:
> 25 But while men slept, his enemy came and sowed tares among the wheat, and went his way.
> 26 But when the blade was sprung up, and brought forth fruit, then appeared the tares also.
> 27 So the servants of the householder came and said unto him, Sir, didst not thou sow good seed in thy field? from whence then hath it tares?
> 28 He said unto them, An enemy hath done this. The servants said unto him, Wilt thou then that we go and gather them up?
> 29 But he said, Nay; lest while ye gather up the tares, ye root up also the wheat with them.
> 30 Let both grow together until the harvest: and in the time of harvest I will say to the reapers, Gather ye

The Prophecy Puzzle

together first the tares, and bind them in bundles to burn them: but gather the wheat into my barn....
36 Then Jesus sent the multitude away, and went into the house: and his disciples came unto him, saying, Declare unto us the parable of the tares of the field.
37 He answered and said unto them, He that soweth the good seed is the Son of man;
38 The field is the world; the good seed are the children of the kingdom; but the tares are the children of the wicked one;
39 The enemy that sowed them is the devil; the harvest is the end of the world; and the reapers are the angels."

Revelation 2:8 – 11

"And unto the angel of the church in Smyrna write; These things saith the first and the last, which was dead, and is alive;
9 I know thy works, and tribulation, and poverty, (but thou art rich) and I know the blasphemy of them which say they are Jews, and are not, but are the synagogue of Satan.
10 Fear none of those things which thou shalt suffer: behold, the devil shall cast some of you into prison, that ye may be tried; and ye shall have tribulation ten days: be thou faithful unto death, and I will give thee a crown of life.
11 He that hath an ear, let him hear what the Spirit saith unto the churches; He that overcometh shall not be hurt of the second death."

The Prophecy Puzzle

These passages represent the time from about 100 A.D. through about 315 A.D. History shows this was a time of severe persecution as described in Revelation. Many people were put to death for their faith. The meaning of the word Smyrna is "myrrh" and I think it shows how God feels about what this church endured for Him. Myrrh is a spice that is crushed in order to release its nice aroma. After that it was used to embalm (preserve) people. The church at Smyrna was crushed even to the point of death for some. I believe their faith pleased God as a fine aroma and through their faithfulness millions of people have heard the gospel and been eternally preserved.

This church fits into "The Parable of the Tares," because it was at this time, after the death of the apostles that false teachers, false doctrines and therefore "false Christians" began to take root within the church. God has said to let them grow until the time of harvest at the end the world. History has shown this to be the case. We each need to examine ourselves and what we believe to make sure we are not a tare (2Cor. 13:5).

Next we have "The Parable of the Mustard Seed" and the church at Pergamos:
Matthew 13:31 – 32

> "Another parable put he forth unto them, saying, The kingdom of heaven is like to a grain of mustard seed, which a man took, and sowed in his field:
> 32 Which indeed is the least of all seeds: but when it is grown, it is the greatest among herbs, and becometh a tree, so that the birds of the air come and lodge in the branches thereof."

The Prophecy Puzzle

Revelation 2:12 – 17

"And to the angel of the church in Pergamos write; These things saith he which hath the sharp sword with two edges;
13 I know thy works, and where thou dwellest, even where Satan's seat is: and thou holdest fast my name, and hast not denied my faith, even in those days wherein Antipas was my faithful martyr, who was slain among you, where Satan dwelleth.
14 But I have a few things against thee, because thou hast there them that hold the doctrine of Balaam, who taught Balac to cast a stumblingblock before the children of Israel, to eat things sacrificed unto idols, and to commit fornication.
15 So hast thou also them that hold the doctrine of the Nicolaitans, which thing I hate.
16 Repent; or else I will come unto thee quickly, and will fight against them with the sword of my mouth.
17 He that hath an ear, let him hear what the Spirit saith unto the churches; To him that overcometh will I give to eat of the hidden manna, and will give him a white stone, and in the stone a new name written, which no man knoweth but he that receiveth it."

These passages describe the church from around 315 A.D. to about 600 A.D. I think it shows very clearly the beginnings of the "political church". Once Emperor Constantine legalized Christianity in 313 A.D. it didn't take long for it to become a tool of those in political power. That, along with the infusing of the Greek and Roman pagan religions, the church was corrupted.

The Prophecy Puzzle

During this time of corruption, there were those who stood against these corruptions, often becoming martyrs because of their stand for the true faith. These are those Jesus Christ makes mention of in Revelation 2:13. Unfortunately, it seems that there were many more who were guilty of the compromises mentioned in the text, than those who were faithful (Rev. 2:14).

It was during this time that the selling of God's blessing through such things as charging money for "church services" began. They also incorporated many of the beliefs of the pagan religions around them into their doctrine. The Babylonian religion can still be found in much of what we consider to be "Christian tradition".

According to *The Babylonian Religion* (From Chuck Missler's, "*Personal Update*"), "*The Origins of our Christmas Traditions*", 12/1/2004:

> "Tammuz, the son of Nimrod and his queen, Semiramis, was identified with the Babylonian Sun God and worshipped following the winter solstice. As the days became shorter and shorter through the winter, they become the shortest at the winter solstice, about December 22-23. Tammuz was thought to have died during the winter solstice, and was memorialized by burning a log in the fireplace. (The Chaldean word for infant is *yule*. This is the origin of the "yule log.") His "rebirth" was celebrated by replacing the log with a trimmed tree the next morning. Sound familiar? (Jeremiah 10 contains an interesting verse which talks about trimming trees, etc.)

The Prophecy Puzzle

> There are numerous other examples. The wassail bowl, the mistletoe (a fertility rite), and others are documented in such works as Alexander Hislop's, *The Two Babylons*. When Babylon was conquered by subsequent empires, this entire religious system was transplanted, first to Pergamos under the Persians, and then to Rome. As the pagan Roman (Babylonian) religious system was integrated with Christian ceremonial observances, many of our current traditions surrounding Christmas emerged."

Some believe this is why we celebrate Jesus Christ's birth on Dec. 25th. It is almost certain He wasn't born then, but it does fit well with these pagan beliefs. This could also explain where we got the "Yule log" and the "Christmas tree" from as well. Other traditions such as mistletoe, infallibility, Mariolatry, and the term "Pontifex Maximus" can all be traced back to pagan Rome.
It was also at this time that the church started to adapt a structure formed after that of the Nicolaitans, where the clergy ruled over the laity.

History also shows that YHWH-God was true to His word and later brought reformers such as Martin Luther to bring the true gospel back to the forefront.

It fits into "The Parable of the Mustard Seed" perfectly. It started out small and grew to be "the world's religion". The birds, which are always evil in the parables, here represent the leaders who brought false, pagan teachings into the church. Even the name "Pergamos," which means "Mixed Marriage" describes how pagan religion and the Christian faith were mixed together.

The Prophecy Puzzle

Next we have "The Parable of the Leaven" and the church at Thyatira:

Matthew 13:33

"Another parable spake he unto them; The kingdom of heaven is like unto leaven, which a woman took, and hid in three measures of meal, till the whole was leavened."

Revelation 2:18 – 29

"And unto the angel of the church in Thyatira write; These things saith the Son of God, who hath his eyes like unto a flame of fire, and his feet are like fine brass; 19 I know thy works, and charity, and service, and faith, and thy patience, and thy works; and the last to be more than the first.
20 Notwithstanding I have a few things against thee, because thou sufferest that woman Jezebel, which calleth herself a prophetess, to teach and to seduce my servants to commit fornication, and to eat things sacrificed unto idols.
21 And I gave her space to repent of her fornication; and she repented not.
22 Behold, I will cast her into a bed, and them that commit adultery with her into great tribulation, except they repent of their deeds.
23 And I will kill her children with death; and all the churches shall know that I am he which searcheth the reins and hearts: and I will give unto every one of you according to your works.

The Prophecy Puzzle

> 24 But unto you I say, and unto the rest in Thyatira, as many as have not this doctrine, and which have not known the depths of Satan, as they speak; I will put upon you none other burden.
> 25 But that which ye have already hold fast till I come.
> 26 And he that overcometh, and keepeth my works unto the end, to him will I give power over the nations:
> 27 And he shall rule them with a rod of iron; as the vessels of a potter shall they be broken to shivers: even as I received of my Father.
> 28 And I will give him the morning star.
> 29 He that hath an ear, let him hear what the Spirit saith unto the churches."

The name of the city in which this church existed was Thyatira and it means "Daughter". It fits very well, because this church represents the "daughter" the mixed marriage of the previous church produced. It is the Roman Catholic Church from the end of the sixth century A.D. up through today.

Rev. 2:26 is the first time Jesus Christ refers to the end by name in the "Seven Letters to the Seven Churches", and more than that it is the only time that "the end" is referred to by name in these letters. I believe this is significant, because I believe it indicates that this church will continue to the end. It is the first of these churches that will continue until the end. By "end" I mean the end of this age, the age of grace; which ends with the rapture. The next age begins with the great tribulation (the last 3 ½ years of the seven-year tribulation).

Jesus Christ does have some very positive things to say about this church (the Roman Catholic Church). He names them in verse 19. This

The Prophecy Puzzle

church has good deeds. The people (the laity), are loving, loyal and faithful. He even states that their last deeds are greater than their first. I believe these last deeds reference to the Roman Catholic Church's strong fight for life for the unborn. The Roman Catholic Church is one of the greatest forces fighting to protect babies from being aborted (murdered). For this they are to be greatly applauded.

But now we need to move onto the negative statements against it. We know from history and the present day structure of the Roman Catholic Church that they did embrace the doctrine of the Nicolaitans, where the clergy rule over the laity.

We see in history that they allowed the actions of "Jezebel". They, like Jezebel (1 Kings 18:13) killed followers of YHWH that would not bow before their authority. They also, like Jezebel, incorporated false gods (1 Kings 16:31 - 33) and beliefs into the faith. They even ended up following Jezebel's example of how to acquire wealth (1 Kings 21:1 - 16). For centuries the Roman Catholic Church received the lands and riches of those their armies concurred and killed.

They have been deceived by Jezebel and have actually embraced her as well. Jezebel is also symbolic of the Queen of Heaven (Jer. 44:17 – 22, Revelation 17). The Queen of Heaven originated in the Babylonian religion. She has over the ages used many names, such as: The goddess Venus, Ishtar, Diana, Asherah, Kwanon, "the Queen Mother of the West", Tara (the "divine Mother of the Tibetan Buddhism"), etc. Today she is presenting herself as "Mary the Mother of God", "the Mother of Nations", "the Lady of Fatima" and **"Our Lady"** by <u>Muslims</u> as well as Roman Catholics. See, "Queen of All" by Jim Tetlow, Roger Oakland and Brad Myers for a complete explanation.

The Prophecy Puzzle

We see that Jesus Christ was true to His word. He has attacked the Roman Catholic Church with the Sword of His Mouth (the Bible). Many people have left the religion after reading and understanding the Bible. While Christ Jesus does make the point that there are true believers within the church; unfortunately, the present official doctrine of the Roman Catholic Church is still filled with false teachings and at best severely clouds the true gospel of grace. The people who are true born again Christians within the church are there despite the teachings of the Roman Catholic Church, not because of them. But as Jesus Christ points out in verses 26 and 27, anyone who overcomes shall rule with Him during the Millennium Kingdom. Remember that one only overcomes by faith in Jesus Christ as a **personal** Savior and LORD (1John 5:4 – 5).

"The Parable of the Leaven" shows how false, pagan beliefs were introduced into the church and like leaven, which always represents sin/evil in scripture, spread throughout the church.

Next we have "The Parable of Hidden Treasure" and the church at Sardis:

Matthew 13:44

> "Again, the kingdom of heaven is like unto treasure hid in a field; the which when a man hath found, he hideth, and for joy thereof goeth and selleth all that he hath, and buyeth that field."

The Prophecy Puzzle

Revelation 3:1 – 6

"And unto the angel of the church in Sardis write; These things saith he that hath the seven Spirits of God, and the seven stars; I know thy works, that thou hast a name that thou livest, and art dead.
2 Be watchful, and strengthen the things which remain, that are ready to die: for I have not found thy works perfect before God.
3 Remember therefore how thou hast received and heard, and hold fast, and repent. If therefore thou shalt not watch, I will come on thee as a thief, and thou shalt not know what hour I will come upon thee.
4 Thou hast a few names even in Sardis which have not defiled their garments; and they shall walk with me in white: for they are worthy.
5 He that overcometh, the same shall be clothed in white raiment; and I will not blot out his name out of the book of life, but I will confess his name before my Father, and before his angels.
6 He that hath an ear, let him hear what the Spirit saith unto the churches."

These passages represent the protestant church, which started near the beginning of the sixteenth century. It seems as if it too will continue on until the rapture / great tribulation. It co-exists with Thyatira (the Roman Catholic Church) until the rapture and great tribulation. I write co-exist, but it is very likely that most, if not all of the formal denominations as well as Islam and other major world religions will unite in some fashion to form a "world religion" by the time the rapture

The Prophecy Puzzle

happens and the great tribulation actually begins. Again I point out that the great tribulation is only the last half of the seven-year tribulation.

We see how the church of Sardis fits into history by looking at many main-line denominations today. Most Protestant churches today have a great history of preaching the gospel of grace, but now are dead. You walk into them and you don't hear anything about the need of a sinner to repent and be born again. You will more likely than not find people comfortably following rules. They have traded Christ Jesus for religion. Many of these denominations completely ignore the Holy Spirit. They are not born-again and therefore will not be raptured, but will have the day of the Lord come upon them like a thief (3:3).

As we look back to their beginning they did indeed reform some of the false teaching of the Roman Catholic Church, but they did not go far enough. They still embraced some false teachings and traditions of the Roman Catholic Church (their work was not complete).

Even with all these problems, there are some in this church that still believe in the gospel of grace and are born-again. I believe the name of the church, "Sardis" reveals that exact truth. It means "remnant."

I think we should also note what is not said here. It doesn't say that this church had been tricked into believing false doctrines; they just left the Author of the Bible behind and only followed His rules.

There is some difficultly in seeing how this church fits into "The Parable of the Hidden Treasure" because its meaning might be different outside of this context. Actually there is an argument within the church of the meaning of this parable. One group sees Christ Jesus as the man finding the treasure and selling all He has to gain the

The Prophecy Puzzle

treasure; while others see people finding the treasure in Christ Jesus and selling all they have to gain Him. In the context of the historic view of the seven churches, I believe the man represents the "reformers" who found the greatest treasure of all in the gospel of grace. Many of them had to "sell" (give up) all they had in the Roman Catholic Church (society/government). They were scorned by family and friends, many even losing their lives in order to hold onto this great treasure. With that said I do believe that in the immediate context in Matthew, the man in the parable is Jesus Christ, but I don't believe that view fits here.

Next we have "The Parable of the Pearl of Great Price" and the church at Philadelphia:

Matthew 13:45 – 46

"Again, the kingdom of heaven is like unto a merchant man, seeking goodly pearls:
46 Who, when he had found one pearl of great price, went and sold all that he had, and bought it."

Revelation 3:7 – 13

"And to the angel of the church in Philadelphia write; These things saith he that is holy, he that is true, he that hath the key of David, he that openeth, and no man shutteth; and shutteth, and no man openeth;
8 I know thy works: behold, I have set before thee an open door, and no man can shut it: for thou hast a little strength, and hast kept my word, and hast not denied my name.

The Prophecy Puzzle

9 Behold, I will make them of the synagogue of Satan, which say they are Jews, and are not, but do lie; behold, I will make them to come and worship before thy feet, and to know that I have loved thee.
10 Because thou hast kept the word of my patience, I also will keep thee from the hour of temptation, which shall come upon all the world, to try them that dwell upon the earth.
11 Behold, I come quickly: hold that fast which thou hast, that no man take thy crown.
12 Him that overcometh will I make a pillar in the temple of my God, and he shall go no more out: and I will write upon him the name of my God, and the name of the city of my God, which is new Jerusalem, which cometh down out of heaven from my God: and I will write upon him my new name.
13 He that hath an ear, let him hear what the Spirit saith unto the churches."

These passages represent the evangelical church, which started with the revivals of the 19th century. With the reawakening in the 1800's came the reasserting of many of the original doctrines of the church, which are mentioned here in this letter. Such doctrines as:

- The Bible is God's word and <u>stands alone</u> as the final authority of Truth ("have kept My word").
- Jesus is God. So many cults in the past 200 years incorporate Jesus, but deny He is the second person of the triune God ("not denied My name") (Christ Jesus' true name is YHWH (Psalm 148:13; Phil. 2:9).
- The gospel of grace. One is saved 100% by grace alone, through faith, not of works so no one can boast (Eph. 2:8 – 9).

The Prophecy Puzzle

- The pre-wrath rapture of Christians - Christians would be spared from the wrath of God (3:10).
- The Millennium Kingdom will be a literal 1000-year reign on earth with Christ Jesus bodily on the throne of David.

This church will exist until the rapture. The Jews who are part of the synagogue of Satan, are those non-Christian Jews who are living during the first half of the seven-year tribulation and will cry out to YHWH when they are attacked by the false Messiah (Hosea 5:15). Those who survive will worship YHWH in the Millennium Kingdom, in the presence of the Christians who were raptured and then reigning with Christ Jesus.

Looking at the "Parable of the Pearl of Great Value" it reveals a truly beautiful illustration of the church. Christ Jesus uses a pearl as His example for a reason. A pearl is started by a small irritation to an oyster. The Christian church began as a small irritation to the Jewish religious leaders. A pearl grows by the oyster's accretion in response to the irritation. The church grew under persecution and largely because of it (People fled from city to city taking and leaving the gospel everywhere they went). A pearl "at the right time" will be removed from its place of birth and growth to bring pleasure to and be treasured by its owner. The church at just the right time will be taken from this earth to spend eternity in the presence of God bringing pleasure and glory to Him.

The name Philadelphia also gives insight; it means "brotherly love" and the church should be identifiable to outsiders, by how its members love each other (John 13:35).

The Prophecy Puzzle

Finally we have "The Parable of the Dragnet" and the church at Laodicea:

Matthew 13:47 – 50

"Again, the kingdom of heaven is like unto a net, that was cast into the sea, and gathered of every kind:
48 Which, when it was full, they drew to shore, and sat down, and gathered the good into vessels, but cast the bad away.
49 So shall it be at the end of the world: the angels shall come forth, and sever the wicked from among the just,
50 And shall cast them into the furnace of fire: there shall be wailing and gnashing of teeth."

Revelation 3:14 – 22

"And unto the angel of the church of the Laodiceans write; These things saith the Amen, the faithful and true witness, the beginning of the creation of God;
15 I know thy works, that thou art neither cold nor hot: I would thou wert cold or hot.
16 So then because thou art lukewarm, and neither cold nor hot, I will spue thee out of my mouth.
17 Because thou sayest, I am rich, and increased with goods, and have need of nothing; and knowest not that thou art wretched, and miserable, and poor, and blind, and naked:
18 I counsel thee to buy of me gold tried in the fire, that thou mayest be rich; and white raiment, that thou

The Prophecy Puzzle

> mayest be clothed, and that the shame of thy nakedness do not appear; and anoint thine eyes with eyesalve, that thou mayest see.
> 19 As many as I love, I rebuke and chasten: be zealous therefore, and repent.
> 20 Behold, I stand at the door, and knock: if any man hear my voice, and open the door, I will come in to him, and will sup with him, and he with me.
> 21 To him that overcometh will I grant to sit with me in my throne, even as I also overcame, and am set down with my Father in his throne.
> 22 He that hath an ear, let him hear what the Spirit saith unto the churches."

The name "Laodicea" means "Rule of the People" and I believe it communicates clearly what this church is all about. It's all about pleasing the people. It represents a segment of the church, which began to really take root around the turn of the twentieth century. It is flourishing today and will exist until the great tribulation (the last half of the seven-year tribulation).

We can see this church all around us today. Churches are preaching a cultural message instead of a message of repentance of sin and faith in Christ Jesus for the saving from hell (a very real place) (Col. 1:20 - 22). They teach we must learn to love ourselves instead of denying ourselves (Mat. 16:24 – 25; 10:38; Titus 2:12). They teach people are good and if we think positive and tap into the good within us we can do anything; instead of the truth that we are evil, helpless and that our only hope is to have the righteousness of Jesus Christ given to us (1 John 1:8; Romans 6:23). If these churches speak of God at all, He is someone or something to use to accomplish their personal goals. In short they

The Prophecy Puzzle

really are teaching the "Eastern Mysticism" / "New Age Religion" under the name of Christianity. If they use the Bible at all, they only manipulated it, taking things out of context to support their false teachings.

This type of church has been becoming more and more common the last few decades. Two people who are known for promoting this type of "movement" or denomination are Eckhart Tolle and Oprah Winfrey. These movements are very dangerous and could very well be a major player in the forming of the one-world religion the false prophet will head up someday. For further study of these "New Age" movements I recommend the book, "A New Earth an Old Deception" by Richard Abanes.

"The Parable of the Dragnet" shows what will happen at the end of the "church age". This church will be doing fine in its own eyes, right up until the rapture. The "good fish", the true Christians will be taken into heaven and those of the Laodicean church, the "bad fish" will be cast back, thrown into the great tribulation and after that the great white throne judgment (Revelation 20: 11 – 15).

Please make sure that you've come to Christ Jesus for forgiveness of your sins and eternal life, not to improve yourself or just this life. Don't be deceived, (Romans 6:23, Col. 2:8 – 10, 2 Thes. 2:10 – 12, Hebrews. 10:14 – 31).

The Prophecy Puzzle

The Prophecy Puzzle

CHAPTER FOURTEEN

The Complete Timeline According to the Book of Revelation

****

I will finish this study on the Book of Revelation by sharing my opinion of what happens and in what order they happen. I need to emphasize that this is only my opinion and that good Christians differ on their understanding of these events. So with that stated I believe the following is the order of the events discussed in the Book of Revelation:

The first thing to happen that will mark the beginning of the end is the rise of a world government (Daniel 7:24). I believe this government to be primarily a revamping of the current European Union (EU), which will one day include much of the Muslim world (the Ottoman Empire)

The Prophecy Puzzle

and even the Americas. The name they go by is not important, but one of the characteristics of this "world government" will be that the world will be divided up into ten regions with a "representative" over each region. Then:

- The first seal is broken (Rev. 6:1 – 2, Dan. 7:24). This is the beginning of the seven-year tribulation. Out of this world government an individual will arise to power. He is often referred to as the antichrist, but I think it is better to think of him as the false Messiah.
    - What will bring him to power will be his ability to bring peace to the Middle East. He will form a peace treaty between Israel and the "world."
        - This treaty will give Israel the right to **rebuild the temple** in Jerusalem and to start the Jewish sacrificial system again.
    - The false Messiah uses religion as well to unite the rest of the world behind him.
    - He uses a false religious system based out of Rome to unite the Gentile world. Over the next three and half years the false Messiah uses this world religious system to control people throughout the world (Rev. 17:3 - 9).
        - Under this religious system it will be for all practical purposes illegal throughout the world to be a true Christian.
            - The Gospel of Jesus Christ will be declared to be hate speech.
            - **Christians** will be **persecuted** and **killed** (Daniel 7:25, 11:32 – 35).
- The second seal is broken (Rev. 6:3 – 4). Probably as little as a few months after the signing of the peace treaty the "world peace" is broken.

The Prophecy Puzzle

- - Many battles breakout around the world with the false Messiah conquering these places as he "restores peace" now through military force.
- The third seal is broken (Rev. 6:5 – 6). Over the following months the false Messiah takes control of most of the world through his military strength. As he does, he also takes control of the resources.
  - He manipulates those resources in order to control people.
    - Hungry dependant people are easier to control and manipulate. He knows that most people will do almost anything to survive, even turn in Christians into the government, even if they are family (Daniel 11:32 – 35, Mat. 24:9 – 12).
- The forth seal is broken (Rev. 6:7 – 8). The effects of war and global socialism are felt.
  - A fourth of the earth falls prey to death from the fighting, famine, disease and wild animals.
- The fifth seal is broken (Rev. 6:9 – 11). At this time, probably shortly past three years into the seven-year tribulation we see this scene in heaven.
  - The people who have been martyred up to this point ask the LORD how much longer it would be before He avenges their blood.
  - His reply is that it would come soon, but more Christians still need to be martyred.
- Shortly after that, at or near the 3½-year mark of the seven-year tribulation the war in heaven spoken of in Rev. 12:1 – 12 occurs.
  - Satan and his angels are forever cast out of heaven **to the earth**.

The Prophecy Puzzle

- - -
  - ○ Apparently somewhere during this time, the anti-Christ is slain and brought back to life.
- The false Messiah turns on Israel, surrounding it with his army (Ez. 38:1 – 16).
  - ○ He puts an end to their sacrifices.
  - ○ He declares himself to be God.
  - ○ He sets up an image to the beast in the Jewish temple, which is soon after indwelled by Satan (Daniel 8:9 – 12, 11:29 – 31, Rev. 12:13 – 17, 13:14).
- The sixth seal is broken (Rev. 6:12 – 17). This triggers the following. The order of them is not clear and some of them might very well happen simultaneously, but the following does happen:
  - ○ Meteors fall from the sky and there is a huge earthquake and the earth's atmosphere is filled with so much dirt and smoke that the sun appears dark and the moon looks red.
  - ○ The Jews in Jerusalem, seeing their predicament call out to Jesus of Nazareth as their Messiah (Hosea 5:15 KJV).
  - ○ Jesus Christ provides escape for the Jews in Jerusalem as they flee through the now divided Mount of Olives to Petra (Zech. 14:2 – 5).
  - ○ An angel flies throughout the world proclaiming the true gospel (Revelation 14:6 – 7).
  - ○ Satan and the false Messiah, along with his cohorts, the world leaders, leave Jerusalem and turn on the world religious system based in Rome (the harlot, Revelation 17:1 – 18).
    - After destroying the false religious system (the harlot), the false Messiah moves his headquarters to Babylon (Zech. 5:6 – 11).

The Prophecy Puzzle

- - Another angel announces the destruction of the harlot (world religious system) (Rev. 14:8).
  - A third angel flies throughout the world declaring that anyone who receives the mark of the beast will be condemned by God (Rev. 14:9 – 11).
    - This same angel also announces that to be a Christian will mean being a martyr (Revelation 14:12 - 13).
  - Somewhere among those events the **rapture** takes place and we see those Christians in heaven (Rev. 7:9 – 17).
    - At the same time the 144,000 Jewish believers are sealed and brought to the temple (Revelation 7:1 – 8, 14:1 – 5).
    - The **two witnesses arrive** at the temple (Revelation 11:1 – 6).
  - Satan being frustrated and angry that he is unable to kill the Jews who escaped to Petra (my guess) turns his hatred toward the 144,000 Jewish Christians in Jerusalem (Revelation 12:17).
    - The two witnesses in front of the temple protect the 144,000 and they smite the people on earth with plagues (Rev. 11:1 – 6).
  - The false Messiah declares that all must worship the image of the beast and have his mark in order to buy or sell anything (Rev. 13:15 – 17).
- Now the seventh seal is broken (Revelation 8:1 -5).
  - The prayer of those under the altar (Rev. 6:9 – 10) is finally answered.
    - The seven trumpets are prepared.
    - They contain the wrath of God.

The Prophecy Puzzle

- - Shortly after that the first trumpet is blown (Revelation 8:6 – 7).
    - One-third of the earth is burned.
- Shortly after that the second trumpet is blown (Rev. 8:8 – 9).
  - A "mountain" falls into the sea, turning one-third of the world's oceans to blood (poison).
    - This could be the Atlantic Ocean because it contains roughly one-third of the world's salt water.
    - Could be the result of a nuclear bomb.
- Shortly after that the third trumpet is blown (Rev. 8:10 – 11).
  - A "star" falls from heaven making 1/3rd of the fresh water on the earth blood (poison).
    - The name wormwood (Chernobyl) could indicate nuclear contamination.
- Shortly after that the fourth trumpet is blown (Rev. 8:12 – 13).
  - The sun is somehow struck resulting in a cosmic disturbance, which all notice, because of the change in the lighting of the earth (Rev. 8:12).
  - An angel announces the **three woes**, which are about to come upon the earth (Rev. 8:13).
- The fifth trumpet is blown (Revelation 9:1 – 12).
  - This happens probably about 5 ½ years into the seven-year tribulation.
  - Satan is given the key to the abyss and releases demonic scorpions (Revelation 9:1 – 3).
    - For <u>five months</u> (150 days) these demonic scorpions sting those who are not sealed by God (Rev. 9:4).
    - The stings are not lethal, but cause so much pain the people want to die (Rev. 9:5 – 6).

The Prophecy Puzzle

- Now **nearing the six year point** in the seven-year tribulation, **the sixth trumpet is blown.**
  - A two hundred million-man army sets out from the East, probably China (Revelation 9:13 – 21).
  - Over the next 391 days this army moves across the land from China to Israel, killing one-third of the earth's population on its way.
    - They will arrive in Israel just in time for the battle of Armageddon.
- The seventh trumpet is blown.
  - The stage is now set for the seven bowls of God's wrath to be poured out upon the earth.

Before we dive into what happens with each bowl of wrath I want to examine the time frame in which they happen. We are not given one here in the book of Revelation, but I believe it is possible that we have been given one in Daniel 12:6 – 12:

> "And one said to the man clothed in linen, which was upon the waters of the river, How long shall it be to the end of these wonders?
> 7 And I heard the man clothed in linen, which was upon the waters of the river, when he held up his right hand and his left hand unto heaven, and sware by him that liveth for ever that it shall be for a time, times, and an half; and when he shall have accomplished to scatter the power of the holy people, all these things shall be finished.
> 8 And I heard, but I understood not: then said I, O my Lord, what shall be the end of these things?

The Prophecy Puzzle

> 9 And he said, Go thy way, Daniel: for the words are closed up and sealed till the time of the end.
> 10 Many shall be purified, and made white, and tried; but the wicked shall do wickedly: and none of the wicked shall understand; but the wise shall understand.
> 11 And from the time that the daily sacrifice shall be taken away, and the abomination that maketh desolate set up, there shall be a thousand two hundred and ninety days.
> 12 Blessed is he that waiteth, and cometh to the thousand three hundred and five and thirty days."

In Daniel 12:7 we are given the often repeated fact that the last half of the seven-year tribulation would be 1260 days, but in verse 11 there is an extra 30 days added and in verse 12 an additional 45 days. Some believe that the bowls of wrath are actually poured out during these extra 30 days mentioned in Daniel, but most believe the bowls of wrath are included in the time span of the seven-year tribulation. I have no problem with either view.

Personally I believe that these "extra" 30 days are not extra, but are part of the 1260. It is possible that the daily sacrifices mentioned in v. 11 were actually stopped 30 days before the attack on Israel (Daniel 11:31) (prior to the middle of the seven-year tribulation). If that is the case these extra 30 days, would simply be the last 30 days of the great tribulation. I think that works the best and it provides a time frame for the bowls of wrath. In the end it doesn't truly matter, so I hope no one gets too upset with my using this hypothesis to provide a time frame for the bowls of wrath. I emphasize that this is just a guess and I'm just trying to provide a possible timeline for these events.

The Prophecy Puzzle

- The **first bowl** is poured out 30 days from the end of the great tribulation (Revelation 16:1 - 2).
  - All the people who had received the mark of the beast and worshiped his image get "loathsome and malignant sores" all over their bodies.
- Seven days later (day 8) the **second bowl** is poured out (Revelation 16:3).
  - The seas of the world become blood (poisonous) and <u>all</u> life within them dies.
- Seven days later (day 15) the **third bowl** of wrath is poured (Rev. 16:4 – 5).
  - All the rivers and lakes in the world are turned to blood (poison).
  - An angel proclaims that YHWH's judgments are right.
- Seven days later (day 21) the **fourth bowl** of wrath is poured out (Rev. 16:8 – 9).
  - The sun burns excessively hot and scorches the earth.
  - The people blaspheme God's name for these plagues and do not repent of their sin.
- Three days later (day 24) the **fifth bowl** of wrath is poured out upon the earth (Rev. 16:10 – 11).
  - The city of Babylon is cast into darkness and anguish.
  - In one hour the throne of the Beast (the city of Babylon) is destroyed. (Rev. 16:19, 18:1 - 24).
- Two days later (day 26) the false Messiah succeeds at killing the two witnesses (Revelation 11:7 – 9).
  - For 3 ½ days the people around the world rejoice. They cry peace, peace because finally those troublesome witnesses are killed (1Thes. 5:3, Revelation 11:10).
- Also on this day (day 26) the sixth bowl of wrath is poured out (Rev. 16:12 - 16).

The Prophecy Puzzle

- - The Euphrates River is dried up making it easy for the two hundred million man army of the "kings of the East" to march toward Jerusalem to fight in "the battle of Armageddon".
    - It could be a result of Babylon (Dubai) being destroyed, but it doesn't really matter.
  - The rest of the world's armies have already gathered there (Ez. 38:21 - 23, Dan. 11:44 – 45).
  - At the end of those 3 ½ days (end of the 7-year tribulation) the two witnesses are resurrected and taken to heaven (Rev. 11:11 – 14).
    - The city of Jerusalem experiences a huge earthquake.
    - A tenth of the city is destroyed and seven thousand people die.
    - The rest of the people in Jerusalem are terrified and give God glory.
  - This is the end of the second woe (Rev. 11:14).
  - The third woe is announced and said to be coming quickly.
- It is now day 30 and the **seventh bowl** of God's wrath is poured out (Ez. 38:21 – 23, Rev. 16:17 – 21, 18:1 – 19:21).
  - Christ Jesus goes to "fight" the battle of Armageddon accompanied by His bride and army of angels (Rev. 19:11 - 21).
  - There is a huge supernatural hailstorm.
  - There is a huge earthquake, which results in the earth being flat except for Jerusalem, which will sit on the only remaining mountain (Zech. 14:10).
- In the 15 days after the battle of Armageddon, the following happens (Daniel 12:11 – 12):

The Prophecy Puzzle

- - All who had received the mark of the beast are judged and die.
  - Clean up begins.
    - The birds of the air help in the clean up by eating the flesh of those killed.
- God magnifies Himself (Ezekiel 38:23).
  - The false Messiah and false prophet are thrown into the lake of fire.
  - Satan is jailed in the abyss for 1000 years.
- The wedding supper of the Lamb is **completed**.
  - All the saints including those who were martyred during the great tribulation are judged.
    - They are rewarded and given the position they will hold while reigning with Christ Jesus during the Millennium Kingdom (Rev. 19:7 – 9, 20:4).
- The Millennium Kingdom!
  - Christ Jesus and His saints reign for a thousand years (Rev. 19:15).
  - Roughly two and half years later the temple is cleansed and the Spirit of God (the Shekinah Glory) enters the Holy of Holies (Ezekiel 43:1 – 5, Daniel 8:14).
- At the end of the 1,000 years, Satan is released and goes throughout the world gathering people to join him in one last battle against God.
  - Many follow after him and are devoured by fire from heaven.
- The earth and the heavens melt away as God the Father approaches (2 Peter 3:10, Rev. 20:11).
- The final judgment.
  - Included in this judgment are all those throughout history who did not believe in and embrace the one true

living God (YHWH) as their Savior and LORD (Revelation 20:12 - 15).

ETERNITY! All things new!

The Prophecy Puzzle

Closing Comments:

The topic of prophecy has been the source of many disagreements over the years, but the best advice I can give is to hope for the best and plan for the worst; remembering Proverbs 3:5 – 6, "Trust in the LORD with all thine heart; and lean not unto thine own understanding. In all thy ways acknowledge him, and he shall direct thy paths."

Another point to make before I close is that if we look at the parables that follow Jesus Christ's discussions of the end-times in Matthew, Mark and Luke they all have one common theme and that is to be hard at work doing the Master's bidding, so we are ready for His return. This is true no matter what you think of the rapture.

I truly hope and pray that this study of the book of Revelation has affected your Christian walk in a positive way and will continue to do so. I would like to close with the following two passages of Scripture:

Colossians 1:9 – 13

> "For this cause we also, since the day we heard it, do not cease to pray for you, and to desire that ye might be filled with the knowledge of his will in all wisdom and spiritual understanding;
> 10 That ye might walk worthy of the Lord unto all pleasing, being fruitful in every good work, and increasing in the knowledge of God;
> 11 Strengthened with all might, according to his glorious power, unto all patience and longsuffering with joyfulness;

The Prophecy Puzzle

12 Giving thanks unto the Father, which hath made us meet to be partakers of the inheritance of the saints in light:
13 Who hath delivered us from the power of darkness, and hath translated us into the kingdom of his dear Son:"

2 Peter 3:11 – 18

"Seeing then that all these things shall be dissolved, what manner of persons ought ye to be in all holy conversation and godliness,
12 Looking for and hasting unto the coming of the day of God, wherein the heavens being on fire shall be dissolved, and the elements shall melt with fervent heat?
13 Nevertheless we, according to his promise, look for new heavens and a new earth, wherein dwelleth righteousness.
14 Wherefore, beloved, seeing that ye look for such things, be diligent that ye may be found of him in peace, without spot, and blameless.
15 And account that the longsuffering of our Lord is salvation; even as our beloved brother Paul also according to the wisdom given unto him hath written unto you;
16 As also in all his epistles, speaking in them of these things; in which are some things hard to be understood, which they that are unlearned and unstable wrest, as they do also the other scriptures, unto their own destruction.

17 Ye therefore, beloved, seeing ye know these things before, beware lest ye also, being led away with the error of the wicked, fall from your own stedfastness. 18 But grow in grace, and in the knowledge of our Lord and Saviour Jesus Christ. To him be glory both now and for ever. Amen."

I hope you were blessed by reading this book and I'd like to recommend my blog, www.prophecypuzzle.wordpress.com for further Bible study.

The Prophecy Puzzle

The Prophecy Puzzle

Bibliography:

Joseph R. Ebenhoe
2008, 2010, 2018

References:
- "An expositional commentary on the Book of Revelation" by Chuck Missler.
- "Daniel the Prophet" by Noah Hutchings
- "Messages from Heaven (DVD) by Eternal Productions
- "Bible Soft PC Study Bible – version 4"
- "Queen of All" by Jim Tetlow, Roger Oakland and Brad Myers
- "Roman Catholicism" by Loraine Boettner
- "The Complete Word Study New Testament" edited by Spiros Zodhiates, Th.D.
- "The Imminent Return of Christ" (CD) by Dr. Robert A. Morey
- "The New Open Bible, study edition" (NASB)
- "The New Strong's Exhaustive Concordance"
- "The Pre-wrath Rapture of the Church" by Marvin Rosenthal.
- "The Ryrie Study Bible" (KJV)
- "Why I Left Jihad" by Walid Shoebat

Printed in Great Britain
by Amazon